KINGSHIP and LAW

in the Early
Konbaung Period of Myanmar
(1752-1819)

A Study of the
Manugye Dhammathat
an eighteenth century
major law book

RYUJI
OKUDAIRA

Kingship and Law
in the Early Konbaung Period of Myanmar
(1752-1819)

A Study of the *Manugye Dhammathat* – an eighteenth century major law book

RYUJI OKUDAIRA

Kingship and Law in the Early Konbaung Priod of Myanmar
(1752-1819)
A Study of the *Manugye Dhammathat* — an eighteenth century major law book

All right reserved. No part of this publication may be reproduced or transmitted in any form or by any means, electronic or mechanical, including photocopy, recording, or any information storage and retrieval system without the written permission of the publisher.

Copy right © Ryuji Okudaira, 2018

Published in Japan by Mekong Publishing Co.,Ltd.
3-7-1 Hongo, Bunkyouku, Tokyo Japan 113-0033

First Published 2018

Basic typeset in Garamond 14Q

ISBN978-4-8396-0309-0 C3022

Dedicated this book to Professor Yoneo Ishii and Professor Than Tun who regrettably passed away before this small book was published.

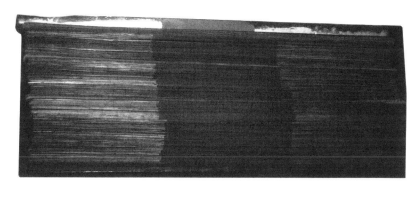
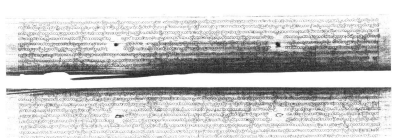

A Set of Palm-leaf Manuscript of a Myanmar Dhammathat or law book

Foreword

Myanmar is widely known as Buddhist State in Southeast Asia, together with her eastern neighbours of Thailand, Laos and Cambodia. Since olden days majority of her population were believers of the Sinhalese Buddhism known as Theravada, the common language of which is Pāli. It has long been noticed, however, that Sanskrit tradition was also adopted as seen in the name of *Manugye Dhammathat* which is nothing but the Burmanized form of *Mānava Dharmashastra.*, although the similarity remains only in the title; its contents having been localized that it has become far from the Sanskritic original.

Despite of a plausible attempt by Dr. David Richardson who translated the *Manugye Dhammathat* into English as early as 1847, it is regrettable that so little has been done until recently to identify the extent to which the text had played in political culture of the subsequent Burmese kingdoms. The contribution of Professor Okudaira who has an admirable proficiency in Burmese, shall be found in the fact that he laboriously scrutinized different law texts thereby a solid foundation has been laid for the subsequent scholars to deepen their understanding of Buddhist polity of pre-modern Burma, all of which was organized upon the *Manugye Dhammathat* as its basis for legitimation.

All future researchers who wish to study the history of not only Burma but also those of other Theravāda Buddhist countries should be grateful to Professor Okudaira for his valuable contributions he made during the past decades in the field of textual study of the *Manugye Dhammathat* as seen in the following pages.

Yoneo ISHII
Emeritus Professor of Kyoto University

Contents

Foreword	7
ABBREVIATION	13
Glossary of Myanmar and Some Pāli & Sanskrit Terms	17
Preface	23
Acknowledgements	27
Introduction	30

Part I   Myanmar 1752-1819

Chapter I   Buddhist Dhamma and Secular Law — 36
- Section 1. Introduction of the Theravāda Buddhism — 36
- Section 2. Formation and Structure of the Theravāda Buddhist State — 37
- Section 3. Buddhist Theory and the Origin of Kingship — 38
- Section 4. Dhamma in the Structure of the Theravāda Buddhist State — 40
- Section 5. Compilation of the law book — 42
- Section 6. Buddhicisation of Manu's Tradition — 43
- Section 7. Dhammathat in the Theravāda Buddhist State — 44

Chapter II   The Genres of Myanmar Law Texts and the Dhammathat — 47
- Section 1. The Genres of Myanmar Law Texts — 47
- Section 2. The Dhammathat as the Major Source of law — 52

Chapter III   Palm-leaf and Parabaik Manuscripts of the Dhammathats — 56
- Section 1. Locations and Conditions of the Dhammathat Source Materials — 56
- Section 2. World-wide Collections of the Dhammathat Manuscripts — 57
- Section 3. Location of Palm-leaf and Some Parabaik Manuscripts at the Major Libraries — 58
- Section 4. Dhammathat in Indigenous Minority Buddhist Groups — 59

Chapter IV The Rise of the Konbaung Dynasty — 61
   Section 1. The Political Situation of the early Konbaung Period — 61
   Section 2. External Affairs — 63
   Section 3. Myanmar Involvement into the English-French Colonial Struggle — 65
   Section 4. Internal Affairs — 68

Chapter V Konbaung Consecration Ceremonies — 73
   Section 1. Origin of the Consecration Ceremony — 73
   Section 2. Theoretical Role of the *Muddha-beiktheik* Ceremony — 74
   Section 3. Establishment of King Badon's Style of the *Muddha-beiktheik* Ceremony — 76
   Section 4. The Ritual of the *Muddha-beiktheik* — 78
   Section 5. A Step toward the Institutionalization of the *Muddha-beiktheik* Ceremony — 80

Chapter VI *Manugye* as the Konbaung *Dhammathat* — 83
   Section 1. Compilation of the *Manugye Dhammathat* under King Alaunghpaya — 83
   Section 2. Characteristics of the *Manugye Dhammathat* — 84
   Section 3. Authorship of the *Manugye Dhammathat* — 86
   Section 4. Date of compilation — 88
   Section 5. A serious problem on several versions of the *Manugye Dhammathat (MD)* — 89

Chapter VII *Manugye* Becomes the English *Dhammathat* — 92
   Section 1. Outline of the history after the death of King Badon — 92
   Section 2. Dr. David Richardson — 92
   Section 3. The Translation of the *MD* by Dr. Richardson — 95
   Section 4. The use of the translation of the *MD* by the British authority — 96
   Section 5. King Mindon's Response: the First Printing press in Mandalay — 98

Part II The *Manugye Dhammathat (MD)*

Chapter VIII Two Different Editions of the *MD* — 102
   Section 1. The 1760 'MS' of the *MD*=The Richardson's Myanmar Text — 102

Section 2. The 1782 MS—A Variant of the 1760 'MS'	102
Section 3. Differences between the 1760 'MS' and 1782 MS	103
Section 4. Insertion of A New Preamble to the *MD*	106

Chapter IX 'Duties of Kings and Judges' of the *MD* (1782MS) — 110
Section 1. New Information added to the *MD* (1782 MS)	110
Section 2. The Duties of Kings	112
Section 3. Duties of Judges	114
Section 4. Witnesses	116

Chapter X Commentary on 'Duties of Kings and Judges' — 120
Section 1. Interpretation of the preamble to the *MD*	120
Section 2. Implication of the New Chapters of *the MD* (1782MS)	125
Section 3. Changes in the Role of the Myanmar Dhammathat in the early Konbaung Period	126
Section 4. Authorship of the 1782 MS	127
Section 5. The Sources of the Eleven Lists	128

Chapter XI 'Early Konbaung Thirty Rulings' and Some Additional Information in the *MD* (1782 MS) — 131
Section 1. Thirty rules added to the 1782 MS of the *MD* (1782 MS)	131
Section 2. Some additional Information described in the Chapter XVI	144

Chapter XII Commentary on 'Early Konbaung Thirty Rulings' and Some Additional Information in the *MD* (1782MS) — 148
Section 1. Insertion of 'the Thirty New Rules' in Chapter III of the *MD* (1782MS)	148
Section 2. Addition of Some Information	157

Part III Kingship and Law in the Early Konbaung Period

Chapter XIII Kingship and Constitution in the Eighteenth Century Myanmar — 160
Section 1. Framework of the Early Konbaung Polity	160
Section 2. Characteristics of the Early Konbaung Kingship	162
Section 3. Propagation of the *Yaza Dhamma* or Royal Obligations	164

Section 4. King Badon's Various Reformations	166
Section 5. Conclusion	170

Chapter XIV   Dhammathats and Law in the Eighteenth Century Myanmar   173

Section 1. Principles of the Judicial Policy	173
Section 2. Legal Procedure	174
Section 3. Proper Use of the Dhammathats	177
Section 4. Judicial Policy Incorporated into the New Chapters of *MD* (1782MS)	178
Section 5. How the Judges Used the Dhammathats in Court	181
Section 6. Conclusion	183

Concluding remarks and Epilogue   186

Footnotes	189
References	214
APPENDIX I	233
APPENDIX II	234
APPENDIX III	236
APPENDIX IV	238
Index	241

ABBREVIATION

AAL	*Alaung Mintaya-gyi Ayedawbon* by Letwe Nawyahta
AAT	*Alaung Mintaya-gyi Ayedawbon* by Twin Thin Taik-wun
ADP	*Atula Dhammathat Hpyathton*
AHP	*Amedaw Hpye Kyan*
AMA	*Alaung Mintaya Ameindaw-mya*
AMGA	*Alaung Mintaya-gyi Ameindaw-mya*
AWD	*Atthathanhkepa Wunnana Dhammathat*
BHHM	*Bama-pyi Hnit-paung Hnit-ya Hmat-tan*
B.L.R.	*Burma Law Report*
CED	*Collins English Dictionary*
CR	*Calcutta Review*
CV	*Cūlavaṃsa*
DBBL	*A Digest of the Burmese Law by Kinwun Mingyi*
DWD	*Dhammawilatha Dhammathat*
DOR	*Dalrymple's Oriental Repertory*
EIGD	*The East-India Register and Directory*

EIRAL	*The East India Register and Army List*
HMY	*Hmannan Mahayazawin-gyi*
HSTH	*Hman She Tak Hswe-daw Zin*
IB	*Inscriptions of Burma*
JASB	*Journal of Asiatic Society of Bengal*
JBED	*Judson's Burmese English Dictionary*
JBRS	*Journal of the Burma Research Society*
KLD	*Kawi Lekkana Dipani*
KBZ	*Konbaungzet Mahayazawin-daw-gyi*
KSD	*Kaingza Shwemyin Dhammathat*
K/W	Kyaw:(back) and Wun(face) of Palm-leaf manuscripts
KWMD	*King Wagaru's Manu Dhammasatthan*
LBK	*Lawka Byuha Kyan*
LMB	*Letwè Nawyahta i Muddha-beiktheik Hkan Ahkan-ana*
LMD (B)	*List of Microfilms Deposited in the Centre for East Asian Cultural Studies Part 8. Burma*
LMBM	*Letwè Nawyahta i Muddha-beiktheik Hkan Ahkan-ana*
L.B.R	*Lower Burma Rulings*
LOA	*A List of the Officers of the Army*
MD	*Manugye Dhammathat*

ABBREVIATION

ME	Myanmar calendar year
MED	*Myanmar-English Dictionary* by the Ministry of Education, Government of the Union of Myanmar
MKD	*Manu-kyetyo Dhammathat*
MMMHK	*Myanmar Mingala Min-hkan-daw*
MMOS	*Myanmar Min Okchok-pon Sadan*
MSHB	*Myanmar-sa Nyun-baung Kyan*
MSK	*Myanmar Swe-hson Kyan*
MTD	*Manuthaya Dhammathat*
MTSD	*Manuthaya Shwemyin Dhammathat*
MV	*Mahāvaṃsa*
MWD	*Manu Wunnana Dhammathat*
MWDD	*Mohaweikhsedani Dhammathat*
MY	*Mahayazawin-gyi* (written by U Kala)
MYD(=MRD)	*Manuyin Dhammathat*
MYK	*Mahayazathat-kyi*
NN	*Niti Niganduwa*
PBW	*Paper relating to the Burmese War*
PD	*Pyumin Dhammathat*
PNTB	Pāli Nīti Texts of Burma

PTS	*Pitaka Thamaing Sadan*
RMD	*Text, translation and notes of the Manugye Dhammathat* by Richardson
ROB	*The Royal Orders of Burma* (edited by Dr. Than Tun)
SEAR	*South East Asian Research*
SMKKS	*Shwebo Myone Kan Kyauksa*
TAS	*Thekkata Abhiṣeka Sadan*
TCD	*Thonze-chauk hsaung-dwè Dhammathat-gyi*
TMYT	*Thwinthin Myanmar Yazawin-thit*
TPTS	The Pāli Text Society
TLS	*Thathana Lingaya Sadan*
UCL	Universities' Central Library (Yangon)
UPUS	*U Po U Shaukhton (Hlyaukhton)*
W.P.D.	*The Working People's Daily*
YD	*Yazabala Dhammathat*
YKHP	*Yezajyo Kondaw Hpyathton* by Yandameik Kyaw Htin
YKM	*Yadanathinka Konbaung Maha Yazawin-Akyin*

Glossary of Myanmar and Some Pāli & Sanskrit Terms

Abhiṣēka (Sanskrit); *Abhiseka* (Pāli); (consecration ceremony)
Abhiseka Sadan (treatise on Consecration ceremony)
Agati. (evil practice)
Agati.-le:-ba: (Four Kinds of Corruption)
Aggan (value)
Akudho Kaung-hmu. (doing demerit)
Akyo:nga:-ba: (The Five Effects)
Alaung-Ariya (Buddha-to-be)
Alon Pyet thint thaw Thet-the Tit-hse Chauk-pa: (Sixteen Kinds of Person Who should be totally dissolved as a witness)
Ameindaw (Royal Order or Edict)
Amyit Taya: Hse-shit hkan:Tahse-shit-htan (the Eighteen Roots or the Eighteen Radical Laws)
Ana (power, authority)
Ana-zo (Executor)
Aparagoyana (the West Island)
Apareikha Niya. Taya: Hkunit-pa: (Seven Factors to Keep Prosperity (of the State from Deterioration)
Apay -Le:-ba: (Four Nether Worlds)
*Apay -ngay*è *:* (the Lower World, in a state of misfortune, Hell)
Aweitza (ignorance, illusion)
Ayudiga-beiktheik (consecration for long life)

Badda Kaba (=Gaba) (the good world, the Present world)
Badein-min Apya:Nga:ba: (the Five Pledges)
Balu: (ogre)
Baya-gati (Fear)
Bayin Ameindaw Pyandan : (king's edict)
Bedan (calamity)

Bedin (prediction, tales of six branches of knowledge)
Beiktheik (Consecration ceremony)
Be: Shit-pa: (Eight kinds of danger/Eight calamities
Boddhisatta (a being destined to attain fullest enlightenment, embryo Buddha, Buddha to be)
Bye-daik (royal secretariat; Privy Council Organized by around the Four-Junior Councillors)

Cakkavattin (Universal Monarch)

Dale.- htondan: upade (customary law)
Danan (property)
Dan Hse-ba: (Ten Types of Chastisement)
Daw: tha.- gati. (Anger)
Dethan (place)
Dhamma (Law of Buddha)
Dhammayaza (king of law)
Dharma (law, moral and religious Duty)
Dharmaśāstra (a code of law)
Dipinkara (=Dibinkaya, Dīpamkara) Buddha

Ekamsika (an order of monks who cover only one shoulder with robe)
Egayit (=Egarit) (Monarch)

Gayuna (compassion)
Gazathana (Elephant's throne)

Hkattiya-beiktheik (consecration for making the government over to the king)
Hsanda-gati. (Personal Desire)
Hkayaing-wun (Deputy Commissioner)
Hkwè-bon (partition of inheritance commentary)
Hkon-daw (a Bench, Lower Court)
Hkon-min: (a Judge for Local Court)
Hluttaw (Council of Ministers, Supreme Court)
Hlut-yon: Nga:-yat (Five Offices for Judicial Affairs in the Capital city)
Hpaya: kyaun:mye (religious land)
Hpaya:-laung: (One striving to attain Buddhahood)
Hpyathton: (=Siyinhton) (judicial rulings, collections of decision by the court)

Hnit-hku.-myauk-thaw: Ne-min: (The Second Sun of the Solar Dynasty)

Kalan (time)
Kaung:-hmu. (meritorious deed)
Kaung:-jyo: (good consequence)
Kudho (virtuous action or Merit)
Kudho- kan (=*kyamma, kama*) (one's deed, word or thought which predetermines one's future),
Kudo-kaung:-hmu. (virtuous action),
kyauk-sa (stone inscription)
kyun (slave)

Let-ma. Yun (executors who carries out his duty without any hesitation)
Let-yon (fighting ability)

Maha-padetha - Taya: Le-ba: (Four Basic Principles)
Makaung:-jyo: (bad consequence)
Maw:ha (ignorance, delusion)
Maw:ha-gati. (Ignorance)
Min:-dan (the king's punishment)
Min:-do. A:-daw Ga:-ba (Five Royal Strength)
Min:-do. i. Pyagade Hkunit-pa: (Seven Royal Fundamental Requirements of a Kingdom)
Min: - do. Kyin. Ya. thaw : Thingaha Taya: Le:-ba: (Four Laws of Assistance by the King)
Min: Kyin. Taya:Hse-ba: (Ten Royal Duties)
Min: Kyin. Taya: Hse-hnit-pa: (Twelve Royal Duties)
Min:nyi Min:tha: (members of the royal family)
Min:taya: (=Just king, Lawful king)
Muddha-beiktheik (consecration ceremony for taking the oaths to govern by laws / Supreme coronation ceremony)
Muddha-beiktheik hkan min: (The king who practiced the *Muddha-beiktheik*)
Mu:daw-mat-taw (King's Counsellor)
Mye-daing (Land officer or surveyor)
Myint.- Mo-Taung (Mount Meru situated in the center of the Buddhist World where the gods (=devas, nats) dwell)
myitta (love, kindness, benevolence)
Myo. i. Asa Le:-ba (Four kinds of (Subsistence for a City)
Myo. i. Inga Hkunit-pa: (Seven Characteristics for a <Strong> City)

Myo.-thugyi: (=dhagyi:) (headman of a town)
Myo.-yon (town's office)
Myo.-wun (governor of a town)

Nat-ein (shrine)
Nauk-yon (Criminal Court dealing with the queen)
*Ne-min- do. i. Ahset-anwe (*descendant of the Sun or the Solar dynasty*)*
Nga:-ba: Thila. (Five Precepts)
nge-jyo nge-na (faults or crimes committed during childhood or youth)
nirvāna (=neibban) (attainment of the final emancipation)
nissaya (a word for word or phrase for phrase translation from Pāli to a vernacular)
nwa: kyaun:dha: (cowherd)

ossa (property)

Papathat (law of vice)
Parabaik (manuscript written on <Shan>paper)
Parupana (Two Shoulders Robe)
Pe (palm-leaf manuscript)
peitta (a departed ghost, one of the four types of hell)
Pitakat Thon: bon (Three Sacred Buddhist Scriptures)
Ponna puroheit)(Brahmin)
Pubhavideha (the East Island)
Pyi-so: (ruler)

Sachi-sama (clerical staff)
Sakka (=*Dhaja*) (the Hindu God Indra which appears in Buddhist Scriptures as *Sakka*)
Sangha (the Religious Order)
Sawbwa (Shan Chief)
Sekkya-wade-min: (=*Cakkavattin*)(the Universal Monarch)
sekkyawala dadaing (boundary wall of the universe)
She.-yon (the East Court or the Criminal Court relating to the capital city)
She.- yon Sadan: (East Court Manual)
Shwe-daik (the Royal Treasury)
Shwe - wun (Officer in Charge of the Royal Treasury)
Sit Inga Le:- ba: (Four Components of the Armed Forces)
Sit-kè (a lieutenant general)

Sit-tan (Inquest collected by the Officers dispatched by the Central Government)
Sit-thugyi: (=Sit-dhagyi:)(Commander in Chief)
Sit-thi Thu-yè (=Sit-the Tha-yè) (warrior)

Taw-kè (forest chief)
Tayama.-taya: Siyin-yè (Judgement for civil law cases)
Taya: Siyinhton (Rulings/Precedents)
Taya Thagyi (=Thugyi)(judge)
Taya-yon-daw (Hight Court)
Thakara-beiktheik (consecration for the prosperity of the kingdom)
thahte-thagywe (richman)
thamadi (Attainment of a concentration of the mind)
Thathanabaing (Primate, Head of Religious Order))
Thathana-daw (Buddhist Religion)
Thekkata Abhitheka Sadan (Sankrit treatise for consecration)
thet-the (witness)
Thenapati (General)
Thon:-ya / Hpan:ya / Let-ya (Prisoner of war)
Thati. (=Dhadi.)(attentiveness /mindfulness)
thattawa (=*dhadawa*)(a sentient being or creature)
Thihathana (Lion's throne)
Thiripawethana-beiktheik (consecration for the increase of reputation)
Tingaha Wuthtu. Taya: Le:-ba: (Four Kinds of Assistance)

Ubout - ne. (Sabbath day)
Upayaza (the Crown Prince)
Upayaza-beiktheik (consecration for appointing the successor of the king)

Weikzaya beiktheik (consecration for victory of war)

Yadana Ko:-ba: :(Nine Gems)
Yaza (=Rāja) (Ruler, King)
Yaza- di - yaza (=(*Rāja-dhi-rāja*)(King of Kings)
Yaza-dhamma (Rules for Royal Observance)
Yaza-niti. (=Rāja-nīti)(Science of political ethics, treatise on politics)
Ywa Lugyi: (village elderly person)
Ywa-thugyi (=Dhagyi) (village head man)

Zan (a super natural power/a certain attainment or state of mind)
Zayat (rest house)
Zeya-beiktheik (consecration for victory of war)

Preface

Okudaira's initial move into the detailed study of individual texts was his 1984 article on Kaingza Manuraja, author of the best-known of 17th century law texts. During the 1630s Kaingza attempted to modernize Burmese law on rational grounds. In the long term only a few of his reforms were successful. Okudaira demonstrated two things: that Kaingza had been constrained by the legal discourse of his predecessors, and that Kaingza had nonetheless found room to innovate within that tradition. Okudaira applied the same method to a different dhammathat in the later part of his contribution to Barry Hooker's *Classical Laws of Southeast Asia* [1986]. Everyone before him who had written on Richardson's *Manugye* (1847) treated it as representative of Burmese Law as a whole. Because *Manugye* was the only dhammathat to have been translated in full into English, it had been misunderstood as Burma's *ur*–text (the work that initiated its entire tradition). Starting in 1986 and culminating with this volume, Okudaira has shown us how to read *Manugye* as a product of its time and place. Its political context was one of dynastic change. Its cultural context was the revival in classical scholarship that a steady rise in the standard of living over the previous century had made possible. *Manugye*'s compilers made decisions as to which bits of written law to put in, and which to exclude. Okudaira explains how their editorial choices reflected the political imperatives of their day.

Alaunghpaya, the founding king of a new dynasty, had his courtiers modify existing theories of law and state so as to justify kingship in a new way. We may respect his endeavours as generating political philosophy, or we condemn them as spreading propaganda. Okudaira's analysis in this volume persuades me towards the former course. The Preamble to *Manugye* (1760) innovates in the same way as the 18 th century Europeans political philosophers innovated, which was by drawing on a fresh classical theme. The Preamble gives much more prominence to the Canonical story of Mahasammata the first king than its predecessor dhammathats. Its author developed the canonical theme into a full-blown sociology of Burma's present institutions of law and state. It was because their society had been plagued by its first thief that Mahasammata was chosen by the populace to be their first king. The people and Mahasammata made an agreement to replace the people's anarchical freedom-from-control with a subjection-to-the-control of Mahasammata. Whether this is fully equivalent to European social contact theory is a moot point, which Steven Collins and I debated a decade ago. But certainly *Manugye*'s elaborate version of the Mahasammata story shares important themes in common with the early modern Social Contract theories produced by Francis Bacon, Thomas Hobbes and John Locke. One of our current debates discusses whether we can talk of an 'early modern' period in Southeast Asian history. It follows from Okudaira's analysis that late eighteenth century Burma was, in this respect at least, early modern. Alaunghpaya's version of the Theravāda Buddhist State shared some social contract sub-theme with Thomas Jefferson's ideas about a constitutional republic, and with Jean-Jacques Rousseau's ideas of popular sovereignty. This invite a comparison between Burma and Europe: we might as well carry it out under the banner of 'early modernity'. Mason Hoadley's recent work on 18 th century law texts of Java has led him to similar conclusions.

Towards the end of the 1980s Okudaira discovered a palm leaf ms. In a Rangoon library that was to double the effectiveness of his methodology. What he unearthed was the full text of a 1782 *Manugye* prepared as a part of King Badon's accession to the throne. Let us call it 'the second edition', though this begs some chronological issues. The second edition manuscript was completed on 25th June 1782, and deposited in the royal library. It must have remained there through most of the nineteenth century, for there are indications that it was consulted in the 1870s by precolonial Burma's last Minister for Law. After the British conquest of Mandalay in 1885, the manuscript was moved to the Bernard Free Library in Rangoon where it escaped scholarly attention for a further century. Badon's second edition of 1782 contains three new chapters, one of which is devoted to political theory. Okudaira relates the innovations of 1782 to the changed political and cultural context twenty years on from Alaunghpaya's reign. In this book he develops a stereoscopic vision, with one eye focused on 1760 and the other eyes on 1782. Thus equipped, Okudaira can show us how Burmese political philosophy developed during the first quarter century of Konbaung rule. He gives us an intellectual history linking changing ideas of law and state to the changing political situation. Fortuitously, Euan Bagshawe has recently made the final stages of the Konbaung evolution available, by putting his translation (2002)of Hpo Hlaing's *Rajadhamma sangaha* online. As recently as the 1980s, Stanley Tambiah and Richard Gombrich could write books on Theravāda politics and statecraft that dealt with Thai, Lankan and Pāli sources, but said nothing about Burma. After Okudaira's and Bagshawe's efforts, there can no longer be any excuses for ignorance of Burma's political theory. This is not just a matter of filling in geographical gaps. The Burmese political tradition seems more elaborate and more constitutional than of Thailand or Lanka.

I mentioned some chronological issue that surround the *Manugye* texts. On the present state of the evidence, Okudaira's hypothesis that the 1782 text is a second edition, and Richardson's shorter version the first edition, cannot be proved beyond all doubt. Probably he is right, but if he were wrong, it would follow that an English colonial officer deliberately suppressed the chapters of rajadhamma lists. Which would raise questions about the trustworthiness of imperial knowledge, especially its knowledge of native law. Was it politically expedient for the English to hide the existence of Burmese political thought? My work on the colonial legal historians of 1880s engages with this issue. Neither John Jadrine nor Emil Forchhammer was entirely scrupulous in their work on Burmese Law; several of their findings were distorted by the needs of imperial propaganda. Maybe Richardson yielded to similar pressure. Or maybe not: he, in the 1840s, was far more knowledgeable about Burmese culture, and sympathetic to it, than were Jardine or Forchhammer in the 1880s. Some useful research on Richardson has appeared recently, but it has not shed light on how he translated *Manugye*. Let us hope that the relevant correspondence will one day turn up in the colonial archives. Okudaira's hypothesis that Badon's text is the second edition is a probability, but it would be useful to have it confirmed as a certainty.

Okudaira is a Japanese historian of the pre-modern Burma. Nonetheless, this volume contains important lessons for those engaged in the construction of Burma's forth-coming constitution. He points to the central place which Mahasammata occupies in early Konbaung theory. This means a central place for social contract sub-theme that is quite incompatible with despotism. Since the eighteenth century (and probably for much longer) Burma has developed an ethics of government and adjudication that draws heavily on the Pāli Buddhist canon. At this stage and times when a new constitution is being planned to be instituted, Mahasammata should be retained with a few adaptations or alterations to suit the place and the time.

Andrew Huxley
Senior Lecturer
Department of Law
University of London (SOAS)
12 January 2008

Acknowledgements

I would like to express my sincere gratitude to all the persons concerned for my study on the legal history of Myanmar. First of all, I owe a great debt of gratitude to Dr. Yoneo Ishii (the late eminent Professor of the Kyoto University, Japan) for his constant encouragement and supervision in all aspects of my Myanmar historical and legal studies from the viewpoint of Southeast Asian area studies. I cannot find the proper words to express my sincere thanks to him for his help and for providing the most valuable 'Foreword' to this book. Sincere thanks also go to Japanese Professors Yoshiaki Ishizawa (former President of the Sophia University in Tokyo), the late Professor Masaji Chiba and Emeritus Professor (of the University of Tokyo) Toshio Yamasaki, the late Professor Genichi Yamasaki (of the Kokugakuin University) and Emeritus Professor (of Tokai University) Nobuyuki Watase in Japan for their generous advice and suggestions for my legal study on Myanmar throughout the1980s and 1990s. I also owe much to Emeritus Professor Katsuro Koga (Osaka University) who has been a constant encouragement for my academic research since my university life began in the1960s. Heartfelt thanks to Professor Kazuo Katayama for his advice in relation to Pāli language and canonical books.

A great debt of gratitude is also owed to Professor M.B. Hooker who generously encouraged my legal study on Myanmar and kindly invited me to contribute to his 1986 publication, entitled *Laws of Southeast Asia* (Vol. I- *Pre-modern Texts*).

In addition, I must pay tribute to the Southeast Asian Studies academic staff at the School of Oriental and African Studies (SOAS), University of London during my stay at the school in 1998-1999, for their assistance and support. Among them, I would like to express my special gratitude to the late Mr. Andrew Huxley, Senior Lecturer (later promoted to Professorship) in the Department of Law (SOAS) who assisted me as a part of the joint researchers on the Myanmar legal history and provided valuable and useful comments and suggestions on my earlier and later drafts, from the viewpoint of Myanmar legal history. He also wrote an invaluable preface to this book which is more than it deserves. My profound gratitude is also given to Mr. John Okell, the then Senior Lecturer in Burmese Studies, who accepted me as a research fellow in the Department of Languages and Cultures of Southeast Asia for his advice in general on Myanmar language and culture. I also wish to express my sincere thanks to Professor Robert H. Taylor (the then Vice Chancellor of the University of Buckingham) and the then Professor (of Anthropology) Andrew Thurton who advised me in many ways and cooperated with my study.

My old friends and scholars, such as Mrs. Ann Alott, the then Senior Lecturer in Burmese language and Culture at SOAS, Dr. Gustaff Houtman (Dutch Antoropologist), Dr. Tilman Frasch (German), Dr. Michael Charney (American, now Professor at SOAS) Dr. Jacques P. Leider (Luxembourger historian), Professor Donald Stadtner (California, USA) and Professor Sunait Chutintaranond of the Chulalongkorn University in Thailand also deserve high praise and thanks for their valuable discussions and comments.

A great debt is also owed to some Myanmar scholars, particularly the late Professor Dr. Than Tun (eminent Myanmar historian), Professor Dr. Hla Pe (SOAS) and U Maung Maung Tin (the late retired Lecturer of Mandalay University), U Aung Than Tun (the late barrister-at–law and legal historian as well), Professor Daw Ni Ni Myint and U Tun Aung Chain, both the former Directors of SEAMEO-CHAT, Professors Dr. Khin Maung Nyunt, U Sai Aung Tun, Dr. Toe Hla, Dr. Kyaw Win, Dr. Khin Hla Han, U Mya Han, U Thein Hlaing, U Kyaw, all from the members of the Myanmar Historical Commission, and Sai Kam Mong, a Shan Historian, Daw Mar Lay in Myanmar language and literature for their valuable comments and suggestions on Pre-modern Myanmar literature, history or legal history.

My praise and appreciation also go to the libraries staff in London and districts in the United Kingdom, particularly to Mrs. Patricia Herbert, retired curator of the British Library, Dr. John Guy, the then deputy curator at Victoria and Albert Museum and Dr. Michael J. Pollock, the then Librarian at the Royal Asiatic Society for their cooperation in providing me with Myanmar source materials. I also owe much gratitude to some Myanmar librarians, such as: Dr. Thaw Kaung, former Chief Librarian of the Universities' Central Library (UCL), the late Daw May Kyi Wynn, who was a librarian there and later curator at the Library of the Northern Illinois University in U.S.A. and the staff of the Library, U Khin Maung Tint, ex-Chief Librarian of the National Library in Yangon and his staff, and also the staff of the other libraries; such as UHRC (Universities Historical Research Centre), the Institute of the Pāli Studies, the Resources Centre for Ancient

Myanmar Manuscripts (RCAMM), the University of Mandalay, and the Cultural Museum in Mawlamyine. Also, special thanks go to the individuals of Myanmar nationals whom I am deeply indebted to.

I owe much to Daw Khin Yi who resided in Japan for more than thirty years and Daw T.S. who resided in U.K. at that time who were well versed in English assisted me a lot in translating Myanmar legal texts into English. I sincerely thank both U Than Kywe, one of the leading artists of Myanmar for drawing several pictures of the mythology on kingship described in the first chapter of the *Manugye Dhammathat,* and U Myint Soe, a Myanmar artist who kindly introduced U Than Kywe to me.

I would like to express my genuine gratitude to both the Japan Foundation and the Matsushita International Foundation for their generous financial support without which I could not have accomplished this research work during my stay in the United Kingdom from 1998 to1999 and the continuous research after the period until today.

Lastly I would like to say sincere thanks to my wife, Yasuko and two daughters: Fumiko and Akiko, who have always been supporting me in my Myanmar studies until today.

Introduction

In 1986, Professor M.B. Hooker published the first volume of a unique book entitled *Laws of Southeast Asia*. It contained a small contribution from me on the Myanmar (Burmese)[1] legal history under the title of 'The Burmese Dhammathat'. My aim, not as a jurist, but as historian, was to provide general overview of the Myanmar Law with a special reference to a pre-modern law book entitled "Dhammathat", particularly from the aspect of legal history. In this book, as Professor Hooker made a useful suggestion that "legal historians to South-East Asia should address their minds to the issue as a specific subject for study in near future" [Hooker 1986: 14]. Inspired by him, I shall address in this book the role the Dhammathat played in the structure of 'The Theravāda Buddhist State'. I shall examine the period from the reign of King Alaunghpaya, the founder of Konbaung dynasty, to the sixth monarch, King Badon (commonly known as Bodawhpaya), during the period from 1752 to 1819 A.D. from the viewpoint of historical research.

The so-called 'Theravāda Buddhist State' has existed for many centuries in mainland Southeast Asian countries, such as Myanmar (Burma), Thailand, Cambodia and Laos, where rulers introduced Theravāda Buddhism as their official religion from Sri Lanka, where this religion was established as monastic Buddhism. Sri Lankan Buddhism had in fact made a major contribution to the formation of the 'Theravāda Buddhist State'. My main interest lies in the 'State' constructed by King Alaunghpaya and perfected under King Badon (Bodawhpaya). Similar state structures had existed in Myanmar since the latter part of the eleventh century of Bagan (Pagan)[2], when Theravāda Buddhism was introduced by King Anawyahta (=Anawrahta) from the Mon Kingdom in the south where it had already flourished.

The Myanmar word, 'Naingan' or 'Naingan-daw' denotes the State. In general, the State refers to the constitution of a sovereign political power, a community that the political power governs, and the territory which the political power and the community occupy. Professor Robert Taylor defined it as "the only institution which is expected to determine its relationship with other bodies and to determine for other institutions in civil society their relationships with each others". He does so commenting on Tilly's view that a state is "an organization which controls the population occupying a defined territory in so far as (1)it is differentiated from other organizations operating in the same territory; (2)it is autonomous; (3)it is centralized; and (4)its divisions are formally coordinated with one another" [Taylor1987: 9]. Indeed, the State in Myanmar from the Bagan period [1044-1287][3] to the Konbaung Dynasty in the 18th and 19th centuries was, as Taylor stated, "determined to ensure that there was no economic and social mobilization outside its control" [*ibid.*: 8]. Unlike the modern Myanmar State, the successive dynasties in the premodern period of Myanmar continually attempted to restrain the local power and to strengthen the power of the central state. The pre-modern State of Myanmar, like other Southeast Asian states, did not occupy a defined territory in a strict sense of territory demarcated by precise borders [See *ibid.*: 10].

Professor Yoneo Ishii defined this style of state as 'the Buddhist State' in which the king-the supreme defender of Buddhism-supported the Sangha (Order of the Buddhist monks), while the Sangha, through correct observance of the precepts, transmitted the Dhamma (Law of Buddha), and the Dhamma legitimated the king [Ishii 1986: 46]. This applies to all the kingdoms of Myanmar. The pre-modern 'Theravāda Buddhist State' of Myanmar functioned by this triangular relationship between the King, the Sangha and the Dhamma. The legitimacy of the king in Myanmar's rule was derived within this trianglular relationship [See also Okudaira 1999: 465]

The Dhammathat is a collection of customary rules and previous court decisions, first compiled during the first half of the thirteenth century in the Bagan period. The original manuscript of the Dhammathat was copied and revised as time went on. The numbers of the Dhammathat gradually increased until the end of the Konbaung Dynasty. Their principal use was to aid a king or a judge in arbitrating Myanmar Buddhist social dispute..

An eighteenth century law book entitled *Manugye Dhammathat* enjoins the king to follow "The Ten Royal Duties", or "The Twelve Royal Duties" [See 1782MS: also see Chapter IX in this book], such as not to do wrong against the Three Gems: Buddha, Dhamma and Sangha, to observe the Five Precepts and other principles. This clearly shows that the legitimacy of rule by a king was traditionally derived from the Dhamma. Nevertheless, the law of the kingdom of Myanmar, which was represented by the Dhammathat was not ecclesiastical but secular in principle. The Dhammathat was not a principal guide for the king to administer the state. In this respect, this book mainly discusses the role which the Myanmar Dhammathat played in a 'Theravāda Buddhist State' structure in the first half of the Konbaung Dynasty from

1752 to 1819. My particular emphasis is on the extra chapters added to the 1782 copy of the *Manugye Dhammathat*.

To speak of *Manugye Dhammathat* meant, until recently, to speak of Richardson's *Manugye*. It is the Myanmar text with English translation and published by Dr. David Richardson[4] in 1847. There is no mention in Richardson's texts of the date of the manuscript which he used for translation. According to John Jardine (the Judicial Commissioner of British Burma in the late nineteenth century), the manuscript which Richardson translated seems to have been copied between 1760 and 1765 [Forchhammer 1885: 19] under King Alaunghpaya or Naungdawgyi. Another version of the manuscript of the *Manugye Dhammathat* which was copied in 1782 at the beginning of King Badon's reign can be found in the National Library in Yangon. Richardson's Myanmar text consists of 14 chapters, while the 1782 version of the manuscripts provides an extra two chapters, adding the kingship and state organizations.

The *Manugye Dhammathat* (1782MS), which has been well preserved in the National Library in Yangon, was mainly used for this study. The focus of this book is on what we can learn from these two extra chapters of the manuscript. Through this analysis, we shall examine the kingship and law during the first half of the Konbaung period. My premise is that the *Manugye Dhammathat* (1782 MS) must have played an important role in the structure of 'the Theravāda Buddhist State'.

I had reviewed most of the major works on the Myanmar legal history conducted by distinguished Europeans as well as indigenous scholars in the nineteenth and twentieth centuries in the section of 'Historiography' in Hooker's *Laws of Southeast Asia*. Some works on the legal history of Myanmar have been written since then, particularly by Andrew Huxley, the late Professor of Jurisprudence, who had been energetically conducting research work on the 'Buddhist Law' in the Theravāda Buddhist countries, especially, Myanmar. The late Professor Dr. Than Tun, a distinguished historian of Myanmar, wrote a thesis on the *Manugye Dhammathat* (1985).[5] The late Dr. Nai Pan Hla, the well-known scholar for Mon history and culture published the Mon Dhammasāt Texts (1992) and Sai Kham Mong, a Shan-learned scholar wrote a book on the Shan Thammasat (2012)[6] also surely deserve special places in the studies of the legal history of Myanmar. Their works offer useful hints for a better understanding of the *Manugye Dhammathat*.

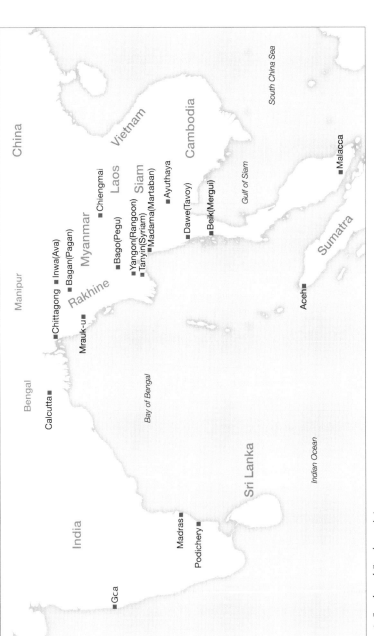

Figure 1. South and Southeast Asia

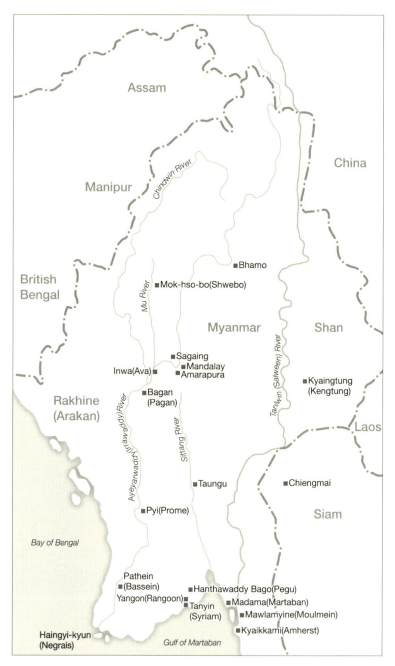

Figure 2. Map of Early Konbaung Myanmar

Part I
Myanmar 1752-1819

Chapter I
Buddhist Dhamma and Secular Law

1. Introduction of the Theravāda Buddhism

It is commonly accepted that the spread of Buddhism to countries outside of India can be dated from the third century B.C., when the Religious Missions during the reign of King Aśoka were dispatched to nine regions under his patronage [MHV XII 3-8: 82]. Out of these regions, Sri Lanka, during the reign of King Dēvanampiya Tissa, was one of the regions to where Thera Mahinda, who is believed as a son of King Aśoka, was sent on a mission [See MHV XIII & IV]. Since then, Buddhism became the accepted religion of the country with the patronage of the King and popular enthusiasm. Thus Sri Lanka gradually became a centre of the Theravāda Buddhism and from there it spread to mainland Southeast Asia, such as Myanmar, Thailand, Cambodia and Laos, etc. Among several schools of Theravāda Buddhism in Sri Lanka, the Mahā-vihāra school, the most conservative one, despite the existence of more progressive schools of Abhayagiri-vihāra and others, has remained orthodox and prominent as the major centre of Theravāda Buddhism under the royal patronage from the twelfth century onwards. This style of state was apparently modeled upon King Aśoka's politics based on Dharma (=Law) [See Sarkisyanz 1965: 23-32; also see Okudaira 1999: 466]. We can call this Aśokan conception of the state as 'Buddhist State'.

In relation to the religious and cultural contact between Sri Lanka and mainland Southeast Asian countries little evidence is found prior to the eleventh century. However, there are suggestions from the eleventh century, there are evidences to indicate that religious and cultural, and even political contact between Sri Lanka and mainland Southeast Asian countries existed. From this century onwards, mainland Southeast Asian countries came into close contact with Sri Lanka, which played an immeasurably important role in the introduction and development of the Theravāda Buddhism and the formation of the 'Theravāda Buddhist State' there [CV II 1927: LXXVI 10-

15: 64-65/ 37-38: 67/ LXXX7-8: 126, etc.; HMY I 1921: 285-28, etc.].
Particularly, the religious intercourse was frequent between Sri Lanka and
Myanmar [CVLX4-7: 214-215/LXX VI 73-75: 70; HMY I: 261, etc.; see
also Godakumbura 1966: 145-162; Hazra *ibid.* 83-130/ Okudaira *ibid.*:
467].

2. Formation and Structure of the Theravāda Buddhist State

Richard Gombrich has stated that the "History of Theravāda Buddhism seen from the point of view taken by the tradition itself is the history of the Sangha" [Gombrich 1988: 87], At first, 'Sangha' referred to communities of Buddhist monks residing in monasteries, and later also came to mean the Order of the Buddhist monks. "The Sangha can be defined as an organization form to provide an environment in which its members could more effectively perform their religious practices" [Ishii 1986: 5]. These practices are not performed haphazardly. They are governed by norms recoginized and upheld collectively by the Sangha or the group members, which are called the Dhamma or doctrines and Vinaya or precepts preached by the Buddha [*ibid.*: 10].

The king was the most powerful supporters of the Sangha in Sri Lanka, and the Theravāda Buddhist countries in mainland Southeast Asia. King Aśoka had long been the model for rulers of all the Buddhist countries, such as Sri Lanka, Myanmar, Thai, Cambodia and Laos, etc. "The kings of Ceylon [Sri Lanka] considered themselves to stand in the tradition and to be responsible to the well-being of the Sangha" [Gombrich ibid.: 160]. The kings of mainland Southeast Asian countries supported the Sangha in various manners, beginning with building monasteries, donating land and other properties to the Sangha. For example, in 1057A.D., King Anuruddha /Anawrahta/ of Myanmar attacked Thaton, the capital city of Mon in southern Myanmar, and brought the sacred relics, *Ti-pitakas* (Pāli Canon)and five hundred monks to Bagan (Pagan), the then capital of Bagan dynasty [See TLS 1956: 92-93; HMY 1921: 271-275] and thereby made a major contribution to the development of Theravāda Buddhism in Myanmar [Okudaira *ibid.*: 468].

In short, a style of the Indian Buddhist state which was established by King Aśoka was transformed into the Sinhalese (Pāli) Buddhist style after introduction of the Theravāda Buddhism to Sri Lanka. This style which we may call 'Theravāda Buddhist Polity' was again transplanted to mainland Southeast Asia and firmly established there. Professor Ishii remarks that this new cultural phenomenon appeared in mainland Southeast Asia after the thirteenth century should be defined as a 'Sinhalization' or 'Pāli-ization' based on the fact that the Theravāda Buddhism was primarily developed in Sri Lanka and that it was transmitted to various places in Southeast Asia through the medium of Pāli language [Ishii 1883: 20]. This phenomenon in mainland Southeast Asia was the one which followed after 'Indianization' since 1st-2nd centuries to 5th-6th centuries [Coedès 1968][7](See Table 1).

3. Buddhist Theory and the Origin of Kingship

The *Manugye Dhammathat* was one of the most popular law books in eighteenth century Myanmar. According to its preamble which is reminiscent of the *Aggañña Suttanta*,[8] it narrates: "the original inhabitants of the world, having eaten the fragrant earth for a long time, became passionately covetous and expressed enmity and consequently the rich soil disappeared. So they were obliged to cultivate crops, each having the share of the land marked off for his own labour. A dishonest person, fearing that his own share would be consumed, stole and ate the share of another. Thus, the first crime was committed. Then, there arose innumerable and endless disputes. In consequence, the people assembled and elected a person who would be able to restore law and order to the community. In this way, the perfect one, whose name was Manu, was elected as their king, and called Mahathamada (corresponding to Mahā Sammata in Pāli). The people gave him power to rule and command revenue. The people conferred upon him ceremonial rites. He was called Mahathamada because he was 'the Great Elected One'. He was called Hkattiya because of his dominion over the land and Yaza as well because of his ability to instruct people according to the laws" [RMD I 1847: 6-7].

Jayasekera, a Sri Lankan legal historian, understands this to mean that "chosen by the whole people Vasetta is what is meant by Mahā Sammata or the Great Elect was the first standing phase to arise for such a one. Lord of the Field is what is meant by Khattiya [Hkattiya]. So Khattiya [Hkattiya] or Noble was the next expression to arise. He charms others by the norms-by what ought (to charm)-what is meant by Raja; so this was the third standing phrase to arise. Thus then Vasettha was the origin of this social circle of Nobles according to the ancient primordial phrase (by which they were known" [Jayasekera 1984: 110]. Sri Lankan kings claimed descent from Mahāsammata and also from Buddha's family who belonged to the Sakyan clan.

Chapter I — Buddhist Dhamma and Secular Law

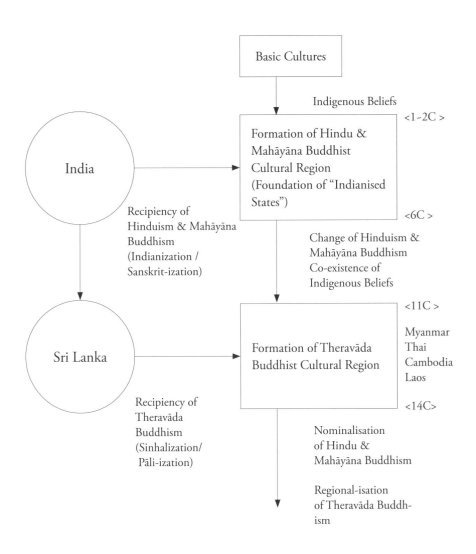

Table 1: Process of the Recipiency of Alien Religious Cultures and their Vicissitudes in mainland Southeast Asia

The Mahā Sammata claim of kings who were not of Sakya descent was probably meant to show that they were Buddhist kings who accepted the Buddhist theory of kingship and they were continuing the Buddhist traditions [Jayasekera *ibid*: 112].

In the first part of the preamble, it seems strange that Manu, the original name for King Mahathamada is given as Manu, a name associated with Hindu idea. As Jayasekera says, it is probable that the laws of Manu or part of it came into the Myanmar legal system through the spread of Sanskrit learning [Jayasekera *ibid:* 112] during the earlier period of the Mon kingdom of Ramaññadesa alias Mon cultural region in southern Myanmar. We find Myanmar kings of successive dynasties claiming descent from Manu identified with Mahathamada in the *Manugye Dhammathat* described as the lineal descendant from the sun (*ne-min: do i. ahset-anwe*) even after the introduction of Theravāda Buddhism into Bagan in the eleventh century [See Okudaira *ibid*.: 471].

4. Dhamma in the Structure of the Theravāda Buddhist State

The constitution of Buddhism is manifested in the belief of three Gems: the Buddha, the Dhamma and the Sangha. The Buddha, whose name before renounciation of the world was Gotama Siddhattha [Siddharta], is the founder of Buddhism. The Dhamma is the entire collection of his teachings, and the Sangha is the association of monks who follows those teachings. Theravāda Buddhism is propagated by the Sangha through communities. Hence, the Sangha's role is of primary importance in such a community as a part of the State that also constitutes a political power exercised by a secular leader who govern the territory where this community is included. Buddhism has a socio-political factor or constituent when 'the Buddhist State' is established under a Buddhist King as a territory where the community follows the Dhamma of Buddha through the guidance of the Sangha. The relationship between the King, the Dhamma, the Sangha in such a 'Buddhist State' is as follows: 'the king supports the Sangha, the sangha transmits the Dhamma, and the Dhamma legitimates the monarchy' [Ishii *ibid*.: 46]. (See Table 2) This type of 'Buddhist State' can be found in such mainland Southeast Asian countries as Myanmar, Thailand, Cambodia and Laos. [also see Okudaira *ibid*. 471-472]. Dhamma basically means the Law or Teachings of the Buddha. Its meaning has been expanded to social custom regarded as not only religious but also moral duty. Taya, a Myanmar word, corresponding to

Chapter I — Buddhist Dhamma and Secular Law

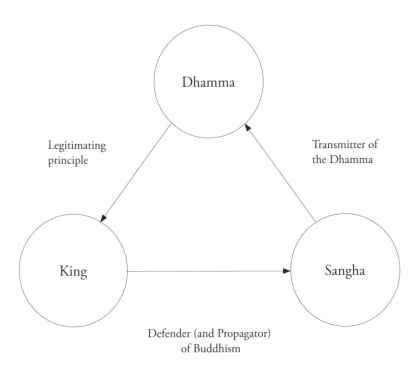

Table 2 : Basic Structure of the Theravāda Buddhist State
[A partial revision of the original source by Ishii (p.81, 1975) and its English translation (p.47) by P. Hawkes (1986)]

Dhamma in Pāli, means 'the laws of the moral world collectively, or any particular moral principle of law, or that which accords with the laws of the moral world, or the established system of just retribution, and even right, equity and justice' [See JBED, 1966: 470]. In the kingdoms which accepted Theravāda Buddhism as the official religion for the rulers, Dhamma functioned as a check on the king's tendency towards despotism. It was the ultimate criterion or standard judgment in the Buddhist society.

5. Compilation of the law book

Dharmaśāstra is the general name of the documents of the ancient Indian Law. Among these, *Mānāva-Dharmaśāstra*, or *Manu-smṛti*, is generally known as the Code of *Manu*. It is said to have been promulgated by Manu, a semi-divine being and law-giver. It contains the customary laws that were in practice among the people at that time. It is more religious than secular. As is well known, the Code of *Manu*, as well as other later forms of the Dharmaśāstra, such as *Yājñavalkya, Nārada, Brhaspati, Katyāyana,etc*, and their commentaries, spread to the surrounding countries, having great impact on the development of the legal history in those countries [Okudaira *ibid*. 468-469]. In the countries influenced by Theravāda Buddhism, such as Myanmar, Thailand, Cambodia and Laos, the diffusion of Dharmaśāstras helped create an incentive to compile the customary laws unique to the various indigenous races. In the process of compiling them, the form of Dharmaśāstras was taken as a model by using their *Vyavahāra*, which deals with the administration of justice proper, as the frame work for the new book of law. At the same time, the Brahmanical elements of Dharmaśāstra were replaced by the Buddhist ones and were written as a book of law for the Buddhist laymen. The result was that Dhammasāt in Mon, Dhammathat in Myanmar, Phrathammsāt in Thai and Phrathammasāt Būhan in Lao, Preah Toammasah in Khmer were compiled in respective countries. [See Table 3] There are frequent mentions of *Manu-smṛti* in the Sri Lankan chronicles such as *Cūlavaṃsa* [CV-pt. II 1953: 154, See Okudaira 1984: 25-27]. However, the Sri Lankans may not have codified their own customary laws [NN 1880: Tambiah 1968: 34].[9]

In Myanmar, the customary laws were probably put into book form by the first half of the thirteenth century [Frasch 1994: 46&53]. Strictly speaking, this law book was not a code but a collection of customary rules and precedents. It was given the name Dhammasatthan or Dhammasattha in Pāli and Dhammathat in Myanmar. Forchhammer suggested that before compilation of the Dhammathat, the Dharmaśāstras were brought prior to the tenth century, to the dominion of the Mons, who were earlier settlers in Myanmar [Forchhammer 1885: 61].[10] Robert Lingat, a distinguished French legal historian, insisted that the Dhammathat was compiled at first in Pāli by the Mon Buddhist scholars either at Bagan or Pegu (=Bago) for the Myanmar [Lingat 1950: 14].[11] This original law book was often copied, revised, and also translated into the vernacular in the succeeding dynasties of Myanmar toward the end of the nineteenth century. Significant numbers of them are known [See PTS 1882 No.1602-1704; TDA: 4-10]. As time went by, they became gradually influenced by Buddhism, particularly during the Konbaung dynasty in 18-19th centuries. In the Myannmar Dhammathat may be found the conceptual nucleus of the traditional law [Okudaira *ibid*.: 469-470].

6. Buddhicisation of Manu's Tradition

The name of *Manu* appeared throughout the Southeast Asian legal literature. In Myanmar, the preamble to the eighteenth century *Manugye Dhammathat* uses Manu as the original name of the first legendary king of the world who was born *Hpaya-laung* (corresponding to *Bodhisatta* in Pāli), belonged to the solar dynasty, and was called 'Mahathamada' (Mahāsammata in Pāli) because he was elected by the people. The same name was applied to a cowherd who was famous for twelve decisions[12] in his village, King Mahathamada appointed him Judge. I shall discuss the relationship between these two characters both called *Manu* in a subsequent chapter. In any case, this legendary story described in the preamble apparently hints that the two legal systems – Hindu and Buddhist – are intermingled in the text. We can not exclude the possibility of influence from Sri Lanka which "the law of *Manu* or a part of it came into the Sinhalese legal system through the spread of Sanskrit learning". In fact, King Mahāsammata was given another name '*Vaivasvat Manu*' and thereby the Sinhalese kings claimed descent from Manu [Jayasekera 1984: 112-113 / see also Okudaira 1999: 471].

Thus, Myanmar law and other Southeast Asian laws owed a certain degree of the debt to Hindu law. However, the surrounding Buddhist culture tended to diminish it. The *Manu-smṛti* or the Hindu code of *Manu* was indeed used as a model, but for legal form rather than legal contents. The *Manugye Dhammathat* contains at the end of explanation of every subject of law, an explanation that "So has *Manu* decided". It was nothing but Myanmar customary law that *Manu* expounded in the Dhammathats like *Manugye*. At first the name of Manu had been impressive and inspiring, but in the context of a Buddhist culture, lost its identity. Kaingza Manu's work, so called *Mahayazathat* shows us how Buddhist ideas were incorporated into the Myanmar law and custom during the seventeenth century. Kaingza explained the Myanmar law invoking the precepts or ideas from Buddhist canon. By Konbaung times, the Hindu *Manu*'s tradition had been thoroughly Buddhicised. [See Lingat 1950: 15-16].

7. Dhammathat in the Theravāda Buddhist State

The Dhammathat, as it has been mentioned, should in principle, be thought of not a code of law, but as collections of customary rules and precedents. "They reflect the social customs of the day, and expound rules of wisdom as guides for kings, ministers, and judges to rule by and for the people to live by" [Maung Maung 1963: 7] And they have done this through all the dynasties of Myanmar from the Bagan period in 11-13th centuries to the fall of the Konbaung dynasty in the late nineteenth century. The Dhammathats mirrored the society of their day. "They do not lay down the "law"; they reflect the customs and the rulers which act and play in society, and when the reflections are clear, the customs and rules are accepted as having binding force". [*ibid*.: 9-10]. They "deal extensively, and freely, with the manners and morals of society, refusing to be confined to the province of pure law"[*ibid*.: 11].

One way of distinguishing law from custom is to say that customary law is decentralized whereas statutory law is centralized creation of law [See Hla Aung 1969: 38]. However, the Myanmar Dhammathat, which is a collection of customary rules and precedents is defined neither as folk law nor as statutory law. It 'changes its character when formalized in law and legal decisions' [See Furnivall 1957: 295]. When the king's judges used it to settle the case before them, it comes to fulfill state function. In this sense, it was no doubt the foundation of the state law and, therefore, was central to the legal life of the country. The reason that collections of legislation were compiled in Myanmar may have been that the compilers of the Dhammatha*t*s always intended jurists to interpret the law book flexibly in accordance with changing time and conditions. The Dhammathats were to be interpreted in terms of the four conditions (*Mahapadetha Taya: Le:-ba:*) (1) *Kalan*(time or period), (2) *Dethan* (place or locality), (3) *Aggan* (value) and (4) *Danan* (nature of the property) [1847: 13; YKH1965: 47].In deciding a case, these four conditions could not be neglected. Myanmar justice sought to mediate

Chapter I — Buddhist Dhamma and Secular Law

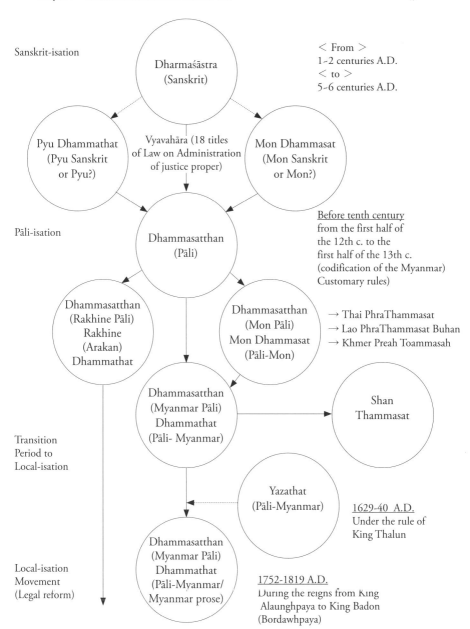

Table 3: Supposed Development of the Dhammathat Literature in Myanmar

and find a sort of compromise between the rival parties [Okudaira *ibid.* 475-476; 1986: 127].

A characteristic feature of Myanmar society is accorded to individual freedom and equality. No one, not even a king, could transcend the law. Since the law was based solely on existing customs, a king was not expected to promulgate legislation. He was expected to maintain law and order, and the people were expected to obey the king or be punished. When a reign came to an end, liability for punishments for some crimes also came to an end, as well as some kinds of civil law suits. The king administered justice because it was his duty and not because of the divine right. Even the king had to obey the law and could be sued [See Htin Aung 1962: 6-7]. Judges who decided cases were of lesser importance than jurists who promulgated the law as if reading it from nature [Furnivall 1957: 132]. Those which had become obsolete were dispensed with. Thus they kept in step with contemporary usage [Aung Than Tun 1961(July)14; See also Okudaira *ibid.* 476-477].

The Myanmar have a saying that the rules of the Dhammathats are overridden by the mutual consent of the contending parties. It was the intention that the Dhammathats were to be consulted in making a decision, but such a decision was subjected to royal authority, and to agreements usually based on local customs[13] [Gywe 1910: iii; see also MMOS III s.350: 59]. One must, however, note that although the power to alter the law was given to the kings, they were respected to follow the general principle of the Dhammathats and were not allowed to hinder their legal principles [E Maung 1970: 5].

The function of the Dhammathats was the peaceful solution of disputes and differences based on morality and ethics. Their basic intention was 'to minimize a serious affair, to mitigate a small one (*kyi thaw: ahmu. go nge aung, nge thaw: ahmu. go pa-byauk aung*)[Aung Than Tun 1970: 39] or '*kyi thaw: ahmu nge ze, nge thaw: ahmu pa lat se*. In other words, it was to 'minimise the full words and ignore the trifles' (*kyi: thi.zaga: go nge aung, nge thi. zaga: go pa-byauk aung*) [ROB IV: ix&229]. A Myanmar legal maxim says: *mwe ma. the dout m.a kyo:* (literally, "The snake does not die: as the stick is not broken", meaning 'Live and let live !'). It is a sort of 'to be fair (or) in fairness' (*taya: hmya.-ta-ye*). These expressions show the characteristic of the Myanmar traditional law. When considered from the viewpoint of the constant principles of justice, the Myanmar Dhammathat is indeed fair and just. Thus, the Dhammathats traditionally were expected to play a major role in the Theravāda Buddhist State to guide both the government and society for better ruling and living, based upon morality and ethics. [Okudaira *ibid.*: 477]

Chapter II
The Genres of Myanmar Law Texts and the Dhammathat

1. The Genres of Myanmar Law Texts

a. Dhammathat

Myanmar has retained more of its source materials on the traditional law than other Theravāda Buddhist countries. Even, however, there have been many losses. These source materials include Dhammathat (law book) and Hkwè-bon (commentary), Yazathat (judicial decision by the king), Hpyat-hton (collection of judicial decision), Sit-tan (inquest by central government) and other legal literature.[14] The media in which these genre appeared include Kyauksa (stone inscription), Pe (palm-leaf manuscript) and Parabaik (writing tablet in the form of accordion folds). Stone inscriptions deal mostly with religious matters and only a few law. Though most of the legal literary works were inscribed on Pe or written on Parabaik, the inscriptions of the Bagan period can provide us with some information on judicial affairs.

For example, in regard to the judicial and legal systems in Bagan, they show that there were three levels of courts: lower courts for preliminary hearings, law court in the capital, and the upper court or appeal court. In addition, there was a criminal court for petty theft cases [IB pl.54/7; pl. 795/19, 27; pl.79/b/17,27, 35; pl. 74/10, also see Than Tun 1959a: 57-58]. Regarding the word Dhammathat or law book, it appears in an inscription of 590 M.E.(=1228 A.D.) reporting a complicated law suit, and is regarded so far as the earliest one which mentions the word Dhammathat [pl II 174=OBI, p.104= UEM No.59, p=170=List 219; see also Frasch 1994: 46&53][15]. An inscription of 611 M.E.(=1249 A.D.), which is one of King Kyazwa's edict pillars, describes a crime and punishment [IB: pl.166a; see Than Tun 1959a: 58; also see 1964: 171][16].

The stone records refer to many disputes over ownership of land between the king or laity and monks, out of which three cases between the king and monks in 595 ME (=AD1235) [IB pl.90], 695 ME (=AD1245) [IB: pl.213b] and 795 ME.(=AD1255) [IB: pl.296] are well known [Than Tun 1959a: 62]. Apart from these, Bagan inscriptions refer to the word *ahmwe* which meant hereditary property like land or slaves and dealt with law suits on ownership of such property [IB: pl74/8-20; see also Than Tun 1958: 43]. An inscription of AD1242 recorded a dispute in which the king himself was involved [Pe Maung Tin in 1960: 433-434] and another inscription described a water ordeal [IB: pl.598a; see also Than Tun 1959b: 184; also see Frasch *ibid*.: 50&53]. Thus, we can catch a glimpse of the judicial affairs in the Bagan period [See more in detail in Than Tun 1959: 171-184; also see Okudaira 1986: 26-29].

As we saw in Chapter I, the Dhammathat was a principal guide for administration of justice and social life in the kingdoms in Myanmar. There are many works on the history of Myanmar literature including two earlier *Pitakat Thamaing* by Uttamasikha in 1681[17] and by the first Maunghtaung Hsayadaw in 1820s[18], *Kawi Lekkana Dipani* compiled by Thiri Maha Zeyathu in 1796, *Pitakat Thamaing Sadan* [Thamaing] published in 1888 by Maha Thiri Zeyathu, *Thoneze-chauk Hsaung- dwè Ein-hmu gan Dhammathat-kyi* and *Thonze-le:-zaung-dwè Amwe-hmu-gan Dhammathat-kyi:* compiled by Kinwun Mingyi U Kaung in 1887 and 1899. These books list roughly 30-80 *Dhammathat*s, some of which have been handed down to the present, though many have been lost[18]. Some of the Dhammathats were versified in the name of Dhammathat Linga. The *Thamaing* (1888) also enumerates ten Hkwè-bons which are mostly a table of inheritance [PTS 1905: 198].

According to Myanmar tradition, some of the earlier Dhammathat works are of great antiquity. For example, according to a Myanmar chronicle, it was the Pyu kings: Pyuminhti and Duttabaung, who had the Dhammathats compiled at first [U Kala 1959: 119&143]. The Pyus were one of the earlier settlers of Myanmar. The *Thamaing* also mentions the three Pyu Dhamathats by the name of *Duttabaung Dhammathat, Atitya Dhammathat,* and *Pyumindi (Pyuminhti) Dhammathat* [Thamaing 1905: 182-183]. But these Dhammathats, if they ever existed, have not been passed down to us today. On the other hand, the Mons who were also earlier settlers in southern Myanmar, have presumably became acquainted with the *Manu-smṛti* or the Hindu Code of *Manu*. Maha Thiri Zeyathu mentioned that there came into being of a Mon Buddhist version of *Manu* in the fifth century [Htin Aung 1962: 8]. However, it is impossible to know, with any degree of accuracy, whether they really existed.

In this regard, we also have to make a careful examination on both the

Dhammathats of *Manawthaya* (*Manosara*) and *Manutheikka* (*Manussika*), which the *Thamaing* mentions as earlier works than *Dhammawilatha* (*Dhammavilasa*) *Dhammathat*, because nothing is mentioned on these two Dhammathats in the Myanmar version of the *Dhammawilatha*. According to Forchhammer, the *Dhammawilatha Dhammathat* was written by Dhammawilatha and considered as one of the oldest Myanmar law books [Forchhammer *ibid.*: 29] mainly on the ground that such description is found in the *Kalyani* (=*Kalyānī*) inscription of the late fifteenth century that the monk Thariputta [Sariputta], a native of Dala in lower Myanmar, was rewarded honourable title of *Dhammawilatha* by King Narapatisithu of Bagan [KI 1892: 8-9; EB Vol.III pt.2: 196]. Furnivall, however, has pointed out that Forchhammer's assertion should be carefully re-examined because the fact is based on, not a contemporary inscriptions, but that of late fifteenth century [See Furnivall 1940: 355].[19]

As a Bagan inscription shows, the exact date of the first compilation of the Dhammathat is not known. It is, therefore, at least from the Bagan period that we can argue with a high degree of accuracy [See Frasch *ibid.*: 45]. We may, therefore, assume that the Dhammathats were revised wholly or partly as time progressed and none seems to survive in the original form. Thus, the dates of compilation of the Dhammathats listed in books on Myanmar legal literature mentioned-above, are sometimes controversial and subject to question. Through a scientific re-examination of stone inscriptions, Pe, Parabaik and other related historical source materials, which are extant today, we can possibly place the chequred legal history of Myanmar into some order [See Aung Than Tun W.P.D. Nov. 1981]. Therefore, re-examination of the dates of compilation of the Dhammathat literature should be made, as Furnivall [1940] and Huxley [1996b/1997a] have cast doubt on Forchhammer's chronology. We need to be aware that the timing of Myanmar legal developments has not yet been settled. Indeed, the task becomes more complex as time goes on [See more in detail Okudaira 1986: 30-31].

b. Yazathat

In modern usage Yazathat is often translated as 'criminal or penal code', but in the pre-modern period of Myanmar, it meant both 'the science of kings' and 'the judicial decisions of the kings'. In other words, the former was the art of governing or more particularly of adjudicating cases, while the latter bore the Dhammathat [Lingat 1950:18]. In fact, the Yazathat, are the two inseparable major factors together with the Dhammathat in the traditional Myanmar law. They are collections of judicial decisions of the kings, or sometimes, of eminent individuals famed for judicial decisions. Forchhammer listed more than twenty-four works of Yazathat, seventeen of which he estimated to be pre-eighteenth century and many of them purely literary works or edifying tales told as popular entertainment [Forchhammer 1885: 76-77]. Some of these did contribute to the interpretation of Myanmar law. Among them, the *Mahayazathat* compiled by Kaingza Manuyaza, a minister to King Thalun [1629-1648], which should more precisely be called Shaukhton ('compilation of learned discourse presented to the king by scholars or ministers) or Hpyat-hton,(only when the king makes decisions basing on the Shaukhton), *Mahayazathat* is reckoned to be the most important of the *Shauk-hton* genre. Under the Konbaung kings, the royal orders were often Yazathats themselves. In order to maintain law, order and peace in the country, the king decreed various orders. Royal orders of the Myanmar kings definitely bore the force of law. They, however, were not always permanent. The new king generally accepted the orders of the predecessor, though he was not responsible for following them. It meant that the orders of the predecessor were superseded by the new king and sometimes were altered or rejected. Local level officers, such as Hkayaing-wun (divisional officers), Myo-wun (the governor of the city), Myo or Ywa-thugyi (town or village headman) issued Hsint-za (summons) to execute the royal orders [Aung Than Tun 1968a:78].

The royal orders have an important position as a major source material for the study of the government system of the kingdoms of Myanmar. Originally they were kept at the Royal Palace Archives known such as Shwe-daik in Mandalay. In 1885 this collection was dispersed. Some of its contents may now be found in the National Library both in Yangon and Mandalay, Burma Historical Research Department, Archaeology Department in Yangon, the Universities' Central Library in Yangon and the University Library in Mandalay and in private hands [See Than Tun ROB Vol.I (1983: vi-viii]. In regard to the publications of the royal orders of Myanmar, *Myanmar Min Okchok-pon Sadan* ("A Treatise on How the Myanmar Kings Ruled") were compiled in five volumes by Bagan U Tin in 1924. Since then it has been highly evaluated as a "Bible" for better understanding on administration under Myanmar kings, though information included in it sometimes tells us merely general ideas. Although it includes many orders of King Badon (=Bodawhpaya), more comprehensive and authentic documents on royal orders have been cherished among historians. No particular documents on the royal orders of Myanmar were published until 1983. More than 7,000 royal orders were collected and published with English summaries in ten

Chapter II — The Genres of Myanmar Law Texts and the Dhammathat   51

volumes by Dr. Than Tun during the years from 1983 to 1990, of which the tenth volume is Index to other nine. It covers the years from 1598 to 1885. According to him, there are only two orders of this kind found prior to the year 1598 A.D.: one is the order of King Kyaswa [1235-1249] dated 1249A. D. engraved on stone and the other is the order of King Mingyi Swa Sawke. [See more in detail Okudaira 1986: 38-41; also see 2003b: 321].

c. Hpyathton

Hpyathton, which is a collection of judicial decisions, also seems to have played an important role in the history of Myanmar legal literature. It may say a collection of Hpyat-sa[20] which is a decision in writing for each case. Forchhammer listed the principal Hyathtons written in Myanmar language up to the compilation of *Mahayazathat* during the reign of King Thalun [1629-1640]. Some of them are anecdotes or decisions attributed to mythical personages who appears as the wise and leraned, such as *Thudhammasayi (=Sudhammacari), Mahawthada (=Mahosadha), Widuya (=Vidhura), Jalakadevi, Julmin*, etc. Many of them, however, are known only by name. But some of them include judicial decisions of the kings or the courts in actual cases [Forchhammer 1885: 75-77]. Although the *Thamaing* refers to altogether 82 Hpyathtons and Dhammathat Hpyathtons enumerate only 34 and under the British period, enumerate altogether 35 including *Yezagyo Hkondaw Hpyathton* which is famous for the collection of decisions at the town of Yezagyo local court [*Thamaing* 1888: 198]. Regarding Hpyathtons which dealt with actual cases, *Duttabaung Hpyathton* by a Pyu king Duttabaung, *Alaungsithumin Hpyathton* by a king of Pagan, *Manuyaza Hpyathton* by Kaingza Manuyaza (a minister to King Thalun in the second Taung-gu dynasty), *Shinkyawthu Hpyathton* by a Judge Shin Kyaw Thu, and *Atula Hsayadaw Hpyathton* by the royal mentor (high monk) to King Alaunghpaya. Among these *Yezajyo Hkondaw Hpyathton* is a rare existing collection of judicial court decisions and give us lots of information on Myanmar law during the Konbaung period. These Hpyathons seems to be of great importance from legal aspect and must have had some influence on the authors of the Dhammathats, and on the court judges in final judgment. They were, actually however, not often used as authorities on Myanmar law during the pre-colonial period [See Shwe Baw1955: 119-120; see also Huxley 1996: 94 and Okudaira 1986: 35-37; 2003b: 32 ; 2014: 45-46].

d. Other Sources

Other important sources on law are mentioned above in a, b, and c, there are some important sources which deal on law, such as *Sit-tan*, which are a report made by officers of central government on local conditions and administration, played an important role in the development of the administrative system in pre-modern of Myanmar. They give us a lot of useful information on Myanmar law. Because the aim of collecting Sit-tans was to determine the boundary issues, taxes, religious lands, etc. which very often caused the related disputes. The evidences of the Sit-tans are, therefore, of great help for the study of local administration and judicial affairs. Historical records do not tell us the origin of the Sit-tan, but we can date it back to Ava period [See Yi Yi 1966: 71]. A large number of the Sit-tan which were collected in the Konbaung period are extant today [MMOS pt2: 108]. Particularly, those collected in 1126 ME (=AD1764), and 1127 M.E.(=1765 A.D.) during the reign of King Hsinbyushin, and those collected in 1145 ME.(=AD1783), 1146ME (=AD1783) and 1164ME (=AD1802) in the reign of King Badon are well known in pre-modern period of Myanmar.[See also Okudaira 1986: 29] In this connection, current research works made by historians, particularly socio-economic historians on the *Thekkayit*, the literary meaning of which is 'dated document' and it includes various kinds of legal disputes and should be studied carefully for better understanding of law and custom in pre-modern Myanmar.[21]

We have to mention the other legal literature, such as law tales[22] and legal maxim.[23] These are, however, very often included in the Dhammathats or Hpyathton literature and not the main legal sources. Therefore a detailed account shall not be given here.

2. The Dhammathat as the Major Source of law

Aung Than Tun, the late well known Myanmar Barrister-at-law asserted that both Indian law books and Buddhist Canon had influenced to some extent on the growth of Myanmar law. The law including the Dhammathat was essentially secular, civil and customary law for the Myanmar people and that this law was based on customs, or habitual practices and other factors, such as royal edicts, judicial decisions, etc. [Aung Than Tun 1961 (July): 14]. Maung Maung, the late distinguished Myanmar jurist stated that the Dhammathats "are not code of law in the strict sense, and there is wide variance among them in content and quality" [Maung Maung 1963: 7]. As he quoted Sir Arther Page, C.J., in regard to a case of Ma Hnin Zan vs. Ma Myaing [13 Ran, 487; see also Ran (1940): 536], the Dhammathat are not sole repository of Myanmar customary law, which is also ascertained from decided cases and the prevailing customs and practices of Burma., referring to a case in Ma Po vs. Ma Shwe Mi [2 UBR 79]. [Also see Chan-Toon 1899: 418-433; 1903: 117]. He continues that "when the rules are uncertain, and there is no proof as to which Dhammathat ought to be followed, or what rule should prevail, or when it can not be shown which rule is the living law and which a dead letter, the then Courts accept a custom that is consonance with equitable principles" [Maung Maung *ibid.*: 10].

John Jardine, the late nineteenth century Judicial Commissioner of British Burma introduced views of the indigenous judges on the Myanmar Dhammathat in his Appendix to a book of Father Sangermano (the first edition in 1833). He essentially states that "--- the tendency of the native judges is to reverence the Dhammathat as was shown in their objections to a proposed statute of distributions as unnecessary. One judge called the Dhammathat the Great Will. Another wrote - It is very just, very subtle, very good, and very clear. All disputes on such matters can be settled by it. It is second sun to the earth. Where then is there a Buddhist who can renounce the Dhammathat?" He continued, "The apparent likeliness to the Hindu law is thus varied by means of Buddhist opinions, and also by the existence of Burmese and other customs, which incorporated in these codes." [Sangermano 1966: 300].

Thus, the Myanmar jurists grasped the ideas and characteristics of the Dhammathat with deep respect, treating the Dhammathats not as a positive, but as a leading guide for the society. They offered mere principles by way of guidance, while the prevailing customary rules were in force in reality. On the other hand, the 18th-19th centuries European residents in Myanmar seem to have mis interpreted the ideas and characteristics of the existing Dhammathats, because they seem to have been unheard to the Europeans at that time. For example:

Captain Hiram Cox, who arrived at Yangon in October, 8th, 1796 and stayed at the capital city of Amarapura returned to Yangon on 1st, November and remained in Myanmar until 24th, April, 1798 as British Resident [Hall 1971 (intro) 6]., He said as follows:

"The Dhammathat is very little attended to, every prince framing a new code when he come to the throne, and every petty magistrate innovating at will" [See Sangermano *ibid.*: 87 on Cox].

John Crawfurd who arrived in Myanmar in September, 1826 as British

Envoy, also stated as follows:

> "Their / Dhammathats's / authority, however, is not appealed to in the courts: and if they are read, it is only curiosity". [Crawfurd 1829: 412-413; also Sangermano *ibid*.].

The Rev. Howard Malcom also describes: "The written code /Dhammathat/, civil and penal, though severe, is on the whole, wise and good, but is little better than a dead letter.--- For all practical purposes it is almost a nullity, being never produced a pleaded form in courts" [Malcom 1839: 256].

Alien eyes in pre-modern period viewed the Myanmar Dhammathat as obsolete and inefficient, probably because of their ignorance of the whole concept of Myanmar traditional law. We must understand the Dhammathat in terms of its loosely structured legal system and the concept of the Theravāda Buddhist kingship. Cox and Crawford suggest that the Dhammathats played little role in the individual law suit. This would support Tilman Frasch, a German historian)'s suggestion that the Dhammathats were more symbolic than practical importance [See Frasch 1994: 49-51]. But it is also evident that the Dhammathats were sometimes referred to by the Judges in the judicial courts in later periods, particularly in Konbaung dynasty [See Okudaira 2001: 151; 2003: 321]. Whether the Dhammathats were used or not largely depended on the ruler's awareness of importance upon them.

For example, one of the judicial decisions that can still be read as Parabaik manuscripts and as book is *Yezagyo Hkondaw Hpyathton*. This collection of the judicial decisions includes those of the local court at Yezagyo from 1150M.E.(=1788A.D.) during the reign of King Badon and after. These decisions, they were passed in accordance with the Dhammathats, Pāli canonical books (Taya-kyan Books on Law of Buddha; Neikpat- Zattaw-Birth Stories of Buddha, Yazathat (Royal decisions), works about courtesy (lawkawut), tales of the six branches of knowledge (bedin)[24], evidence, etc. [YKHP 1965: 2, 10, 26, 34, etc.] In regard to the Dhammathat, *Manuthaya* [*Manusara*] *Shwemyin, Dhammawilatha* and other several Dhammathats were cited and used for judgements [*ibid*: 18-19, etc.]. According to the Royal Orders for the appointment of Judges, they were requested to make judgment in accordance with the law of Dhammathat. They were also requested to make judgment, referring to *Manu-dhammathat* first, if not applicable, then, *Kaingza Manuyaza Hpyathton* which was compiled in the time of our ancestors. In other words, precedents shall be taken into consideration in making a judicial decision [See SNTOA 1975: 72; HLHMT 1960: 21; YKHP *ibid.*91; (ROB (21, June, 1819)(T)ROB VII: xii & 332].

To sum up, at least during the Konbaung period,the Dhammathats did play a substantial role even in individual law suit. They also played a significant role for the maintaining the king's claims to the legitimacy. *Dhammayaza* or *Mintaya* ("Just king" or "Lawful king") was one who observed the 'Ten Royal Duties' [See Chapter IX a.2] and other royal duties and ruled the country in accordance with the law. Early in Myanmar legal history, the ancient Sanskrit Dharmaśāstra or Pāli Dhammasatthan (or Dhammasatta) had their own kind of legitimacy. By Konbaung time, it had evoked into something larger and different, because so many Myanmar customary rules, royal orders, and previous decisions had been stirred into the original text.

According to Forchhammer, "Every Burmese or Talaing [Mon] monarch endevoured to preserve exisiting law (but not hereditary institutions) and to enact and enforce new ones suitable to the customs and usages of the people from whom they were intended. But subsequent weak rulers, or a change in dynasties, reduced the body of law promulgated by the predecessors or members of subverted dynasties to a dead letter; it was set aside and then forgotten" [Forchhammer 1885: 91]. Thus Myanmar kings could revise or newly compile the Dhammathats to suit to changing time and conditions and preserve or abolish the laws promulgated by the former kings. They, however, paid respect to the Dhammathats and instructed to decide a case in accordance with the Dhammathat [See ROB (19 August, 1758)(T)ROB III:53 & 214; AMA-Apaing-hka 16: 258-259; etc.].[See also Okudaira 2003b: 323]

Thus, the Dhammathats were law for all time, while the royal promulgations were only law when the king ruled, though the succeeded king could follow them if he liked. It is therefore, the Dhammathat literature served as the major source of Myanmar law.

Chapter III
Palm-leaf and Parabaik Manuscripts of the Dhammathats

1. Locations and Conditions of the Dhammathat Source Materials

A fairly large number of the Dhammathats had been compiled since the Bagan period until the end of the nineteenth century at the fall of the Konbaung Dynasty. Unfortunately, many Dhammathats and related legal documents were lost, at least twice by war: the first time when the Mons rebellions annihilated Inwa (=Ava), the capital city of the second Taungu dynasty in 1752 [See Furnivall 1940: 370] and the second time when the Mandalay Palace was ransacked by the British troops in 1885 [See MSMB I 1991: xiii]. In addition, some of them seem to have been lost during the British colonial period and the Japanese military occupation [See Okudaira 2006: 43].

The Dhammathats and other legal documents were traditionally written on palm-leaf manuscript (Pe) or folded paper (Parabaik). There are few materials before the nineteenth century because of the frequent occurrence of fire, bad whether, damages caused by such as insects and bookworms, loss by war or fire, inferior collection and storage methods, etc. [See Yi Yi 1961: 248]. Dr. Thaw Kaung, a learned librarian of Myanmar said that "no palm-leaf manuscripts have survived for older than about 300 years" [Thaw Kaung 2005: 52-53]. Most of the manuscripts of the pre-eighteenth centuries seem to be either illegible or incomplete; some not in a good condition. On the other hand, Parabaik were used for mainly drafting, note, etc. It is said that it will last at most one hundred and fifty years [See Yi Yi 1962: 10] and legal documents which exist today are mostly from the latter half of the eighteenth century to the end of the Konbaung dynasty.

Quite a few of the Dhammathats and the related legal documents inscribed on palm-leaf are still extant. In a manuscript culture there seem to be very few original documents written by the author himself. Most of them are written by copyists. The bulk of these are located in Myanmar, but there are few in India, Europe, (such as United Kingdom, France , Germany, etc.) and possibly elsewhere in some unexpected countries.

Major Michael Symes who was dispatched, as the chief of the mission, to the kingdom of Ava by the Governor-General of India in 1795 described in his Account as follows:

"The Birmans generally call their code Derma Sath, or Sastra *[Dhammathat]*; it is one among the many commentaries on Menu; I was so fortunate as to procure a translation of the most remarkable passages, which were rendered into Latin by Padre Vincentious Sangermano, and, to my great surprise, I found it to correspond closely with a Persian version of the Aracan code, which now in my possession. ---" [Symes 1800: 303].

Vivian Ba who resided in Paris reproduced a portrait of Sangermano holding up a page:

"The Barnabite Father, Vincent Sangermano, who was a great European Historian of Burma. Others all drew from his "History of Burman Empire". He is seen here with a leaf from one of the manuscript books he took with him back to Italy. He spent 25 years in Burma and returned to Italy in 1808 with a Burmese student who later became a famous surgeon in Rome" [Vivian Ba 1965: 40].

Another passage in Syme's Account says that:

"His Majesty was thereupon pleased to order a handsome copy of the Razawan *[Yazawin]* or History of their kings, and of the Dhirmasath *[Dhammathat]*, or Code of laws, to be delivered to me from the royal library: each was contained in one large volume written in a beautiful manner, and handsomely adorned with painting and gilding." [*ibid.*: 422][See also *ibid.* 43-44].

2. World-wide Collections of the Dhammathat Manuscripts

The historical facts that some Dhammathat texts were taken abroad by Sangermano and Symes suggest that foreign libraries may possess them. The majority of the Dhammathats and other legal source materials which are existing today are located in Myanmar, particularly in the National Library and the Universities' Central Library both in Yangon. Some are preserved in other Universities' libraries, research or public institutions and Archaives, such as Universities Historical Research Centre (UHRC) at the University of Yangon Campus, Pāli Studies Library (Pāli Thutethana Sa-kyi-daik) at Kaba Aye, Resource Centre for Ancient Myanmar Manuscripts (RCAMM) at

Botahtaung, all in Yangon, the University of Mandalay Library and other museums and libraries in the districts, such as the Taungdwingyi.[25] A few are possessed by Buddhist monasteries throughout the country and some of them still in private hands. The number of the legal source materials, particularly in the Universities' Central Library (UCL) in Yangon has been increased particularly in the past twenty years because of their highly motivated collection. [See also Okudaira *ibid*.: 44].[26]

In libraries outside of the country, some of the Dhammathats and the other legal source materials have been preserved in libraries, such as the Oriental and India Office Collection of the British Library in London, United Kingdom; Bibliotheque Nationale (BN) in Paris, France; the Library of the Asiatic Society of Bengal in Calcutta, India. etc. A list of the Dhammathat and Hpyathton manuscripts with their number and location is given in Appendix IV so that we could get rough information about the existing source materials on the Myanmar legal literature. As to the publication of the Dhammathat literature, some of the major Dhammathats and Hpyathtons were printed from the middle of the 19th century to the 1960s [*ibid*.].[27]

3. Location of Palm-leaf and Some Parabaik Manuscripts at the Major Libraries

Between the 12th-13th centuries of the Bagan period and the end of the nineteenth century of the Konbaung period, scores of the Dhammathats in different title had been compiled and inscribed mainly on palm-leaf and some on parabaik manuscripts. These different titles usually exist as copies or later editions, of the original. Mostly these are to be found in Myanmar, where the vigorous effort of librarians and scholars has preserved and catalogued them. This has been particularly true since the 1990s, when a Government Program for preservation, conservation and studies on old manuscripts was initiated.[28]

Regarding the collection of the Dhammathats and other old legal literatures, we have noticed that the number of palm-leaf and parabaik manuscripts has much increased at UCL since 1980s. The number of the palm-leaf and parabaik manuscripts which has now preserved at UCL has reached about 146 items while the number in 1980s was about 65. On the other hand, other libraries in Myanmar has not increased their holdings since 1980s. One example is the number of the National Library in Yangon which in the 1980s was the most in preserving the palm-leaf and parabaik manuscripts of the Dhammathat and other legal literatures. Likewise, the Library in the University of Mandalay which still has the same or a bit less holdings of palm-leafs and parabaiks. Recently, it has been UCL that has led the field.

As the Appendix IV indicates, the total number of the manuscripts of the Dhammathat and other legal literatures except of private hands are roughly three hundred including both the complete and incomplete. The most popular Dhammathat judging by the number of surviving palm-leaf copies, *Manuthaya* (*Manusara*) *Shwemyin* (about 30copies) and the *Manuwunnana* (=Manuvannana) (about 25 copies). Next come *Manu, Manuyin* (*Manu Reng*), *Manugye,* and *Attayathi* (*Attarasi*), *Wineikhsaya Pakathani* (*Vinicchaya Pakasani*) (about8-13), then come *Wagaru, Dhammathat Kuncha, Kozaung-gyop, Kaingza Shwemyin* and *Yazabala* (about 3-4): least popular are *Wineikhsaya* (*Vinicchaya*) *Bedaka, Wineikhsaya* (*Vinicchaya*) *Yathi, Hsonda Manu, Manawthaya* (*Manosara*), *Pyumin, Kyetyo, Kyannet,* which survive in one or two copies each. Apart from these, there are lots of the Dhammathat manuscripts, the title of which are not clearly mentioned. These are tentatively excluded from counting as number. In addition, there will be a few more old legal manuscripts which are in personal hands or keeping at other libraries or monasteries in rural areas.

Regarding the Dhammathat and old legal literatures which have been well preserved in abroad, We estimate their total number to be roughly one tenth of those in Myanmar. Some important complete copies among them, such as the *Dhammawilatha* (1749 A.D.), held by the British Library in the United Kingdom which is the oldest surviving Dhammathat manuscript and some others in full set. The Bibliotheque Nationale in Paris, France, has preserved some of the legal literatures. The Asiatic Society of Bengal in India, which is regarded as a part of the Professor Desai's collection[29] has altogether nine legal manuscripts [See Appendix IV].

Many copies of the Dhammathats and other legal literatures whether in Myanmar or abroad, are incomplete and or undated. This can cause serious problems for reconstructing her legal history. One such is the influence of *Dhammawilatha Dhammathat* upon the 1782 re-compilation of the *Manugye Dhammathat..*

4. Dhammathat in Indigenous Minority Buddhist Groups

The other indigenous minority races, such as Mon, Rakhine (Arakan) and Shan have the same legal genres as the Myanmar Dhammathats. In regard to the Mon Dhammasāt, some of the manuscripts were collected and published under the title of "Eleven Mon Dhammasāt Texts" by Nai Pan Hla, a well known Mon Scholar in 1992.[30] In addition, probably there exist some more manuscripts, particularly in some monasteries in the Mon state.[31] On the other hand, although investigation has not been thoroughly made yet, the existence of altogether fourteen items of the Shan Dhammathat (Thammasat) manuscripts have already been found and published in 2012 in Japan by Sai Kham Mong, a well-known Shan historian.[32] As to Rakhine Dhammathat, it is said that two Dhammathats have survived, one written in Pāli in the name of *Kyannet* and the other in vernacular called *Ketyo* which is another version of *Dhammavilatha* [See Huxley 1996: 102-103]. No investigation, however, has been made yet on the existence and location of the Rakhaine Dhammathats [Okudaira 2006: 45].

Chapter IV
The Rise of the Konbaung Dynasty

1. The Political Situation of the early Konbaung Period

Myanmar history has seen four major dynasties within eight hundred and forty years: Bagan Dynasty [1044-1287], Taungu Dynasty [the first Taungu Dynasty 1486-1599; the Second Taungu (=Nyaungyan) Dynasty [1605-1752] and Konbaung Dynasty [1752-1885]. This book focuses on sixty-seven years beginning from the foundation of the Konbaung Dynasty by King Alaunghpaya to the death of the Sixth King Badon [1752-1819].

In 1740, Nga Tha Aung led a rebellion in Bago (=Hanthawaddy Pegu) against Ava (=Inwa), the capital city of the Second Taungu Dynasty [(T)ROB III: 13]. The main cause of rebellion was exploitation in the form of overtaxation by a Myanmar governor [See Koenig 1990: 12]. After they had consolidated power in the southern provinces based at Bago, the new Mon regime began to attack the northern rival at Ava, which had been beset with various rebellions in northern Myanmar as well. Ava was now totally besieged by enemies and was incapable of fighting against them effectively. A massive Mon invasion led by King Banyadala from Bago finished off the capital city of Ava [See KBZ: 85-90] during the dry season in 1752-1753.

Ava had fallen and with it Taungu Dynasty collapsed. Maha Dhamma Yaza Dhipati, the last king of the Second Taungu Dynasty was taken to Bago with more than thousand courtiers and subjects whom the Mons later killed [KBZ: 104-106]. He became known to posterity as 'Hanthawaddy Pa Min' (=King who was taken away to Hanthawaddy). The Mon had annihilated the Restored Taungu dynasty, also known as the Second Myanmar Empire. The Mon, however, made some strategic errors. They did not attack the areas of Mu and lower Chindwin, where the Myanmar still retained military potential [See Koenig *ibid.*:12]. This gave the Myanmar a chance not just to redeem themselves, but to attack the Mon strongholds in the South.

A number of local and district Myanmar leaders in the area took advantage of the available manpower to resist the Mons. Best equipped such leaders was U Aung Zeya, who was born in the family of successive village headman (ywa-thugyi) at Mok-hso-bo and later changed his name into Alaunghpaya. He renamed Mok-hso-bo as Shwebo. He raised his army, and collected weapons, troops and transport from the neighbouring forty-six villages [SeeKBZ: 18]. While defeating his rivals, he systematically organized his growing supporters, the rivals and regained the capital city of Ava in 1753. Victor B. Lieberman skillfully described King Alaunghpaya's strategic ability in battles, referring to Konbaung chronicle as follows: he "was a superb tactician who combined resolution and flexibility. Enemies found it impossible to contend with ever-changing mix of behind-the-lines cavalry raids, ambushes, and frontal assaults. He was also a methodical organizer, subjecting his men to specialized training that may have been unusual by Burmese standards" [Lieberman 1984: 236; also see KBZ I: 18].

Captain George Baker described in his journal of a Joint Embassy as an Ambassador from the Honourable East India Company to the King of Buraghmahns [Burman][33] in 1755, observed and portrayed King Alaunghpaya as follosws:

"--- he is about 45 years of age, about 5 feet 11 inches high, of a *hale Constitution*, and *sturdy,* though *clean, make* and of a *Complexion, full as dark* as the *generality* of *Buraghmahn,* his *Visage somewhat long,* though not thin, nor *prominent,* and *coarse features,* a little *pitted* with the *Small Pox,* his aspect somewhat grave, when *serious;* and, when *seated* in his *Throne,* I thought he supported *Majesty* with a *tolerable grace*; his *Temper---* is *hasty*; and *disposition, severe, rather cruel*: ---"[DOR 1808: 70-71].[34]

Alaunghpaya ascended to the throne and built the new capital city in Shwebo in 1753 and drove the Mon forces from Upper Myanmar in the following year. Local rulers, such as Min or Sawbwa of the Danu, Kachin, Kathe (Manipur) and the Shan were brought under his control. King Alaunghpaya himself marched to Pyi (Prome) in lower Myanmar and occupied Hinzada and Dagon (renamed as Yangon) in 1755. He began a military campaign against Bago (Hanthawaddy) in March of the same year. Bago was completely surrounded by Myanmar stockades and finally fell on 6th May, 1757. The following year, he regained Tanindayi (Tenasserim) from Thailand and incorporated Madama (Mouttama/Martaban) and Dawe (Tavoy) into Myanmar in 1760. King Alaung-hpaya further advanced to Thailand and laid siege to Ayuthaya [Ayutia] in April, 1760. However, he raised the siege of Ayuthaya and hastened back to Yangon. On the way back

Chapter IV— The Rise of the Konbaung Dynasty   63

to Yangon, King Alaunghpaya died at Kin Ywa [See ROB III: xxii-xxxiii]. According to an another chronicle, he died at Madama (=Martaban) due to illness [AAL 1961: 23].

2. External Affairs

King Alaunghpaya's campaign on the south-eastern frontier which aimed at defeating the Ayuthaya Dynasty turned into a dismal failure. It was the first of a series of operations in 1767 with the third King Hsinbyushin's war to the death against Ayuthaya [See Koenig *ibid*.: 16]. Under the fourth King Singu and the fifth King, Hpaungga-sa Maung Maung (who seized the throne only for a week and was executed by Prince Badon), there were no campaign against Ayuthaya. However, the sixth King Badon (commonly known as Bodawhpaya) who took over the throne in February, 1782, expanded an active policy in both internal and exteral spheres.

He launched two major military campaigns. One conquered Danyawaddy (=Dinnyawadi) *Pyi-gyi* (kingdom) in Rakhine (Arakan) and the other attempted to destroy the Thai kingdom. As for the Campaign against Rakhine, on 16th October, 1784, King Badon appointed the Crown Prince as Commander-in-Chief and ordered him to take over Danyawaddy upon the pretext of restoring proper conditions in Rakhine for the prosperity of Buddhism (*thathana-daw*)[ROB (16, October 1784) (T)ROBIV: 388]. On 2nd January, 1785, Mro-haung (=Myo-haung), the capital city of Rakhine fell and King Mahasamata deserted his kingdom. However, he was captured shortly after and taken by the Crown Prince of Myanmar to Amarapura, the new capital city of Myanmar, with his royal families and subjects, Brahmans, over twenty thousands of captives, various kinds of weapons together with the Mahamuni Buddha Image [(T)ROB xxvii; KBZ: 8-10, 16-17].

After only a few months' campaign under the leadership of the Crown Prince of Myanmar, the whole area of the independent country of Rakhine was brought into the Myanmar domain. After four hundred years of independence, Rakhine now became a directly ruled province of the Konbaung King. "The concrete motives behind the annexation other than general imperial aggrandizement, was undoubtedly to strengthen the material strength of Myanmar power for the upcoming large operations on the eastern frontier. Requisitions of men and supplies came immediately after the annexation" [Koenig *ibid*.: 23; KBZ II: 37] Indeed, men and supplies were sent from Rakhine towns and villages to the Madama (=Martaban) Route for the campaign against Thailand [KBZ II: 37].

The other campaign under King Badon, which was of a larger scale, was to annihilate the Thai kingdom. It began from Beik (Mergui) on 4th July, 1785. According to the Konbaung chronicle, this campaign was of such a large scale that it consisted of five routes (via Chiengmai /Ywa-haine /Dawe (Tavoy)/ Beik(=Mergui) and Htaraik-the King's route) and altogether 200,000-300,000 soldiers (out of which 100,000 soldiers were attached to the king's route, over 30,000 soldiers each for the rest of the four routes). King Badon's personal participation in the campaign against Thailand evidences how serious his imperialistic ambitions were. However, after fierce fighting they were successively defeated in a series of battles from 1785 to 1786. The king himself returned from his unsuccessful expedition against Thailand in February, 1786. Another campaign against Thailand launched in September, 1786, but was repulsed again by Thai troops. It was evident that the major reason of the failure was an extreme shortage of provisions (*myo-yeik-hka*). Consequently, the successive defeats of 1785-1786 and 1786 brought heavy loss both in men and materials to the Myanmar kingdom [KBZ: 22; also see (T)ROB IV: xxiv-xxvi].The failure of the military campaign against Thailand, as will be told later, forced King Badon to give greater priority to internal projects.

Myanmar and China traditionally had had occasional diplomatic relations as well as military contacts since the Bagan period. During the first half of the Konbaung period battles occasionally broke out between Myanmar and China, particularly during the reign of King Hsinbyushin: Chinese attacked Keng Tung in December, 1765 and attacked Bhamo in December, 1766; Chinese invaded Myanmar northern territories again in December, 1767 and Myanmar troops were dispatched against Chinese invaders within a few days; Again Myanmar troops were dispatched against the Chinese invaders in October, 1769 [See (T)ROB III: xxxiv-xxxv].

Koenig asserted that the battles between Myanmar and Chinese invaders of the late 1760s resulted in important consequences for Myanmar. To sum his views up, (i) Myanmar arms had emerged superior to that of Chinese in the border area and a Myanmar controlled equilibrium was reestablished for the first time in over three decades; (ii) local affairs of the border area, in the end, were usually adjudicated by the Myanmar authorities; (iii) the fact that Myanmar victories in the battles against Chinese invasions while simultaneously maintaining control of northern Thailand and besieging Ayuthaya demonstrates the vitality and strength of the administrative and military system built by King Alaungphaya; (iv) the Chinese and Thai campaigns of the 1760s also had the benefit of leadership by a cadre of able officers who cost their blood in the internal conflicts of the 1750s, under whose effective leadership, Konbaung military capability reached its peak in the 1760s [Koenig *ibid.*: 19].

No further intercourse between China and Myanmar occurred until a curious flurry of diplomatic missions between 1788 [KBZ II: 64-68 and 1796 [KBZ II: 98-99]. However, diplomatic activities between both states ceased until 1823 because King Badon was angry at the duplicity of the Chinese Shans of Kaingma and the Sawbwa of Bhamo. In collusion with Chinese officials in Yunnan they duped the Burmese court into sending missions to Peking, which the emperor was able to portray as a tribute missions [Koenig *ibid.*: 18].[35]

On the other hand, the western border area gradually became unsettled after annexation of Rakhine to Myanmar in 1784. Some of the Rakhine people fled to the Chittagong District which was sparsely populated and adjacent to the territory of the British East Indian Company. Some of the Rakhine who had fought against Myanmar rule remained in the territory of Rakhine. Thus the annexation of Rakhine resulted in a creation of a common, but sensitive frontier with the domain of the British East Indian Company in India. Indeed, the border incident over the Rakhine rebel leaders opened a new phase in Anglo-Myanmar relations [KBZ II: 10-18]. This Anglo–Myanmar interacttion later definitely became one of the major causes of the 'First Anglo-Burmese War' in 1824 which broke out under the Seventh King Bagyidaw.

A letter from the Governor-General in Council to the Secret Committee of the Court of Directors of the East India Company dated on 21st November 1823, a year before the war, presents an official view of the British India on the war. The following clarifies the situation.

"---for some years past the Burmese have gradually been encroaching on the Southeastern frontier of Chittagong, and advancing pretentions to the jungles frequented by our elephant hunters, through unquestionably situated within the established British boundaries" [PBW 1825: 1].

3. Myanmar Involvement into the English-French Colonial Struggle

As for French and English relations with Myanmar, the Mon rebellion in 1740 caused them to abandon their enterprises in 1742 and 1743 respectively, though the ventures by both continued in modest way. "The destruction of the English factory at Syriam (=Tanyin)) in 1743 brings down the curtain upon the East India Company with Burma" [Hall 1968: 241]. However, both the Myanmar and the Mon eagerly wanted English material. During the period–throughout 1740s and 1750s–they attempted to obtain canon, muskets, and ammunition through negotiations with French and English, where the Mons were invariably more successful because of her favourable geographic position [Lieberman 1984: 212].

In 1749, the French re-opened relations with the Mons who desperately needed military support. This French involvement with the Mons urged the English East Indian Company to counter by securing a new spot for the trade expansion in Myanmar.

"In 1753, when a foothold was sought on the opposite shores of the Bay of Bengal, the spot chosen by Fort St. George for the erection of a new factory was not Syriam (Tanyin) but the island of Negrais (Haing-kyi-kyun), a place deemed safe from intrusion than the Burmese port." [Hall *ibid*.: 241]. On 26th April, 1753, David Hunter's expedition arrived on the island of Negrais (Haing-kyi-kyun) and anchored off the spot previously recommended by Thomas Taylor as the best site for a settlement. However, it soon became evident that the spot was of little value [See *ibid*. Appendix: Tragedy of Negrais: 297].

On 13th March, 1755, Captain George Baker from the Pathein (=Bassein) trade depot accompanied a Myanmar envoy to Negrais island (=Haing-kyi-kyun). Henry Brooke, Chief of Negrais, who succeeded David Hunter after his death at Negrais, welcomed the Myanmar envoy. However, the negotiation of the envoy with Henry Brooke was unsuccessful in acquiring sufficient military supplies [See (T)ROB III: xxiii; xxvi]. On 6th October, 1759, Armenian intrigues brought about the massacre of the whole factory staff at Negrais, and again the British East Indian Company ceased its operations in Myanmar.

Being released from the 'Seven Years War' between England and France, the English were again free to trade in Myanmar, though neither Negrais Island (=Haing-kyi-kyun) nor Pathein found favour in their eyes. Even Thanyin (=Syriam) was no longer attractive to them, Yangon had already eclipsed its importance [See Hall *ibid*.: 24]. Thus, the contact between the Konbaung Dynasty and the English Indian Company ceased due to problems caused by the negotiation of Negrais Island in 1761, when the matter on the release of the Negrais prisoner ended, save for the withdrawal of Robertson and Helass from Pathein (Bassein). Both Madras (=Chennai) and Culcutta (=Kolkota) considered it worse than useless to make any attempt to obtain redress for

Chapter IV— The Rise of the Konbaung Dynasty   67

injuries. In consequence, official relations between the Konbaung Dynasty and the English Indian Company, did not resume until 1795, when the mission of Symes to the court of Ava was dispatched [See *ibid*.: 353; also Symes 1955: xxv-xxxv].

On the other hand, French interest in Myanmar was soon revived after the British Indian Company withdrew, though its power collapsed in India after the defeat of "War in Prassi" in 1757 and "War in Wandewash"in 1760. Negotiation between France and Myanmar were successful for the release of the French nationals captured by King Alaunghpaya and the renewal of the ship-building and commerce. That is to say, in 1766, a French mission from Pondicherry, headed by one Lefèvre, visited the Court of Ava asking the release of French prisoners who had still survived from the capture of ill-fated Galetee and Fulvy off Syriam (=Thanyin) ten years ago and also the renewal of privileges of trade granted in the days of Dupleix. Two years later, this mission returned to Myanmar with its objective fulfilled. Shortly afterwards, a small French establishment for building and repairing ships was opened at Yangon [Hall *ibid*.: 353]. As a consequence, France was the only European country permitted to maintain a formal establishment in Myanmar. However, because of the entry of France in the war for American Independence in 1778 the venture at Yangon was left inactive and finally it was abandoned in 1784 at the early stage of the reign under King Badon [See Koenig *ibid*.: 24-25]

Thus, the relations between Myanmar and each of the two major European powers-English and French differed in the first half of the Konbaung period. Koenig divided this period into two: the first was the period characterized by the primary English and French interest in the shipbuilding potential of Myanmar, with only the second interest in trade and by Myanmar and Mon leaders' interest in obtaining European munitions and arms, which encompassed the years 1695-1761 for the English and 1713-1784 for the French.

This period began with the Rakhine border incident of 1794 and ended with the death of King Badon in 1819. The English attempted to re-establish a modest position in Myanmar, though Myanmar-Anglo relation was incessantly occupied by the Rakhine problem toward which Myanmar's sense of grievance suspicion of English motives was increasing and reached a climax as a result of the Chin Pyan episode. This Myanmar feelings against the Rakhine problem seemed to have stemmed from the procedural blocks to communication that were so prominent a feature of the journals of English envoys [Koenig *ibid*.: 29].

Thus the Rakhine problem followed by subsequent events on Myanmar–

British India border area provided the immediate cause of war between Konbaung state of Myanmar and the British Indian Company as described above.

4. Internal Affairs

Turnining our eyes to internal affairs, the first half of the Konbaung period in the eighteenth and nineteenth century Myanmar, as Koenig suggested, falls roughly into two broad phases: the first phase was from the rise of King Alaunghpaya in the early 1750s to the death of Hsinbyushin in 1776; the second phase, through a transition period which covers the whole tenure of King Singu being the period under the reign of King Badon for thirty seven years [See Koenig *ibid.*: 30-31].

In the first phase, the central government paid careful attention to the organization and augmentation of its resources, where she framed a policy in such a manner that left the kingdom in a general healthy condition both administratively and demographically [*ibid.*]. During the reign of King Alaunghpaya, ties between the central administration and local administrations were weak because of poor communications between the capital city and rural areas, though the court and central administrative structure was fairly well organized. Accordingly, King Alaunghpaya ruled over the country through chieftains belonging to ethnic groups and Wuns or local governors who were appointed by the king who took oaths of allegiance [See Maung Maung Gyi 1983: 118]. Since the time of King Anawrahta of the Bagan period, Buddhism had traditionally played an important role in contributing to the unification and centralization of the state. Under the rule of King Alaunghpaya, there is evidence that shows how both the Myanmar and rival Mon kings showed great concern about Buddhism for the purpose of unification and centralization of the state.

In the exchange of correspondence of the Myanmar King Alaunghpaya with the Mon King Binya Dala (Banyadala), the former sent a message to the latter on 16th June, 1756 that "when two kingdoms became one like water that cannot be cut into two halves, it would be good in the name of love and compassion (*myitta-gayu.na*) on all being." [ROB (16 June, 1756) (T) ROBIII: 30; 159]. On the other hand, the latter made such a response to the Myanmar King on 28th June, 1756 that two capital cities of Hanthawaddy (Bago) and Ratanasingha (Shwebo) would prosper and that Buddhism would also expand like a waxing moon [ROB (28, June 1756) (T) ROB III: 31&161]. Replying to the Mon king, the Myanmar king sent such a letter on the same day, dated on 28th June,1756 that the Mon king should accept the offer of friendship or alliance for the benefit of both kingdoms referring to the cue of Bhuridhatta Jataka [ROB (28, June 1756) (T) ROBIII: 32&162].

Through this correspondence between the two Kings of Ratnasingha and Hanthawaddy, the Mon King had the impression that King Alaunghpaya was amenable to peace term and that both the people of the two different places of Ratnasingha and Hanthawaddy would soon restore friendship between them [*ibid.*: 36&171/172]. Thus, both the Kings proved to be defenders and promoters of Buddhism. King Alaunghpaya himself commanded vast resources and exercised almost unlimited powers and thus he was in an unparalleled position to promote the adoration of the three gems: the Buddha, the Dhamma and the Sangha. The faithful performance of this royal function not only strengthened ties between the capital city and local regions, but also served to promote unification among the various ethnic groups of the country such as the Burman (Myanmar), Mon, Shan, Rakhine, and others, who professed faith in Buddhism [See Smith: 1965: 3; also see Okudaira 1989: 69-70].

Although King Alaunghpaya implemented the careful administrative and demographic measures, he had left the task incomplete, mainly because at the age of forty-five years he died an untimely death on the way back to Yangon from Thai expedition. He intended to eradicate many of the old corrupt practices and abuses at the local and official levels that had succeeded from Taungu Dynasty and the internal war period. The two major problems which had been troubling for the first half of the Konbaung Dynasty, were the need to make central control over local sphere *de facto* as well as *de jure*, and the need to strengthen royal control over crown revenues and services. Faced with mounting evidence of the erosion of central control over officials and resources, reams of edicts were issued and kingdom-wide cadastral, revenue, and population surveys were launched in 1765 under King Hsinbyushin and twice in 1783 and 1802 under King Badon.

The fall of Hanthawaddy in 1757 marked the beginning, not only, of the end of the division of Myanmar into two ethnic and regional entities, but also, of the assimilation of the ethnic groups into the Myanmar population, for which we may call it "Myanmar- ization" (=Burmanization). Particularly, the Myanmar-isation movement of the Mons in the South was accelerated, though many fled to Thailand and sporadic risings occurred in 1758, 1774 and 1783, among which the exodus in 1774 was the most serious [See Koenig *ibid.*: 31-32].

In the second phase, King Badon appeared to have begun his rules in a realm that was in a relatively healthy condition. The King was given appraisal by an English envoy in 1795 as follows:

"The Birmans, under their present monarch, are certainly rising fast in the scale of Oriental nations. Their laws are wise, and pregnant with sound morality; their police is better regulated than in most European countries." [Symes *ibid.*: 122-123]

The above description proves that King Badon was a Great King of Law (*Maha-dhammayaza*). It is generally accepted that King Badon was one of the most powerful and successful rulers in the history of Myanmar. The annexation of Rakhine enhanced the reputation of King Badon in the kingdom of Myanmar [See Desai 1961: 98]. In fact, no other Myanmar king had ever conquered Rakhine since King Narameikha founded Mrohaung (=Myohaung) and decided it as the capital city of Rakhine. He was also successful in retaining Tanindayi (Tenasserim) and Dawe (Tavoy).

During the reign of King Badon, one of the most significant historical events were the *Muddha-beiktheik* ceremonies[36] which were performed twice in 1783 and 1784 in succession. The *Muddha-beiktheik* was a consecration ceremony, whereby a person became qualified to be a genuine king. It was strongly connected with the legitimacy of kingship. According to the Buddhist tradition, those kings who did not perform this ceremony, did not deserve to be called 'Great King'. Only when a king performed the ceremony, he was qualified to protect Buddhism, and competent to govern the territory endowed with juristic power, etc. [See MMOS I s.163: 239]. In reality, it did not function fully under Myanmar monarch. A good number of kings did not perform the ceremony. Kings, actually, could rule for life, even though not formally endowed with proper powers, without lustration and oaths. More important was an actual physical possession of the palace and the throne. More practically, it also depended upon a network of a loyalty oaths.

Thus, the chief function of the *Muddha-beiktheik* ceremony in the Myanmar kingdoms was to magnify the king's authority in the Court, to glorify his position and to strengthen his own self-confidence. He would have to see himself as a strong, unchallengeable, and successful king before he ventured upon the ceremony. In effect, it could not only be a manifestation of his pomp and power, but also a way to protect himself against those who might revolt against him.[37] King Badon unlike his predecessors attached great importance to the observation of these coronation ritual. He collected and studied the *Muddha-beiktheik* documents, consulting with Maung Htaung Hsayadaw, a Buddhist Primate [TAS 1976: hka], referring to the *Abhiṣeka* ritual from India so that he could observe the ritual in an outstanding manner compared to other kings in the past [See LMBM 1985: preface]. These practices of the *Muddha-beiktheik* by King Badon were just self-glorification to make a gesture of his confidence in administration in the atmosphere of the magnificent ceremony [See Okudaira 2000: 128].

On the other hand, toward the end of eighteenth century, Myanmar economic situation began to decline in growth. The failure of the military campaigns against Thailand both in 1785-1786 and 1786 was, as Koenig pointed out, "the real beginning of a long downward spiral" [Koenig *ibid.*: 33]. It is said that around 40 percent of the men who were conscripted for the Thai expeditions were lost due to enemy action, disease, starvation, and desertion [KBZ II: 22-39]. The Myanmar economy began to decline in growth. "These decisive reversals were followed by a decade of intensive construction of public works, while foreign policy lay relatively dormant." [Koenig *ibid.*: 33]. Construction of the massive Mingun Pagoda [KBZ II: 102-119], which became a virtual obsession with Badon, began in 1790 and was only abandoned in 1802 after twelve years of heavy labour requisitions. The repulse of the Thai invasion of Dawe (Tavoy) in 1791-93 involved over forty thousand men. However, what was probably the largest and the most onerous requisition came in 1795, when there was virtually a general mobilization of the entire empire for major expansion of the Meikhtila tank and canal system [KBZ II: 91-95].

Every district, including Rakhine, was ordered to send a specified draft of men to work on the project. The next round in the war with Thai and from 1797 to 1804 brought with it the necessity of raising new armies of conscripts with each dry season. Coupled to constant drain on labour for military and corvee purposes were heavy taxation and special imposts. The cumulative effect of the withdrawal of large numbers of men from the demographic pool between 1785 and 1804 was to disturb significantly the social and agricultural organization of realm. Once removed from their native locale for military service or corvee labour, few men returned, be it from disease, starvation combat, or desertion. As such the constant withdrawal of labour from the agricultural sector, had a log-term as well as short-term effects on productivity.

Michael Symes who was dispatched again by the Governor General of India to the Court of Ava in 1802, sent a letter to J. Lumsden, Chief Secretary to Government dated on 2nd September 1802, in which he described the situation of the Ava Kingdom as follows:

"It has unfortunately happened that we have come here in a season of scarcity, and the arrival of an Envoy from the British Government has already tended to enhance the price of every article. At the capital the want of grain is severely felt." [Hall 1955: 125]

To make the situation worse, a great famine which was caused by a severe drought from 1802-1803, 1805 in the dry zone reached its overall Myanmar was so severe that resources were inadequate to sustain large bodies of people. Amarapura was almost completely destroyed by arsonist's fire in 1809 and also the royal palace was destroyed in March, 1810 [(T) ROB IV: xxx]. Even though the people of the capital city of Amarapura, had been reduced to eating tree leaves and wild herbs, through the height of the troubles. King Badon had maintained his residence at Mingun, ten miles away to the north along the Ayeyarwadi (=Irrawaddy) River side until the Crown Prince died on 12th October, 1809 and Price Sagain (Later King Bagyidaw) [(T) ROB IV: xxix]. became the Crown Prince. King Badon occupied the New Palace on 10th May, 1815 [(T) ROB IVxxxi]. The kingdom also suffered a series of earthquakes between February and September in 1812 [KBZ: 188]. King Badon, however, retained his powerful reign until his death on 5th June, 1819 at the age of 75 years old, though social unrest was fatally brought about the various parts of the realm.

Chapter V
Konbaung Consecration Ceremonies

All the countries that have or had kingship have or had their coronation ceremonies. The 'Theravāda Buddhist State' is a form of political integration favoured by mainland Southeast Asian countries such as Myanmar, Thailand, Laos and Cambodia etc, where Theravāda Buddhism was introduced mainly from Sri Lanka. This Buddhism was originally introduced from India to Sri Lanka in the 3rd century B.C. as one of the King Aśoka's Missions headed by Reverend Mahinda, together with the model of consecration (coronation) ceremony during the reign of King Dēvanampiya Tissa. The consecration ceremony called *Abhiṣeka* in Sanskrit was observed for the King [MVXI 77-81] which seems to be the first ceremony in the history of Theravāda Buddhist kings.[38]

Although the afore-mentioned consecration ceremony means a sort of 'coronation ceremony' in western terminology, the term *Abhiṣeka* was not used in the sense of a 'crown'. Aryapala, a well-known Sri Lankan scholar, gave such a warning that "the use of the word 'coronation' by most writers when actually they mean the *abhiṣēka* [*Abhiṣeka*](anointing), is quite misleading. These writers no doubt refer to the inauguration ceremony in the current terminology" [Aryapala 1968: 372]. The Pāli terminology of *Abhiseka* in the Theravāda Buddhist countries in Southeast Asia, such as Myanmar has been used in the same meaning corresponding to Sinhalese *Abhiṣēka*.

1. Origin of the Consecration Ceremony

The preamble to the *Manugye Dhammathat* in Chapter I-pt.1 explain how the original inhabitants of the world conferred upon *Manu* the three kinds of Beiktheik [*Abhiseka*]. He was called Mahathamada, because he was worthy to be chosen by many; he was called Yaza, because he was capable of instructing men; he was called Hkattiya because he was the lord of land. These three kinds of consecration rituals were essential factors for becoming a king

[RMD1847: 4-24; 1782MD: ki./k-ki/w]. There were fourteen kinds of consecration during the Konbaung Dynasty [See MMOS I 1963: 247-248] which treats three kinds of consecration ritual mentioned above were regarded as the top three. Although the preamble do not refer to "*Muddha-beiktheik*" consecration as a Mahathamada consecration, it seems to be the same. Mahathamada refers to the king who had conferred on him the so-called *Muddha-beiktheik* ceremony. Mahathamada was unanimously elected as a king by all the inhabitants of the world.

Thus the second and third ranks of consecration ceremonies were *Yazabeiktheik* and *Hkattiya-beiktheik,* which were observed probably immediately after a king took possession of the throne.[39] *Muddha-beiktheik* was the most significant, elaborate and complex of them. Traditionally it was to be observed five years after the king ascended the throne [MMOS *ibid.*: 241]. In theory, a king who did not practice this ceremony was not regarded as legitimate. In theory if the king did not perform the *Muddha-beiktheik* ceremony, he was neither genuine, nor just [*ibid.*: 240]. In actuality there were not a few kings during the pre-modern period of Myanmar who did not. Of greater importance was the actual physical possession of the palace, throne and the kingship. Some Konbaung kings, such as King Badon, King Bagyidaw[40], King Thayawaddy, King Mindon and King Thibaw performed the *Muddha-beiktheik* ceremony. In particular, King Badon who reigned for thirty-seven years and King Mindon whose reign lasted twenty-five years, both performed this ceremony twice each during their reigns [LMB Zagalet-hsaung: 1]. King Badon, however, seems to have performed the *Muddhabeiktheik* five times [ROB (18 March, 1795 (T)ROB V: 624], though no historical records are given in detail except two performances in 1783 and 1784 in succession as mentioned in Section 4.

2. Theoretical Role of the *Muddha-beiktheik* Ceremony

a. Essential requirement as a 'Great King'

As we have seen, '*Muddha-beiktheik* was the most important ceremony among other Beiktheik rituals, because it was strongly connected with the legitimacy of kingship. According to the traditional theory, those kings who did not observe this ceremony were not regarded as genuine ones and were not worthy of being endowed with any titles, and did not deserve to be called 'Great King'. Not being endowed with Five Effects (*Akyo: Ga:-ba:*) [41], he would be considered sinful. Only when the king observed this ceremony, would he be qualified to protect Buddhism, be competent to govern the territory endowed with juristic power, and properly entitled to request a part of the profits of produce (*louk-hkun*). Consequently, the king's endeavour would be fruitful, because observation of *Muddha-beiktheik* was a merit-making as well as a happy event. Thus it was the occasion for the king to promise to abide by the various royal laws [See MMOS I, s.163: 239; Okudaira 2000a: 125-126]. Theoretically those kings who did not observe it were not entitled to Dhamma-yaza (King of Law), but they were in fact regarded as a lawful if they ruled justly over the kingdom of Myanmar.

b. Restraint of Despotic Rule by the King

The consecration oath taken by the king conveys the meaning that he is the guardian of the people. He was requested to love them as if they were his own offspring. The oath bounded the king to the Sangha headed by the primate (Thathanabaing). It impressed on the people's minds that the king was the defender and promoter of Buddhism [See Thaung 1959: 175]. This shows a bilateral relationship involving rights and duties between the king and the people. It acted as a check on the king's tendency towards absolute rule and despotism. The people recognized his right to rule as long as he ruled rightly. When a king acted against the people's will, they could admonish him, sometimes with exceptional severity. In one case, the people banished the king from the kingdom. In another case, they banished the crown prince. In extreme cases when people did not approve or accept the king, they put to death the reigning king and replaced him with a new king [MMOS II: 5]. Nearly always these irregular successions stayed within the ruling dynasty. The king replaced by his uncle, his sun or his brother. When a coup attempt failed, the leaders were either exiled or executed [See also Okudaira: *ibid.*126].

c. Acknowledgement of Legitimacy of Kingship

The *Muddha-beiktheik* was a consecration ceremony whereby a person became qualified to be a genuine king. Throughout Myanmar's successive dynasties, it was the essential qualification for kingship. At least one *Muddha-beiktheik* ceremony was required to qualify a *de facto* ruler who had seized power as a *de jure* or 'legitimate' king. Theoretically it was the people who entitled a person to ascend the throne as the legendary first King *Mahathamada* was chosen by the people as the king. Kings were expected to rule till their death if they could. Sometimes they could not, and were killed by sons or brothers. As we saw a king was expected in principle to test his popularity at least once during his reign. He did so making an appeal to the people that his rule so far had been just. The people had the right to request that the king whom they had selected themselves should govern them lovingly like he treats his own children, and respect holy men and monks. This is the message of the Ten Royal Duties (*Min: Kyin. Taya: Hse-ba:*), Four Laws of Assistance by the king (*Min:-do. Kyin. Ya. Thaw: Thingaha Taya: Le:-ba:*)[(42)]. Following the Theravāda Buddhist tradition, the Myanmar kings aspired to be called Dhammayaza (King of law). This was the best possible qualification for ruling over the lay and ecclesiastical world. King Badon, whose reign lasted for more than thirty-seven years, underwent the supreme coronation of the *Muddha-beiktheik* twice in 1783 and 1784 in succession. This reflected his prestige he acquired after conquering of Rakhine. Though his later campaigns failed, he enhanced stability of his rule by excluding his rivals [See also Okudaira *ibid.*: 126-127].

3. Establishment of King Badon's Style of the *Muddha-beiktheik* Ceremony

It is generally accepted that King Badon was one of the most powerful rulers in Myanmar history. The boundaries of the country reached their utmost limit as the result of his conquests and annexation of Rakhine (Danyawadi) in 1784 and in 1785 respectively. The annexation of Rakhine enhanced the reputation of King Badon, because no other Myanmar king in the past had ever conquered Rakhine. He also succeeded in retaining Tanindayi (Tenasserim) and Dawe (Tavoy). His reign extended over thirty-seven years. King Alaungsithu ruled longest for fifty-five years and next, King Narapatisithu in the Bagan period ruled as long as King Badon. King Badon asked Maung Htaung Hsayadaw to write about proper practice of the *Muddha-beiktheik* ceremony. He told his scholars what sources to follow, and which recently imported Sanskrit text on consecration to translate [See *Thekkata Abhitheka Sadan* (TAS) 1782 in HSTH]. In this regard, Michael Charney, who is a historian of pre-modern period of Myanmar, emphasized the contribution of Nyanabhivaṃsa who was a young Budhist monk and expert in Sanskrit literature to the translation of the Sanskrit text of *Abhiṣeka* into Myanmar [Charney 2006: 46]. In this regards, Huxley asserted that "Being close to the Manipur border sharpened local skill in Sanskrit. These conditions produced an efflorescence of monastic talent that the Prince of Badon drew on when he fought his way to the throne in 1782" [Huxley

2007: 431].

According to Bagan U Tin, King Thalun [1629-1648] in Nyaunyan Dynasty performed the *Muddha-beiktheik* ceremony as did King Dattarāja [1153-1165] in the Danyawaddy Kingdom of Rakhine [MMOS pt.1, s163: 240]. King Dattarāja's ceremony, at least clearly demonstrates the bilateral contract orally exchanged between the king and the *Thahte-thagywe* or rich men [See San Shwe Bu 1917: 181-184]. We are told of King Thalun's consecration ceremony in *Hmannan Maha Yazawingyi* [See HMY III: 214-219] or the consecration record [YMS: 1-15]. It took in 995M.E. (=1643A.D.) after four years of enthronement modelled upon King Aśoka who performed *Abhiṣeka* ceremony in four year's time after he ruled over the whole country. Although it is not clear whether King Thalun and the rich men exchanged their bilateral contracts, he seems to have done it if we follow U Tin's account [MMOS pt.1 s 163: 240].

Kings who did not practice the *Muddha-beiktheik* were called *Thamanya Min* (=*Thaman-min,* ordinary king), while those kings who practiced the ceremony being called *Muddha-beiktheikta-min* (or *Muddha-beiktheik-hkan-min*), king who went through the ceremony). [MMOS pt.1 s.163: 239-240]. The latter, as we have seen, did not followed a fixed patten [Furnivall 1925: 142]. King Badon's larger project was to collect literary works for his Library in the new capital city of Amarapura. At the suggestion of Maung Htaung Hsayadaw the king dispatched a study mission including ten Brahmins to obtain the copies of treatises on *Lawki Kyan* (Book on worldly affairs) from Calcutta (Kolkota) [TSA 1976: hka.]. Before that, Maung Htaung Hsayadaw translated the Bengali version of the Sanskrit *Abhiṣeka Sadan* (Treatise on Consecration Ritual) into Myanmar under the title of *Thekkata Abhitheka Sadan* in1782 [AHP 1961: dha.]. King Badon impressed on his scholars under the Maung Htaung Hsayadaw how important it was that his consecration should be bigger and more authentic than the haphazard ceremonies put on his predecessors [See AHP: 28-31; 48-49; 51-52; 62-64, etc.; LMBM 1985: preface]. Thus King Badon's two consecrations of 1783 and 1784 constructed from the various precedents a new standard model which his successors would follows [Okudaira 2000: 125]. This model was compiled and recorded by Maung Htaung Hsayadaw under the title of *Yadanapura Sadoukhta.Myo.ti Nan: ti Mintayagyi Muddha-beiktheik Sadan* [AHP: preface:na.] in prose when he left the monkhood (Primate) to serve as a lay minister. Poems describing for the *Muddha-beiktheik* ceremonies were composed by Thet-pan Atwinwun and Letwè Nawyahta in Mawgun (Record of a significant event meant to last) genre.

4. The Ritual of the *Muddha-beiktheik*

King Badon's ceremony was extremely elaborate and lasted for a week. It began with the selection of the place to build a temporary building known as mandat where the ceremony was to be performed. In brief it was mainly composed of three parts, viz; (a)attendance of Buddhist monks and Brahmins (*Ponna-do.*), (b)a petition made to the King to rule in accordance with the law by Princesses(*Min:thami:-do.*), Brahmins and Richmen (*Thu-gywe= Dhagywe*), and a speach delivered by the King to the subject [LMB, See also MMOS I: 243-246, Thaung 1956: 171-185; Yi Yi 1961: 85-129; Okudaira 2000: 122]. He underwent the *Muddha-beiktheik* ceremony twice, first on 17th May, 1783 AD (=1145M.E.) on the day of the transfer of the capital city from Inwa (=Ava) to Amarapura. His second ceremony was on the 2nd June, 1784 A.D. (=1146 M.E.) on the day when the Royal Residence for the Crown Prince was built in the Palace ground. The two ceremonies were similar and included these features.

a. Attendance of Buddhist monks and Brahmin:

When the arrangements were completed, the Lord, King of the country, attired in the robes like those of the Brahma kings, with the Queen also dressed in the robes like those of the queen of the Nat King, set out together on the bejeweled Palanquin. When they reached the *Mingala Mandat* (auspicious temporary building), the Thathanabaing (Head of the Buddhist Order) and twelve Ponna Puroheit (Brahmins) brought forth the *Pitakat Thon-bon* (Three Sacred Buddhist Scriptures). After these were placed in the *Sihathana* (Lion's throne) temporary building, he then washed his head in the *Gazathana* (Elephant's throne) temporary building. After that, the King and Queen seated themselves on a guilded platform made of fig wood.

b. Petition to the king to rule in accordance with the law by Princesses, Brahmins, and Rich-men respectively:

The eight princesses dressed as celestial beings prostrated before the King and Queen. Then with both hands they held a bejeweled right whorled conch, filled with water from the sacred Ganges, and placed it respectfully above the King's head. Then the chief of the Princesses proclaimed: "Oh Lord King, may you be steadfast in the laws practiced by the Mahathamada, the first King in the world; Oh Lord King, may you never be wrathful in dealing with the lords of the kingdom, may you protect all the people, may you love and pity all of them as if they were your own offspring, may you regard the lives of all the people as you would your own; Oh Lord King, may you abstain from greed and anger, may you eliminate the evil *Mawha* (ignorance); Oh Lord King, may you only utter noble words, may you only perform deeds of grace, may you pursue only glorious deeds", and after they finished the proclamation, they poured the Beiktheik water over the King's head.

Then, the eight Brahmins performed this in the same manner, held a bejeweled right-whorled conch with both hands, filled with water from the sacred Ganges, and placed it respectfully above the King's head, and the chief of the Brahmins recited, "Oh Lord King, may the faith increase in glory, may you love and pity all the living beings as your own sons, may you keep and guard the prosperity of all the living beings as your own, may you always follow such things as never be wrathful in dealing with the Lords of the kingdom, observing the laws, listening to the words of the learned, guarding the kith and kin", and after they poured the Beiktheik water over the King's head.

After that, the eight Richmen recited the invocation in the same manner as the Princesses and the Brahmins, and they proclaimed, "Oh Lord King, may you take what is due to you according to the law, may you stay away from the lawless ones and evil men."

After that, the Richmen implored again, "Oh Lord King, may you receive our Beiktheik water, may you practise according to our words, and may you look after the people with justice by enjoying the wealth of one-tenth of our products; Oh Lord King, if you should practise according to our word, may you prosper both in this world and the world after that. May you glory increase every day like the rising sun and waxing moon, may the kings of many countries bow their heads before you, may there be no thieves and robbers in the country, may the faith increase in glory, may the people daily bless you, and may you live long to rule over us. If you should be heedless to our petition, and if the consecration oaths which virtuous kings take be broken by you, may the world be in turmoil, may great storms arise and great earthquakes crumble the earth, and the fires of hell burst aflame on earth, may evil omen and witches, and souls in torment hover over the palace and cause fear and trouble, may the cobra, and viper and tiger roam and devour you".

c. A Speech delivered by the King to his subject

The king reciprocally delivered a speech to acquaint his subjects with the fact that he was fully aware of his rights and duties and said, "I have given all kinds of Dana (alms), and so I have attained this position of the king. If I should seek the prosperity and welfare of the people and sacred monks of the country and if I should ask for not more than one-tenth of the people's products according to the traditional custom, and if I should hold myself apart from the evil men who are the enemies of religion, if the monks respects novices and people of the country as I would respect my sons and daughters born of me, then may body be free from all the diseases, may I live long, may I be victorious over all my dangerous enemies, and may white elephants and treasures be bestowed upon me." [See AHP: 54-64; MMOS I s.166, 167 & 168: 243-246; MMMHK 1905: 1-18; San Shwe Bu 1917: 181-184]. (Aforementioned a. b. and c. are extracted from Okudaira *ibid.*: 123-124)

5. A Step toward the Institutionalization of the *Muddha-beiktheik* Ceremony

a. Substantial Meaning of the *Muddha-beiktheik* Ceremony

In U Tin's book on the *Muddha-beiktheik* ceremony, the Myanmar Monarchy was essentially dependent upon popular acceptance. The ceremony enhanced the exchange of oaths between the king and the people at the ceremony. This is, of course, a part of the standard account of Myanmar kingship, deriving from very old legends in Indian tradition [See Heesterman 1957: 114-122], and it describes the theory rather than the practice. In theory this standard *Muddha-beitheik* ceremony was essential to a king's legitimacy. In practice this was often not the case.

Many, if not most, kings did not undergo the ceremony. Kings actually, could rule for life, even though not formally empowered with proper powers, without lustration and oaths. Of more practical importance was actual physical possession of the palace throne-room and the network of loyalty oaths. Thus, the chief function of the *Muddha-beiktheik* ceremony in Myanmar kingdoms may have been to magnify the king's authority in the palace to glorify his position and to strengthen his own self-confidence. He would have to see himself as a strong, unchallengeable and successful king before he ventured upon the ceremony. In effect, it would not only be a manifestation of his pomp and power, but also self-protection against those who might revolt against him [Okudaira *ibid.*: 127-128]

The ceremonial rite which was performed at the time when a new king ascended the throne was theoretically not enough to make rule. At this stage, he was only a ordinary king. The word '*Muddha-beiktheik*' appears probably for the first time in source material on King Badon's ceremony in 1783. It might be conjectured that the '*Muddha-beiktheik*' ceremony itself was performed like *Datharaja* in Rakhine, but the same terminology was not always used, nor was the ceremony always fully performed, before the time of King Badon. It is even possible that the *Muddha-beiktheik* ceremony was fully performed by King Badon, and that the terminology of '*Muddha-beiktheik*' was probably first invented during his reign. Though the *Muddha-beiktheik* ceremony aims to increase legalisation and the legitimacy of kingship, it also functioned to magnify the glory of kingship[43] [Okudaira *ibid*.: 128].

b. "Institutionalisation" of the Myanmar Consecration Ceremony

In a Theravāda Buddhist State and loosely structured society such as Myanmar, kings could change the style of the *Muddha-beiktheik* ceremonies. We could say that the *Muddha-beiktheik* ceremony was not well "institutionalised" yet before the Konbaung period. However, the method of *Muddha-beiktheik* ceremony practised by King Badon was followed later by Konbaung kings such as King Bagyidaw [See AHP: preface (Na.); also see LMB: preface (Zaga-lethsaun)], Thayawaddy [KBZ II: 249-251] and Mindon [YBMS: 1-8]. The method of the *Muddha-beiktheik* ceremony practised by King Badon was recorded under King Bagyidaw. King Badon impelled the institutionalisation of the full-scale consecration ceremony more formal. He made the *Muddha-beiktheik* ceremony was more formal. On the occasion of the *Muddha-beiktheik* ceremony performed by King Bagyidaw, Maha Dhamma Thingyan carefully arranged the ceremony comparing and collating eighteen books on the consecration ceremony [See AHP: *ibid.*] and this arrangement contributed to the establishment of a full consecration ceremony in Myanmar [Okudaira *ibid.*128-129].

c. Feature of the Theravāda Buddhist State under King Badon

The *Muddha-beitheik* ceremonies practiced by King Badon consequently served to promote the institutionalisation not only of the ceremony itself, but also of the state organization as a whole. They were connected to his reforms in administration, the legal system and religious affairs, etc. His prestige as the first Myanmar king to conquer Rakhine (=Yakhine=Arakan) in 1784-1785 increased his legitimacy. He was the first Myanmar king to rule nearly the whole territory of the present day Myanmar. The 1782 version of the *Manugye Dhammathat*, which was evidently revised from the original one compiled under King Alaunghpaya around 1756, seems to be almost only one

Dhammathat describing the relationship between the State and Religion, in other words, kingship and Buddhism, or the king and the Sangha. King Badon also introduced a new religious policy: the establishment of the Religious Council which consisted of twelve members of senior monks headed by Thathanabaing (Head of Religious Order).Thus the Theravāda Buddhist State which was founded again by King Alaunghpaya reached its zenith during the period before the failure of military campaigns against Thailand in 1785-86 under the reign of King Badon. The institutionalisation of state organisation was further advanced, and the *Muddha-beiktheik* ceremony was enhanced and recorded. Theoretically its major function was to magnify the king's authority in the Royal Palace, to glorify his position and to strengthen his own self-confidence. Our analysis of *Muddha-beiktheik* ceremony demonstrates an important aspect of the structural features of the Theravāda Buddhist State: the gap between theory and practice [Okudaira *ibid.*129-130].

Chapter VI
Manugye as the Konbaung *Dhammathat*

1. Compilation of the *Manugye Dhammathat* under King Alaunghpaya

In 1752 shortly before the capital city of Ava of the Second Taung-gu dynasty fell under the attack of Mon invaders and King Maha Dhammayaza Dhipati [Dibadi] was taken to Hanthawaddy Bago, one of the most firmly based local Myanmar leaders, whose name was U Aung Zeya of Mok-hso-bo (later Shwebo) known as King Alaunghpaya, systematically commanded his rival leaders, well organized the population under his control and repulsed the Mon invaders from northern part of Myanmar and finally destroyed the capital city of Hanthawaddy Bago in 1757. Mok-hso-bo was renamed Shwebo, and U Aung Zeya proclaimed himself as the King Alaunghpaya of Myanmar in 1752. His consecration took place in 1753 at Ratnasingha alia Konbaung Shwebo. As Lieberman pointed out, King Alaunghpaya was content to resurrect the administrative structure of the Second Taungu Dynasty with only minor changes [See Lieberman 1984: 230] at least during the opening years of the Konbaung Dynasty [Okudaira 2000b: 181].

King Alaunghpaya, as the first king of a new dynasty, needed all the legitimacy he could get. He encouraged prominent priests and laymen to study every branch of learning be it written in Pāli or the vernacular Myanmar language. He initiated a 'Revival of Learning' which included the study of Myanmar traditional law. Under his patronage, eminent jurists, such as Reverend Atula Hsayadaw, Judge Letwe Beiknandhu, and Minister Kyone-wun Bhumma Zeya, emerged [Frchhammer 1885: 90-91]. Thus despite obstacles, the first half of the Konbaung period was one of the epoch- making stages of Myanmar legal history [Okuaira 1999: 478; 2000b: 181].

Regarding the traditional law books known as Dhammathat, Forchhammer's account is as follows: King Alanghpaya asked Zonda Hsayadaw, a monk of Zinpyugyun [Shinbyu-gyun] of Salin-myo, to prepare *Manuyin Dhammathat* [the Original *Manu Dhammathat*] in Pāli. It revived the ancient law of Dhammathat and purpoted to set forth the ancient law of *Manu* as contained in the *Wagaru, Ko-zaung Gyop* and others. The old texts written in Pāli prose were reproduced in Pāli verse. Thus, during the first half of King Alaunghpaya's rule, the only Dhammathat was recensions of the previous ones. But in 1755, *Manuyin Dhammathat* was translated into the vernacular language of Myanmar mostly in Nissaya style which was a word for word translation from Pāli, by Tezothara, a monk of Ratnashingha (Konbaung Shwebo) [See Forchhammer 1885: 92, 96].[44] Forchhammer saw this as a step towards the compilation of a new law book, which was called *Manugye* [*Manu+Akye*: elaborated version of *Manuyin Dhammathat*]. According to one source, it was compiled in 1756 [*ibid*.: 96], after King Alaunghpaya himself attacked and annihilated Hanthawaddy Pegu (Bago), the capital city of Mon and enlarged his Royal Palace of Ratnasingha (Shwebo) in 1755. The *Manugye Dhammathat* [abbreviate as *MD* in the following] was compiled by Kyone-wun Bhumma Zeya under the request of King Alaunghpaya [*ibid*.]to restore law and order and to improve the administration. In addition, the Myanmar Encyclopedia (MSK) describes that the *MD* was composed of 'eighteen portions' in Myanmar prose basing on ten volumes (hse *dwe:*) of the Pāli version of Hindu origin of the code of *Manu* [MSK II: 112].[Okudaira 2000 b: 181] Supposed process of compilation and its later copies of the *MD* is shown in Table 4.

However, the *MD* seems to have been compiled as a symbol of King Alaunghpaya's new dynasty rather than practical in the law courts. No evidence has been found of any royal orders proclaiming the *MD* as the standard for judicial decisions.[45] On the other hand, King Alaunghpaya issued the Royal order that the king and ministers should study various Dhammathats for a similar case [ROB III (19 August 1758): 53-54; 214]. In regard to this Order, Than Tun commented as follows: "*Manuyin* is the Dhammathat and *Manu Kye [Manugye]* becomes a work which explained the Dhammathat. *Manothara Shwe Myin* is the digest of law in a gold-edged notebook. Judges were told to make a good study of three Dhammathats"[ROB VII: xvii-xviii].

2. Characteristics of the *Manugye Dhammathat*

The *MD* was written in vernacular language of plain Myanmar prose with a little Pāli mixed. As Harvey says, "it is neither a code nor a digest, but rather an encyclopaedic record of existing laws and customs and of the rulings preserved in the former Dhammathats" [Harvey 1967: 238]. In other words,

Chapter VI— *Manugye* as the Konbaung *Dhammathat*

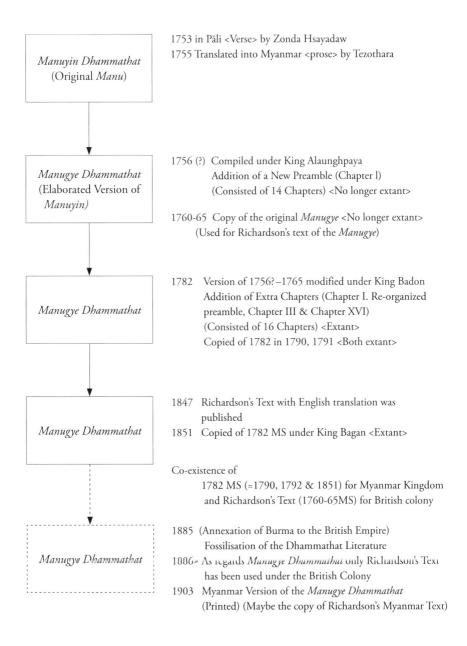

Table 4: Process of Compilation and Copies of the *Manugye Dhammathat*

it is an explanatory works on the existing laws and customs embodying Myanmar culture. Because of its authority over earlier works, it obtained a commanding position throughout the Konbaung period and even to the the British colonial period. It is characteristic of the *MD* to be deeply influenced by Buddhism. The rules contained in the *MD* claim the support of the Buddhist Canon. It was influenced by the rules of *Kaingza Manuyaza Hpyathton* (or more accurately called Shaukhton) [See Lingat 1950: 20], more popularly known as *Mahayazathat* which was compiled by Kaingza Manuyaza, the seventeenth century minister to King Thalun. [Okudaira *ibid.* 182]

Why then, did King Alaunghpaya request Kyone-wun Bumma Zeya to compile such a law book for laymen as incorporated by the precepts of the Buddhist Canon? We may assume that the previous Dhammathats before King Alaunghpaya were all written in pure Pāli or Pāli-*nissaya* (word by word translation to vernacular language) prototype and it was also too difficult for the people to understand the laws and customs explained in Pāli or Pāli-Myanmar' [*ibid.*].

However, when it came to the reign of King Alaunghpaya, the King seems to have requested rewriting of the Dhammathat in more plain and popular manner so that people could understand the laws and customs easier and the king could rule over the country in more efficient way. In other words, the *MD* explained the Myanmar laws with frequent quotes from Buddhist Jātaka stories from Sutta Pitaka and Vinaya Pitaka, so as to make the Dhammathats more attractive to the Buddhist Myanmar. Because of this development, King Alaunghpaya's rule was an epoch-making period in the history of Myanmar legal literature.

Who was the *MD*'s author? U Gaung's Digest [p.8] describes neither the name of the author nor the year of completion. Neither do the surviving complete set of palm-leaf manuscripts [1144M.E.=1782A.D./1152M.E= 1790 A.D./1153 M.D.= 1791A.D./1213 M.E.=1851A.D.]. I shall reopen the question of when the *MD* was written and by whom in the following sections.

3. Authorship of the *Manugye Dhammathat*

Already noted, *Pitakat Thamaing Sadan* by Maha Thiri Zeyathu in the late nineteenth century describes that the *MD* was compiled by a minister (amat) who was awarded two titles of Kyone-wun Bumma Zeya (because he was a minister in charge of the palace moat at the capital city of Shwebo) and Maha Thiri Ottama Zeya Thinjyan ("Highly honoured") [See SMKKS: 3L] by

Chapter VI— *Manugye* as the Konbaung *Dhammathat* 87

King Alaunghpaya. This has been confirmed by *Myanmar Sweson Kyan* ("Encyclopedia of Myanmar") [See MSK II 1955: 112 & MSK VIII 1963: 425-426]. But it says that "apart from the fact that he was awarded two titles during the reign of King Alaunghpaya, so far nothing has been known about him in detail including his birth date and place of birth, etc" [MSK II *ibid.*: 112]. No royal order regarding the compilation of the *MD* has been found. It is rather strange that for such a prominent person as him no information has been found until today. MSK says that "the *MD* or the Decisions of the Hemit Manu is so well known that it will not be an exaggeration to say that almost all the natives of Myanmar are familiars with his name. The name of Minister Kyone-wun Bumma Zeya's work is mentioned as a great book of law in the history of Myanmar literature"[*ibid.*]. It is essential for the present and later scholars to study and discuss this subject. Regarding the judicial circle during the reign of King Alaunghpaya, there were some distinguished law experts, such as the Judge Letwe Beiknanthu, Atula Hsayadaw and Kyunwun Bunnma Zeya, etc. Letwe Beiknanthu compiled *Wineikhsaya Pakatani* (*Vinicchaya Pakasani*) *Dhammathat*. Athula Hsyadaw made decisions for difficult cases for almost ten years as requested by King Alaunghyaya. Likewise, the Minister Kyone-wun Bunnma Zeya wrote the *MD* in almost pure Myanmar prose based on the ten volumes of the famous *Manu Dhammathat* in Pāli compiled by the Hermit Manu. We do not dispute that Kyone-wun Bumma Zeya was the author of the original *MD*. But why did he, the minister of palace moat of the capital city compile a law book? This is unusual. As has been described in the aforementioned MSK, it is quite possible that he compiled the law book independently or he may have been assisted by a certain monk who has specialized in law of the Dhammathat such as Atula Hsayadaw, etc. This assumption comes from the fact that Kaingza Manu Yaza, the minister to King Thalun in the Restored Taungu dynasty, compiled the *Maha Yazathat* (=*Kaingza Manu Yaza Shaukhton*, also called *Kaingza Manuyaza Hpyathton*) with the help of Taunhpila Hsayadaw [*Maha Yazathat* 1222M.E. =1860: hsaw/K-hsan/W]. We have no evidence regarding the relationship between Kyone-wun Bumma Zeya and other contemporary law scholars, such as Atula Hsayadaw, the Judge Letwe Beiknanthu who seems to have written the *Dhamma Wineikhsaya* [*Vinicchaya*] *Dhammathat* (=*Dhamma*) in prose[46] or the minister U Tun Nyo (the Twinthintaik-wun) who wrote the *Kandaw- pakinnaka-linga Dhammathat* (=*Kandaw*) in verse probably during the period in his monkhood which coincides with contemporary period [See Digest 1903: 8], or by other learned monks, etc. However, it can be safely conjectured that they were in contact with each other. Doubtless it was the monks who were the forerunners and distinguished scholars even in the Dhammathat field of secular law. Monks were well versed in Pāli and also in Pāli Dhammasattan literature. They certainly influenced the lay jurists. And perhaps the lay jurists influenced them.

4. Date of compilation

According to the PTS [p.188], the *MD* was compiled during the reign of King Alaunghpaya who founded Yadanatheingha-myo (=Shwebo) in 1115M. E. (=1753A.D.) and the Digest [p.8] does not have any fixed date of compilation. Forchhammer described the year as around 1756 [Jardine Prize 1885: 96]. Furnivall follows the Forchhammer's view [1940: 364]. Dr. Maung Maung, who is the author of *Law and Custom in Burma and the Burmese Family* (1963) mentioned 1752 for the date of compilation in 'A List of Dhammathats' [See Appendix I]. According to Forchhammer, as has been mentioned, Zonda Hsayadaw who was a monk of Zinpyugyun [=Hsinbyu-kyun], Salin-myo, prepared the *Manuyin* (=*Manu Reng*, Original *Manu*) in Pāli verse in 1753 and it was translated into Myanmar prose by the monk Tezothara in 1755 [Forchhammer *ibid.*: 92; see also Furnivall *ibid.*: 362]. Forchhammer continues, "In the year 1756 Alompra [Alaunghpaya] requested Mahasiriuttamajaya /Mahathiri Outtama Thinjyan/., the minister of military works, to compile a code comprising the customary law and usage in force in his dominions; he wrote the well-known Manu Kyay [*Manugye*]---." [Forchhammer *op.cit..*: 96]. Aung Than Tun described that it was compiled between 1758 and 1760 [1961: 15]. Thus Forchhammer gave the definite date of 1756 for the compilation of the *MD*, although PTS and Digest and the surviving palm-leaf manuscripts do not give a date. From where did Forchhammer get the information? It is chronologically very possible that it was compiled in the year immediately after the *MD* was translated into the vernacular in 1755. However, we do not find any authentic records on both dates of *Myanmar* translation of the *Manuyin* and the *Manugye*. So far, we have not found any instructions or orders by King Alaunghpaya for these.

The available historical records say that: King Alaunghpaya began to establish a capital city at Mok-hso-bo on 21st, June 1753. Then, he constructed the city of Shwebo on 26th, June 1754, the palace construction of which was completed on 12th, September of the same year and celebrated the occupancy of the new palace at Shwebo. In March, 1755, King Alaunghpaya began military campaign against Hanthawaddy Mon rebellions and declared

Chapter VI— *Manugye* as the Konbaung *Dhammathat*   89

the victory over them at Dagon where he renamed it as Yangon on 2nd, May in the same year. As soon as he came back to the capital again at the beginning 4th of February, 1756, he left the capital for military campaign in lower Myanmar to attack Hanthawaddy (=Hantharwadi). It was after when Hanthawaddy was completely surrounded by his troops on 8th, March 1757 and finally fell on 12th, May that King Alaunghpaya left Hanthawaddy on 2nd, July and went back to the capital in October in the same year. Therefore, King Alaunghpaya was away from the capital for almost one year and half. During that time, the Crown Prince administered the capital city on behalf of the King. Then, King Alaunghpaya began to enlarge the capital city of Shwebo to the Greater Shwebo, after the conquest of the kingdom of the Hanthawaddy on 24th, October 1757. During the year of 1756 King Alaunghpaya was in the midst of military campaigns. It is more likely that the *MD* was compiled in the year 1757 for commemoration of the conquest of the Hanthawaddy and new expanded capital city [See (T) ROBIII 1985: xxii-xxx]. Aung Than Tun's suggestion that it was compiled between 1758-60, is equally plausible.

5. A serious problem on several versions of the *Manugye Dhammathat* (*MD*)

Unfortunately we have no manuscript of the *MD* written by its author. If we had it would solve many problems of textual criticism. According to MSK [II: 112], it says that Kyone-wun Bumma Zeya compiled the *MD* only in prose, dividing into 'eighteen portions' (*hse.shit pain: pain: ywe.*) of the ten volumes (*hse-dwe:*) of the original *Manu* (*Manu Kyan Yin*) written in Pāli. Possibly it has been handed down verbally by those who were acquainted with the original *Manugye*. Then, what does 'the eighteen portions' means? Does it indicate the eighteen chapters or volumes? Otherwise, the eighteen roots (*amyit-taya:hse-shit hkan:*), i.e. the eighteen radical laws which were originally introduced from the Sanskrit Dharmaśāstra? If it means the eighteen chapters or volumes, could it be possible that surviving texts of the *MD* is composed of eighteen volumes (*atwe:*)? It is apparent that 'the eighteen portions' implies 'the eighteen roots' because any Dhammathat used not "pain:", but "atwe:" for chapter or volume. In addition, the *Manuyin* which was a model as the Original Code of *Manu* for compiling the *MD* divided the law into 'eighteen roots' from the original Manu in Pāli composed of ten volumes [*Manuyin:* 1878: 2]. The Richardson's text which Forchhammer used for his article is a palm-leaf manuscript inscribed between1760 A.D. and 1765A.D. [*ibid.*: 19] For reasons unknown to us it is possible that he did not clarify the exact date of copying of the manuscript, either due to lack of reliable authority on the subject or for lack of time. This consists of the fourteen volumes (chapters). Forchhammer says that 'The Manu Kyay [*Manugye*] is divided into 14 chapters' [*ibid.*: 96]. He apparently used 1874 (Second edition) of Richardson's translation for his article. He seems very likely that he never used any of the four versions of 1782/1790/1791/1851 *MD*, though Kinwun Mingyi used the *MD* (1782MS) for his Digest.

In addition, the first Richardson's Myanmar text with full translation was published posthumously in 1847 a year after his sudden death in 1846 at Amherst (=Kyaikkami) in the British Tenasserim. Though he once visited Ava, the Myanmar capital, he is unlikely to have seen the *MD* (1782MS). Why didn't he mention the copy date of the manuscript he used? Is there any possibility that it was incomplete one and is some parts of it missing? If we accept the explanation of 1847 (First edition) at the end of the fourteenth chapter, it is likely to be a complete one. It says: "Here ends the fourteenth and last volume of the great work of Menoo." But this clause which consists of nine lines was not described in the Myanmar text and was apparently added in English translation. We do not find any Myanmar text corresponding to the English translation. But strangely enough, Myanmar paragraph which consists of the nine lines is added in the second (1874) and fourth (1896) editions. What does it signify? Is the first edition incomplete? Or did the editor of the 1874 edition wish to affirm that it was a complete one? We have no conclusive answer. Anyhow, due to lack of the original palm leaf manuscript (1760-65) of the Richardson's text, it makes us difficult to compare both the Richardson's printed text and 1782 MS (palm-leaf manuscript) as we will mention below.

Except the *MD* (1760-65 MS) used by Richardson there is another manuscript of the *MD* which seems to be revised in 1782. This is apparently a variant (different version) of the original *MD*. This fact also caused a serious problem until present on relationship between Richardson's Myanmar text and 1782MS. The Richardson's text with full English translation dominated the whole British colonial period in Myanmar, while 1782MS as well as the same line of the manuscripts of 1790, 1791 and 1851 had been used until the fall of the Konbaung Dynasty and then had been almost forgotten. Kinwun Mingyi U Gaung used the1782MS in the 1890s, but after that it gathered dust until its modern rediscovery.

The *MD* (1782MS) includes omissions of words, phrases and even paragraphs

Chapter VI— *Manugye* as the Konbaung *Dhammathat*

in many places and is also found repetition of words, but it gives us much information on Myanmar traditional law which is not included in the Richardson's text. Judging from the contents of the *MD* (1782MS and comparing with the Richardson's text, We surmise that 1782ME was written later than the Richardson's Myanmar text. Dr. Than Tun conjectured that the *MD* (1782MS) is not the work of a single author and that it was compiled at various periods in time [See Than Tun 1985: 28-43].

Considering various possibilities, it is conjectured at present stage that the original *Manugye* was similar to the Richardson's text (1760-65 MS) which consisted of fourteen chapters, while 1782 MS was revised between the period of 1760-65 and 1782. Or it is more probable that 1782MS was newly revised at the beginning of the King Badon's reign in 1782.

Chapter VII
Manugye Becomes the English *Dhammathat*

1. Outline of the history after the death of King Badon

King Badon's conquest of Rakhine (=Yakhine) in 1784-85 enhanced his reputation. However, it also destroyed the buffer state that had separated from the East Indian Company in Bengal. In June, 1819, when King Badon's thirty-seven years reign ended at his death, his grandson, Prince Sagaing, was peacefully enthroned under the name of Bagyidaw. King Badon had proclaimed Prince Sagaing as the heir-apparent to the exclusion of his sons, soon after his Crown Prince Upayaza died in March, 1809. Many influential princes, such as the Prince of Taungu, the Prince of Pyi (Prome) were either executed, or poisoned, or deprived of their estate. King Bagyidaw was called 'a palace king' meaning one who spent his time inside the palace. He left his duties to his brother-in-law, having no interest in administration or the world outside the confines of the palace [See Desai 1961: 113]. In June, 1821, King Bagyidaw moved the capital city from Amarapura to Ava and completed his new Palace in March, 1824. A few weeks later, war broke out between the people of Myanmar and the British. Though Maha Bandula, the commander-in-chief, fought bravely against the British, finally King Bagyidaw's kingdom was defeated. The British annexed Assam, Rakhine and Tanindayi (=Tenasserim) in 1826 under the agreement of the Yandabo Treaty.[47] King Badon's failure in the Thai campaign in 1785-1786 became a serious drain upon the resources. King Badon and his successor King Bagyidaw thus looked to expand their domain westwards. This is what led the dynasty into the war with Britain in 1824-26, 1852 and 1885. In the last of these wars, the Konbaung dynasty fell.

2. Dr. David Richardson

During the King Bagyidaw's rule, the British surgeon, David Richardson translated the *MD* into English. He was born in London in 1796 to Scottish parents and became a doctor. He joined the Madras Army as a surgeon in 1823, just before the outbreak of the first Anglo-Burmese war. During the war, he was transferred to Myanmar and was active in lower Myanmar. After the war, he began to take an active part in Tenasserim (Tanindayi) provinces, especially Amherst (=Kyaikkami) and Moulmein (Mawlamyine) until his death at the age of forty-nine. He spent mostly as an administrator and very often as a diplomat as well as an explorer under the Government of British India or the Commissioner of the Tenasserim Provinces in the South [See Langham-Carter 1966a: 207, more in detail see Grabowsky & Turton 2003: 23-30; also see Okudaira 2000b: 183]

The first 'Anglo-Burmese war' was terminated by the Treaty of Yandabo in 1826. Under this treaty the whole country located to the South of Martaban (Moutttama/ Madama) was ceded to the British Government and it constituted the Province of Tenasserim which consisted of four districts: Mergui (=Beik), Tavoy (=Dawe), Ye (which was, before long, amalgamated with Tavoy) and Amherst (=Kyaikkami). Shortly after Amherst was selected as the capital of Amherst district, the Biritish Government decided that Moulmein (=Mawlamyine) had greater commercial and military advantages. It became the headquarters of Amherst district as well as the Province of Tenasserim [See Furnivall 1939: 7]. The British Government had been endeavouring to develop the trade of Moulmein (=Mawlamyaine) [Desai 1939: 285]. Major A.D. Maingy who was then the Commissioner of the Province of Tenasserim dispatched a mission to the Shan Chieftains at Lampang (=Labaung) near Chengmai (=Zimme) and Dr. Richardson was selected to lead it because of his language ability in Myanmar, Thai and Shan [Langham-Carter *ibid.*209; more chronological survey made by Grabowsky & Turton *ibid.*: 30-32] [Okudaira *ibid.*]

Dr.Richardson started exploring several regions to the north of Moulmein (=Mawlamyine) in 1829, visiting Shan Chieftains [See Blundell 1836: 601-625]. In search of trade possibilities he went back to the same places in 1834 [*ibid.*: 687-696] and 1835 [*ibid.*: 696-707]. He left Moulmein with Lieutenant Mcleod who was on a mission to Yunan via the Lao or Shan States, on 13th December, 1836. They traveled to the north together on the fourth mission to the Interior of the new settlements in Tenasserim (=Taninthayi, Tanindhayi) Provinces. Shortly after they had left Moulmein, they separated: Richardson took the usual route to Mainglongyi, while Mcleod heading for Chiengmai. This time also, Richardson, after visiting Karen territories and Shan Provinces went to Ava [*East India* 1869: 104-157; also see Grabowsky

& Turton *ibid.*: 32-34; See also Okudaira *ibid.*183-184]. When Richardson requested, through Henry Burney, who was the Resident to the court of Ava that the new King Thayawaddy (=Thayarwadi) permit him to enter the capital city of Ava from the Shan States, he was refused at first. In the end, though the king relented, received the British mission headed by Dr. Richardson courteously, he would not recognise Burney as the Resident. Burney closed the Residency at Ava. Dr. Richardson, with 250 westerners including British residents and the American missionaries, left Ava for Moulmein and arrived there on 25th August, 1837 [*East India ibid.*: 137-147; also Desai 1939: 285-325; Grabowsky & Turton *ibid.*: 32-34].

On 12th September, 1837, Blundell, the then Commissioner of Tenasserim Provinces, sent a copy of Dr. Richardson's report to the British Government of India, commenting on his excellent work which had, however, been nullified under the new King Thayawaddy (=Thayarwadi). The British mission finally closed the office in 1840. The Provinces of Tenasserim of the British Government were obliged to reduce trading with Myanmar. Then, Blundell turned his attention to Siam and deputed Dr. Richardson to visit Bangkok in December 1838. Dr. Richardson visited Bangkok, the capital city of Siam in January in 1839, where he had discussions with the King Rama III and the Minister for Foreign Affairs and left in March in the same year [See Richardson 1839-1840: JASB 8(96)1016-1036; 9(97)1-3; 9(99)219- 250; also see Langham-Carter 1966a: 217; Turton 1997: 177; see in detail Grabowsky & Turton *ibid.*: 34-35]. Apart from /his/ diplomatic visits through expeditions as seen in the above for more than ten years, Dr. Richardson had held a number of different appointments. First he was appointed to Assistant Surgeon of the medical establishment with the Madras Army in 1823 [EIGD 1823: 269], he was later promoted to Surgeon with the Army in 1836 under the instructions of the Civil Commissioner in the Tenasserim Provinces and in Medical Charge Talaing Corps at Moulmain [*ibid.*1839: 81]. He was in charge of the medical services of the station of Moulmein and later he was posted to medical charge of the civil establishments and jail at Amherst. In addition, he was a medical officer to the various Madras regiments in the Moulmein garrison [Langham-Carter 1966a: 217]. He was promoted to Principal Assistant to the Commissioner of Tavoy (=Dawe) in July, 1845 [EIR&AL 1846: 112] and was the Commissioner of Tenasserim Provinces in December, 1845 for a short time. Soon after that, he died in Moulmein in 1846 [Okudaira *ibid.*: 184].

3. The Translation of the *MD* by Dr. Richardson

Dr. Richardson died suddenly [CR 1847: 94] at the age of forty-nine probably due to weakness after his long and arduous journeys and frequent bouts of malaria [Langham-Carter 1966a *ibid.*: 218]. He was buried in a monastery compound to the east of the Kyaikthalan Pagoda in the city of Moulmein [Langham-Carter 1947: 31].[48] He was highly reputed as a pioneer mainly as a diplomat as well as an explorer, though his death prevented him from attaining higher positions. Let us not forget another of his works, his translation of the *MD* which was originally compiled around 1756 under the reign of King Alaunghpaya. Richardson seems to have painstakingly translated the law book from Myanmar to English under such difficult circumstances mentioned above. Unfortunately, we do not know exactly how he set about this work [Okudaira *ibid.*184]. Richardson was a man of ability: "Richardson's personal capacities and personality served him well in his public role as a diplomat or 'officer' to use his own term. Of clear importance are local knowledge and growing experience of the Shan, Burmese, and Karen in matters political, economic, and social" [Grabowsky & Turton *ibid.*: 42; see more in detail on Richardson *ibid.*: 39-42]. Wayland, a contemporary of Richardson, simply mentions the fact that the *MD* was translated into English by him [Wayland 1853: 110]. We do not know whether he was ordered by his superiors to translate *Manugye* nor how he got the manuscript, nor why he, rather than a legal specialist, translated the Dhammathat. Why did he choose the *MD* rather than any other law book? When did he carry out the work? How well could he understand the complicated Myanmar customary law? Which version of the *MD* was on his desk? [Okudaira *ibid.* 185]

Richardson's translation of the *MD* was published in 1847 by American Baptist Mission Press in Moulmein. It says: 'it was translated from the Burmese by Dr. Richardson, Esq., Principal Assistant to the Commissioner Tenasserim Provinces'. This remarkable work is a posthumous publication, the last service which Richardson performed for the British Government. Mr. A.D. Maingy who was the Commissioner for the Provinces of Mergui (=Beik) and Tavoy (Dawe), organised a committee to draw up a suitable legal code. Richardson was neither a professional jurist nor administrator, but a mere assistant surgeon with the army at that time. He, however, was regarded as a good speaker of Myanmar and Thalaing [Mon] languages. He himself described in his letter to his father in London, dated 29th April, 1827 at Moulmein that "---as I speak the Birman better than any officer in force except one" [Langham-Carter 1966b: 236]. Langham-Carter endorsed his description in such a manner that "Richardson settled down happily in Moulmein, becoming fluent in the Myanmar and Thalaing languages and getting to know the local inhabitants and also his Commander-in-chief" [*ibid.*: 237]. Therefore, he was possibly selected as a member of the said committee as a language expert, who was accordingly familiar with native custom [Okudaira *ibid.* 185]. We can conjecture that the British administrators needed to understand the native customary law, and chose Richardson for the project because he was one of the best Myanmar language experts among British officers. Possibly he had help from Myanmar scholars who were well acquainted with the Myanmar law and custom.

Perhaps the *MD* was chosen because the British administrators found it by chance somewhere in Tenasserim provinces. The second possibility is that it came from Dr. Adoniram Judson[49] who established his Baptist mission at Amherst in April 1826 and who had profound knowledge of the Myanmar language. Judson was invited to accompany Mr. John Crawfurd, the British Envoy, to negotiate a commercial treaty with the Myanmar King [E. Judson 1883: 288]. The third possibility is that Richardson obtained a manuscript of the *MD* at the Court of Ava either directly from the King Thayawaddy (=Thayarwadi) or from a Minister, because very often law texts were given by the Myanmar kings to foreign missions. The fourth possibility is that a British administrator discovered that the *MD* was one of the most popular law books in Ava and it was written almost entirely in plain Myanmar prose making it easier to translate, or the *MD* was the most extensive of all the Dhammathats, dealing with both civil and criminal aspects of Myanmar customary law and reflecting various aspects of Myanmar social and cultural life at that time [Aung Than Tun 1981: 30th November (WPD)]. Thus Europeans came to know about the *MD* and it became very popular among them. It was authoritative in the law courts throughout both the Konbaung and British period. In this respect, Dr. Richardson's contribution to the legal world in and outside of Myanmar is beyond measure. His painstaking effort and elaborate translation of such a voluminous and complicated oriental law book into the language of English deserves our highest appreciation [Okudaira 1986: 42-43; *ibid.*186]

4. The use of the translation of *MD* by the British authority

The first edition of the *MD* was published at the American Baptist Mission

Press in Moulmein in 1847, a year after he died. The second and fourth editions were published by the Mission Press in 1874 and 1896, both in Yangon (=Rangoon), while the third edition published in 1891 is supposed to have been missing [See TCD I: iii]. The Myanmar texts with English translation of 1847, 1874 and 1896 editions have almost the same content, though there are minor differences among them such as the difference in number of pages caused by different typographical composition settings, spelling variations and, as mentioned earlier, an additional clause for Myanmar text in 1874 and 1896 [See Table 6]. Hence the 1891 edition (which is missing) is probably the same, because there are no serious difference between the 1874 edition and the 1896 one. In addition, the Myanmar text was published at the Hanthawaddy Press in Rangoon in 1903, which has obviously the same Myanmar text that was used in the Richardson's translation. These differences are negligible. Richardson's translation is extraordinarily elaborate and voluminous, though there are unfortunately some mistranslations, most of which are due to conflicting rules contained in the *MD* itself. This is the reason why Gywe referred to *Manugye* as 'the victim of a mistranslation' [Gywe 1919; xxiv]. Mistranslations sometimes appear due to misinterpretations of terms relating to the Myanmar culture[50] [Okudaira 1986:43]. There are also minor and unavoidable errors in his translations, but such mistakes are typical of translation work. As a whole, however, the contents of the *MD* are skillfully transmitted into English by Dr. Richardson. Thanks to his translation, the *MD* became a ready reference material and was given authority over all the other Dhammathats need not be consulted [*Ma Hnin Bwin v. Shwe Gone* in L.B.R. Vol. VIII 1948:1-16]. Later, however, the supreme Court reversed this decision by demonstrating that the translation of the *MD* had errors and that the original work itself contained inconsistencies through borrowing from other sources [*Dr. Tha Mya v. Daw Khin Pu* in B. L.R.1951: 108] [Okudaira 1986.: 43-44; 2003b: 186-187].

The omission of the copy-date of the Myanmar manuscript used by Dr. Richardson caused a further serious problem. The Myanmar Dhammathats were mostly transcribed on palm-leaf (Pe) in which the date of transcription was usually described in the colophon of last page, while the date of compilation of the original one is very often omitted [See Feuhrer 1883: 333; also Okudaira 1986: 62]. Accordingly, we can assume that the manuscript of the *MD* used by Richardson would have been given in the colophon. Nevertheless, Dr. Richardson omitted it from all editions of his book. This has caused a crux in the study of the pre-modern history. Given how the Myanmar manuscripts were handed down from period to period, it is doubtful whether the printed text precisely matches the contents of the original or its copies. Therefore, not only the technical errors of transcription but also whether matter has been interpolated at different periods should be examined [See Okudaira 2003b: 187].

5. King Mindon's Response: the First Printing press in Mandalay

The *MD* continued to be copied in palm-leaf form even after 1847

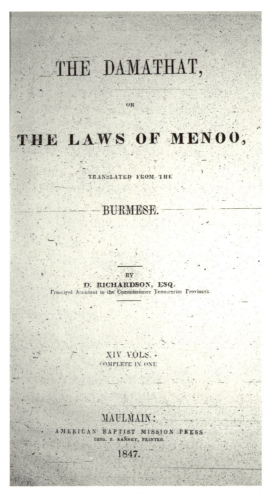

(The first Burmese Text of *MD* with the English translation by Richardson)

appearance in print. Some palm-leaf manuscripts of 1860s and 1870s are extant today at the Universities' Central Library and the National Library, both in Yangon, but these are only a few Chapters of the *MD*.[51] In addition, recently it was confirmed that the palm-leaf manuscript of the *MD* copied in 1213 M.E. (=1851A.D.) during the reign of King Bagan was existing in complete set. It is therefore possible to conjecture that the *MD* was still in use in the form of a palm-leaf manuscript in the kingdom of Myanmar under the reign of King Mindon, while the 1847 publication of it with the translation was applied in the British judicial administration in 'Lower Burma'. This fact shows that the 1782 MS was constantly authorized in the kingdom of Myanmar, while the Richardson's text being authorized in the British colony [See Figure 3].

King Mindon, second to the last King Thibaw of Konbaung Dynasty, was interested in European civilization. He invited European mechanics and engineers to the capital city of Mandalay. He encouraged the establishment of various kinds of factories for industrial development in his kingdom. For example, King Mindon introduced European printing machines to the city of Mandalay. In 1874 (=1236ME) *Nepyi-thaw thathinsa* [*Nepyidaw dhadinza*] ("The Capital Newspaper") was published weekly in the same manner as it was published in Yangon under the British dominion and this was the first newspaper in the kingdom of Myanmar [BHHM 1969: 121] The year of the first publication coincided with the publications of the second edition of the *MD* with English translation by Dr. Richardson at Hanthawaddy Press in Yangon. Thus, King Mindon was considerably influenced by the European technology seen in 'Lower Burma', such as Yangon, Moulmein and others. Information about European technology directly arrived from India and Europe. King Mindon ardently responded to the foreign influence in his environs. However, no palm-leaf manuscript of the *MD* was printed by the Myanmar government. Apart from the *MD* other major Dhammathats, such as *Manuwunnana* (=*Manuvannana*), *Manuthaya* (=*Manusara*) *Shwemyin*, *Manuyin* (=*Manu-Reng*), *Wineikhsaya Pakathani* (*Vinicchaya Pakasani*), *Waru* (*Wagaru*) were printed in succession during the latter half of the 19th century.[52] All these Dhammathats omitted the years of printing from the palm-leaf manuscripts. This can still causes serious problems, when discrepancies appear between the printed books and the palm-leaf manuscripts.

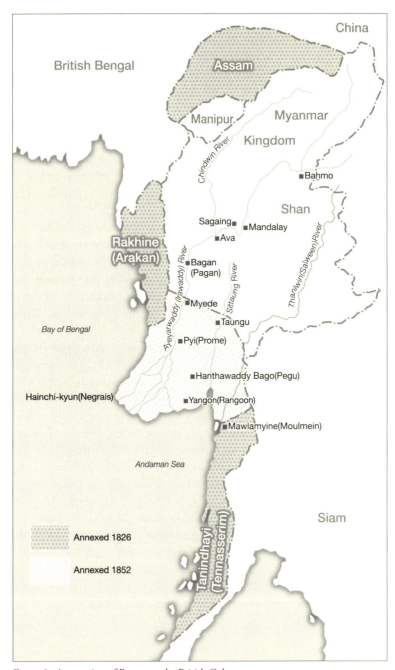

Figure 3: Annexation of Burma to the British Colony

Part II
The *Manugye Dhammathat (MD)*

Chapter VIII
Two Different Editions of the *MD*

1. The 1760 'MS' of the *MD*=The Richardson's Myanmar Text

The *MD* was compiled around 1756, a year after King Alaunghpaya came back from the Hanthawaddy campaign and expanded the capital city of Shwebo. As far as we can tell this original manuscript of the *MD* no longer survives. Dr. Richardson does not tell us the copy-date of the manuscript which he used for his English translation. Forchhammer estimated that it was compiled between the years 1760-1765 [Forchhammer 1885:19].[53] John Jardine, who was the late nineteenth century Judicial Commissioner of Burma, described in his Preface to the second edition (1885) of *A Description of the Burmese Empire* by Father Sangermano that the *MD* which Richardson used for his translation was the manuscript of the 1760 [Sangermano 1966: xxxv]. It is, however, unlikely that this is correct. It is not unlikely that Jardine's '1760' was shorthand of 1760-65. If accepted 1760 as correct, it is still unclear whether it was copied under the reign of King Alaunghpaya or King Naungdawgyi, because the date is shown only in the Christian era, and King Alaunghpaya died on 11th May, 1760. Tentatively, we regard the Myanmar text of Dr. Richardson as the '1760 version' of the *MD*. We cannot prove that the 1760 version of *MD* would be a copy of the original *MD* compiled probably in 1756. At least the copy-date is close to the date when Kyone-wun Bhummazaya wrote the original.

2. The 1782 MS—A Variant of the 1760 'MS'

In regard to the *MD*, one complete set of palm-leaf manuscript is extant at the National Library in Yangon. This manuscript was copied in 1144 M.E. (=1782 A.D.), immediately after King Badon (=Bodawhpaya) was enthroned. The Universities' Central Library (UCL) has also preserved three other copies of 1790, 1791and 1851 manuscripts of the *MD*. But these are apparently recopied from the 1782 version and accordingly there are no major differences except their colophons in the last pages. It means that the 1790, 1791 and 1851 versions are in line with the1782 version. We may, therefore, possibly surmise that there are two lines of the *MD:* one is the 1760-65 'MS' which was used for English translation in the Dr. Richardson's Myanmar text printed in 1847, 1874, 1891 and 1896 and also Myanmar text printed in 1903 at Hanthawaddy Press and used in the British colonies: the other is the 1782 MS and its recopied versions of the 1790, the 1791 and the 1851 in the Myanmar Kingdom. In other words, we may tentatively name *for convenience sàke* that the former is the 1760MS and the latter 1782MS. In short, we have two complete sets of the *MD*: one is the Richardson's Myanmar texts [1760 MS], the other is a version of 1144M.E. [1782 MS].[54] It is noteworthy that there were at least two different textual tradition of the *MD*: one is that of the line of 1760 'MS' and the other of 1782MS and both of them co-existed till the end of Konbaung period.

3. Differences between the 1760 'MS' and 1782 MS

Since the *MD* (=1760MS) was translated into English by Dr. Richardson and published with Myanmar text in 1847, it has become popular. When people say the *MD* they mean Richardson's text. No one seems to have noticed the existence of 1782 MS, though Kinwun Mingyi U Gaung [See Aung Than Tun 2006], who was the Chief Minister to both King Mindon and King Thibaw, actually used this version in his book popularly called *Digest* [DBBL 1898: (i)][55] Dr. Forchhammer, however, did not discuss this version in his Essay for the Jardine Prize, nor mention it. He did not list this version even in his reference of source materials [See Forchhammer 1885: 108-109]. It is evident that he used certain portions of the Richardson's English translation in 1874 (2nd edition) of the *MD* text for his account on the Dhammathat [*ibid.*: 17-20]. During the 1980s we traced the palm-leaf manuscripts of the *MD* in the Dhammathat lists of the public and Universities libraries in Myanmar, and we found only one complete set of palm-leaf manuscript at the National Library in Yangon. It seemed as if this manuscript and accordingly later versions of 1790, 1791 and 1851were awaken from its slumber since the end of nineteenth century. At the same time we felt that all the jurists, historians, and any other scholars in and out of Myanmar who had been interested in the Dhammathat literature had relied fully upon the Richardson's text and that they had long been ignoring the 1782 MS. Accordingly, it seemed very likely that they had never compared it with Richardson's text (=1760 MS). At first a typed copy[56] of the 1782 MS was made by the librarians of the National Library and brought to our notice. Thus the 1782 MS was brought to light probably for the first time in our century. Instantly we found that the 1782 MS consisted of 16 Chapters, while Richardson's text had only 14 Chapters. This difference seemed to us to be of extreme importance. Those who copied the 1782 MS are not mentioned anywhere in the manuscript. We knew that the scribe seems to have started immediately after King Badon ascended the throne and was finished on the fourteenth day of the waxing moon of Waso in 1144 M.E., corresponding to 25th June, 1782 A.D. Dr. Than Tun also asserted that the 1782 MS and the Richardson's text (1760 MS) were different from each other [Than Tun 1985: 28-43]. [Okudaira 2000b: 188][See Table 6]

We had been speculating for several years on the possibility that Richardson's text could be a revision of the 1760 MS. In other words, it was used in judicial administration for the Tenasserim provinces where were then under British rule, omitting certain portions of the 1760MS. However, taking account of the fact that Richardson transcribed such phrase that "Here ends fourteenth volume of the great work of Menoo", it is unlikely that Dr. Richardson revised the original, though it is evident that he omitted the transcription date of the 1760 MS. It would, therefore, seem that the added Chapters (I-pt.2, III & XVI) of 1782 MS are not included in 1760 MS. [*ibid.*: 189].

On the other hand, the added pt.2 of the Chapter I and Chapter III in 1782 MS end in the colophons in such sentences "finished pt.2 of the Chapter I" and " --- finished the Chapter III--- on 3rd of waning of the month of Kason, 1144ME *[=1782AD]*" respectively, while some Chapters (V, VII, VIII, IX, XIV & XVI) end in use of "---finished to make copy" respectively and another Chapters (I-pt.1&3, II, IV, VI, XII & XIII) end in "---finished" and the rest of the Chapters (X & XV) end not using any word for completion of the works respectively. Through this, it may be possibly conjectured that at least pt.2 of the Chapter I and Chapter III were added at the beginning of the reign of King Badon, though it is in question whether the Chapter XVI was added at that time.[57] At best we can say that the 1782MS was compiled at the time of King Badon's enthronement and represents the authors' thoughts on Myanmar kingship at a precise historical moment. At worst it was compiled between 1752 and 1782 and represents one man's vision of early Konbaung Dynasty kingship [See Okudaira & Huxley 2001: 252]. However one is inclined to support the former hypothesis than the latter one, taking

Chapter VIII— Two Different Editions of *MD*

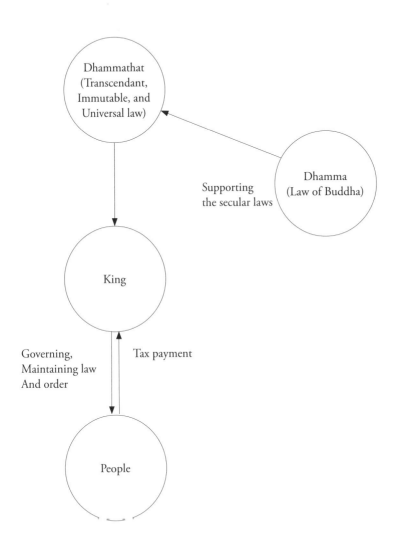

Table 5: The Dhammathat as Secular Law supported by Law of Buddha

account of King Badon's various reformations particularly on legal aspect.[58]

4. Insertion of A New Preamble to the *MD*

Each of the many Dhammathats, which were compiled between the time of the Bagan Dynasty and the fall of the Konbaung Dynasty, has its unique style of preamble concerning a mythical story on royal authority, the outline of which is similar, but not entirely the same. There are various forms of preamble, such as those of the *Wagaru Dhammathat* in the late thirteenth century, which is extremely short, and of the *MD* in the eighteenth century, which is quite long. Some of the preambles, which are suitable to compare with that of the *MD* are such as *Manawthaya* (=*Manosara*), *Kaingza Shwemyin, Manuyin,* etc. On the other hand, the story of *Manu* who became a judge is disregarded in the preambles of *Mohawishsedani* (=*Mohavicchedani*) and *Aṭṭathanhkeip* (=*Attasanhkepa*) *Wunnanakyan*. Apart from the *MD* the preambles of the other Dhammathats are mostly not detailed and elaborate on descriptions of the myth of kingship. For example, the preamble of the *Dhammawilatha Dhammathat* gives much space for the description about administration of justice which is not dealt with in the Richardson's text of the *MD* and is dealt with in the second part of the Volume I of its 1782 version. However, the description from the beginning of the world up to the Great Elect of King Mahathamada is omitted in the *Dhammawilatha Dhammathat*.[Okudaira 1994: 60-61].

In the preambles of the Dhammathats, such as *Manothaya* (=*Manosara*) [MOTD: 3-9], *Pyumin* [PD: 1-45], *Khaingza Shwemyin* [KSD34-44], and *Manuyin* [MYD: 3-5], the outlines of the mythical stories are very similar, though they are, to some extent, different in setting. These are in relation to the king of the abode of Brahma who died there in the previous world, and who was reborned in this world as a direct line of King Mahathamada and his two sons, namely: Thubhadya and Manu (or Manuthaya= Manusara, or Manawthaya=Manosara), who later brought the science of astrology and the Law Book (Dhammathat) respectively from the boundary wall of the Universe (*Sekkyawala-dadaing*). The preamble of the *MD* does not mention this aspect in detail. On the other hand, the preambles of other Dhammathats, such as *Pyumin, Manuthaya* and *Manuyin* do not refer to such idea that King Mahathamada was regarded as the second sun who belonged to the solar dynasty, and that he was legally appointed as king through ceremonial rites, being called by the people as Mahathamada, Hkattiya and Yaza. Concerning the so-called "Twelve Decisions" by a young cowherd (later Manu), and "Seven Decisions" by him after he had been appointed as Judge Manu by the King Mahathamada, the *Dhammawilatha Dhammathat* dealt with the process of accepting the position of Judge in detail [DWDb: 27-28]. But among the contents of the seven days' decisions which Manu dealt with, only the seventh day's decision is referred to [DVD (ii): 28].[*ibid.*: 61].

The preamble of the *Dhammawilatha Dhammathat* does not refer to the twelve decisions. Those of *Pyumin* [PD: 3-4] and *Manuthaya* [MTSD: 3] describe in detail the fact that the Dhammathat was compiled in the Magada language[59] by three respective persons: King Pyumin who was a descendant of King Mahathamada, Thagyamin or King of Celestial abode, and a kingly revered monk. The *Manuthaya* also describes that the Dhammathat was brought to Zabudipa (=Zambudipa, South Island)[60] and that it was translated into the Ramañña (Mon) language by Reverend Buddhagotha (=Buddhaghosa) [MTSD: 3]. No reference to this is seen in the *MD*. But the preamble to the *MD*, as a whole, described the mythological story on kingship in most elaborate and detailed manner.[*ibid.*: 61-62].

The preamble of the *MD* which consists of the myth on royal authority, is not actually an original work, especially relating to the first part of the story on Great Elect of King Mahathamada.[61] Its characteristic feature, however, is that it narrates the tradition of administration in the Theravāda Buddhist society in accordance with law, combining the first part on the Erection of King Mahathamada and the second part on the Story of Manu into single myth. The *MD*, like other Dhammathats, commences with words for worship of Buddha. This is followed by a preamble which consists of two parts. The first part narrates the period beginning with the emergence of the present world (*Badda Kaba=Gaba*) and continuing up to the election of King Mahathamada [RMD 1847: 1-8; 1782MD: k/K-ki/K]. The second part tells the story of Manu, a counselor, as well as a minister to the King, who after resignation from his post because of a misjudgment, became a Yathe (=Rishi) or hermit and attained a supernatural power and then traveled to the boundary wall of the Universe, where he found the Dhammathat and presented it to the king for promulgation [*ibid.*: 9-24; 1782MS ki./K -hka./W; *ibid.*: 58]. [See Table 5].The outline of the preamble of the *MD* is as follows:

a. The first part of the Preamble- Great Elect of King Mahathamada

The opening describes the creation and destruction of successive worlds. That is the emergence of the present world after the previous ones had destroyed seven times by fire and once by water. After this, a description of the site of the Bodhi tree where a succession of Buddha attained enlightenment is presented. Then it deals with a discourse on Buddhist ontology. It reads like a modification of a Buddhist religious work.[62] The first living beings whose existence in the celestial state had ended, appeared in this world and were called Byahmas or Brahmas. At first they enjoyed heavenly bliss like birds flying with radiant bodies in the expanse of the heavens. They descended to the earth. But when they ate the products of the earth, they developed heavy bodies and were compelled to remain on the earth. The preamble continues with a detailed description on the emergence of the sun, moon and stars, while describing the process of formation of the present world and introducing the structure of the Buddhist cosmos.[63] These original inhabitants of the world, having eaten the fragrant earth for a long time, became passionately covetous and harboured hostility towards one another, and consequently the rich soil disappeared. So they were obliged to cultivate crops, each having a share of the land marked off for his own labours. Then, the first crime was committed.

There arose innumerable and endless disputes. In consequence, the people assembled and elected a man who was born as *Hpaya-laung* or embryo Buddha, who was honest, wise, and trustworthy and who would be able to restore law and order to the community. In this way, the perfect one was called Mahathamada. The people offered to give him a tenth of their products, requesting him to restore law and order. In return, they gave him the authority to rule and command. The people conferred upon him three ceremonial rites of enthronement, called Beiktheik.[64] He was called Mahathamada because he was the great elected one. He was called Hkattiya because of his dominion over the land and finally he was called Yaza because of his ability to instruct people according to the law. The original name of King Mahathamada was *Manu*, who is the lineal descendant from the sun (*Ne-min:i. Ahset-anwe*). He was also called the second sun (*hnit-chein myauk thaw ne-min:*), who enlightens all. Among the rulers, Mahathamada is the first. He is a man of power, glory and authority. Therefore, nobody dared to infringe upon the rules he laid down.

b. The second part – Story of Manu

The author of the *MD* added the story of a counselor called 'Manu', who was well versed in the art of administering justice. King Mahathamada began to rule the country, making the boundaries of districts, cities, towns and villages. The people, however, were dissatisfied and dispute arose. King Mahathamada, therefore, honoured a young cowherd of about seven years of age who had great wisdom and who was famous for his 'twelve decisions' in his village.[65] Then he was requested by the King to dispense decisions on all judicial cases in the country. The cowherd at first hesitated to accept the burden of his office and the responsibility of making judgments, replying to the King that he was afraid of undertaking the responsibility of giving the decision of all cases in the country, because he thought that it was humanly impossible to be free from misjudgment.[66] Then, King Mahathamada, having fixed a certain term in years and months, begged the cowherd that he should undertake it. So, the cowherd, making his obeisance to the King, agreed to enter the court and to decide cases for seven days[67] with the King's authority. The name of *Manu*, which was originally that of King Mahathamada, was bestowed on him by the King and he was appointed a counseller, judge as well as minister. On the seventh day as a judge, as he had predicted before the King, he made a misjudgement on the cucumber case.[68] Although he corrected his wrong decision, he was afraid of continuing as a judge. Manu asked the King to allow him to become a Yathe (hermit). He, then, traveled to a rock cave in the hills and remained there, spending his days in meditation. Then, attaining a supernatural power (*zan*)[69], ascended into the realms of heaven. On the boundary wall of the Universe, he found the Dhammathat, which was engraved in letters as big and prominent as elephants, buffaloes, oxen and horses, covering a variety of subjects. It included decisions approved by men of great learning, which could help to solve many problems, and could bring about peace and well-being to the people of the world. Yathe (Manu) learned the Dhammathat by heart and brought back to the earth and after inscribing on a golden plate presented it to King Mahathamada, desiring that it might be beneficial to all the people on the earth in future. [Aforementioned a. and b. are extracted with a little modification from Okudaira 1994: 59-60]

Chapter IX
'Duties of Kings and Judges' of the *MD* (1782MS)

1. New Information added to the *MD* (1782 MS)

The Richardson's text consists of only 14 Chapters, while the 1782MS provided 16 Chapters. That is to say, Pt.2 of Chapter I, Chapter III and Chapter XVI of the 1782MS are not included in Richardson's text. Chapter II & III of the Richardson's text were moved to Pt.3 of the Chapter I and Chapter II of 1782MS respectively; Chapter IV, V, VI, VII, VIII & IX are the same Chapters with those of the 1782MS. Chapter X and XI of the 1782 MS correspond to Chapter X in Richardson's text. Chapter XII, XIII and XIV of the 1782 MS correspond to XI, XII and XIII in Richardson's text respectively. Chapter XV of the 1782MS corresponds to XIV of Richardson's text. Chapter XVI of the 1782 MS summarizes the contents of the whole work from Chapter I to Chapter XV and then it emphasizes the importance of qualification of the judges speaking figuratively on gold. Not all of this is included in Richardson's text. A table of comparison is given in Table 6.

The preamble of the 1782MS consists of Pt.I which is almost the same with the original preamble of the *MD* (=Richardson's text) and of Pt.II which was probably newly inserted in the 1782MS and of Pt.III which was moved from Chapter II of Richardson's text. Pt.2 of Chapter I describes about politics, particularly the duties of kingship and law concerning the processes of dispute settlement [hka./kyi: wun:]

It is an original and valuable source for political theory in eighteenth century Myanmar. Here follows its text:

a. Concerning Politics — The Duties of Kingship
1. Twelve Royal Duties [*Min: kyin. Taya: Hsehnit-pa:*]
2. Ten Royal Duties [*Min: kyin. Taya: Se-ba:*]
3. Seven Characteristics for a (Strong) City [*Myo. i. Inga Hkunit-pa:*]
4. (Another) Seven Characteristics for a (Strong) City [*Myo. i. Inga Hkunit-pa:*]

5. Seven Royal Fundamental Requirements of a Kingdom [*Min:do. i. Pyagade Hkunit-pa:*]
6. Four Components of the Armed Forces [*Sit Inga Le:-ba:*]
7. Four Kinds of (Subsistence) for a City [*Myo. i. Asa Le:-ba:*]
8. Five Royal Strengths [*Min:-do. A:-daw Ga:-ba:*]
9. Seven Factors to Keep Prosperity (of the State from) Deterioration [*Apreikha. Ni.ya. Taya: Hkunit-pa:*]
10. (Another) Seven Factors to Keep Away from the Deterioration (of the State) [*Apareiha Niya. Taya: Hkunit-pa:*]
11. Four Kinds of Assistance [*Tingaha Wuthtu Taya: Le:-ba:*]

b. Concerning Law - Processes of Dispute settlement
12. Four Types of Persons Who Should Pass Judgment to Deputize for Kings [*Min: do. Koza: Hta: Ywe. Siyin Ya. Thu Le: -ba:*]
13. Five Judges [*Taya:-thugyi: Nga:-ba:*]
14. Six Types of Persons Who Should Not Pass Judgment [*Ma. Siyin Se Thint Thu Chauk-pa:*]
15. Seven Types of Persons Who Should Behave Like a Stone Pillar [*Kyauksa-taing Ke-tho. Kyint Ya. Thu Hkunit-pa:*]
16. Four Nether Worlds [*Apay Le:-ba:*]
17. Eight Kinds of Danger [*Be Shit-pa:*]
18. Ten Types of Chastisement [*Dan Hse ba*:]
19. Eleven Kinds of Person Who Should Be Witness [*Ti. Ya Thet-hse Tit-ba:*]
20. Sixteen Kinds of Person Who Should Be Totally Dissolved as A Witness [*Alon: Pyet thint thaw Thet-the Tit-hse Chauk-Pa:*]
21. Twenty-eight Types of Witnesses who Should be Removed from the Bunch (Group) of Witnesses [*Pyet Thint Thi Ahkaing Hma. Pyet Ya Thi Thet-the Hnit-hse-Shit pa:*]
22. Five Miscellaneous Kinds of Witness [*Thet-the Apya Nga:-ba:*]
23. Ten Percent of the Property in Question entitled to Witness [*Thet-the Hkan do. Sa:Ya.Thi Hse-zu. Tit-su.*]
24. Twelve Kinds of Qualities of the Law Books [*Dhammathat-do. i. Gon Apya Tit-hse Hnit-pa:*]

[I-pt.2: hka./K-hki./W; See Than Tun 1985: 29-38; Okudaira & Huxley 2001: 249]

The text gives more detailed explanation of each item on these twenty-four lists as follows.

2. The Duties of Kings

In regard to List 1, these are: (1)Not to transgress against the Three Gems (*Yadana Ton:-ba:*), (2)To avoid ignorance(*Aweitza*), (3)To be well-disposed towards charitable donors, (4)To provide long-term support to scholars, (5) To give alms to those in immediate need, (6)To follow the customs like Dhammathat faithfully, (7)To adopt the policy of following precedent, (8) To keep the stories well in mind (*pon-byin go pyu.*), (9)To observe the five precepts of Buddhism (*Pinsathi Nga:-ba:*), (10)To control anger, (11)To identify the twelve kinds of misdeeds (*A-kudho*) and (12)To govern the populace and the monks [I-pt.2: hki/W-hki/K].[70]

As to List 2, these are: (1)To give alms, (2)To observe the precepts, (3) To be generous, (4)To be honest (*Hpyaunt-mat thaw Hnalon:*), (5)To be kindhearted (*Nu-nyant Thein- mwe thaw Hnaloun:*), (6)To adopt a moderate style of life, (7)To avoid anger, (8)Not to persecute (*Hnin:-ban: Hneit-set*) the people, (9)To be tolerant, and (10)Not to be oppressive (*Chouk-hcye Chin Kin:*) These are what the king should observe [I-pt.2: hki/K].

Regarding List 3, (1)An disputed single ruler, (2)Alliances with other rulers, (3)A minister (*Amat*) who can pass judgment over affairs of state and village disputes, (4)A granary full of the Seven Kinds of Paddy (*Zaba:-myo: Hkunit-pa:*) which are like the Ten Kinds of Jewels (*Yadana Hse-ba:*)[71], (5)A strong moat, ditch, embankment, and a cat-walk on the fortified gateway of the city wall, (6)An extensive territory (*Taing-ga:*) and (7) Elephant (regiments), cavalry (regiments), chariot (regiments) and infantry soldiers [I- pt.2: hki./K].

As to List 4, these are: (1)A strong city, (2)Wide passage for soldiers on the fortified battle-field (3)Various armaments such as the lance, (4)A fighting force organized into soldiers and commanders, (5)Men to guard the gate, (6) Strong gate posts inside the walls and (7)Strong gate posts outside the walls [I- pt.3: hki/K].

As regards List 5, these are: (1)A king, to act as lord of the country, (2) High officials, to carry out the king's wishes and perform their duties, (3) Small villages, inhabited by virtuous persons, (4)A strong city surrounded by three moats, (5)Punishments that benefit the crime, (6)Ample stock in granaries and sufficient supply of water in tanks and ponds, (7)Alliance with other kingdoms [I- pt.2: hki/K].

On List 6, these are: (1) Elephants, (2)Horses, (3)Chariots (*Yahta:*), (4) Foot soldiers [*ibid.*].

Regarding List 7, these are: (1)Seven varieties of rice, (2)Cattle-fodder, (3)

1782 MS		RICHARDSON'S TEXT (Printed from 1760-65 MS)					
		1847 (1st ed.)		1874 (2nd ed.)	1896 (4th ed.)		
Chapter		Page	Chapter	Page	Chapter	Page	
I	pt.1	ka/K-hka./W	I	1-24	1-26	4-26	
	Pt.2	hka/K-gi/W					
	Pt.3	gu/K-ga./W	II	64-108	65-109	65-110	
II		nge/K-hsu./W	III	25-63	26-65	26-65	
III		hse/K-zaw:/W					
IV		zaw/K-jyaw/K	IV	109-127	109-127	110-128	
V		jyan/K-Nyan/W	V	128-145	128-147	129-148	
VI		nya:/K-htaw:/W	VI	146-178	146-182	148-183	
VII		htaw/W-da:/W	VII	179-220	182-226	183-227	
VIII		na/K-fa/W	VIII	221-243	226-250	227-251	
IX		ti/K-tan/W	IX	244-257	250-263	251-264	
X		ka:/K-du./W	X	258-313	264-321	265-322	
XI		du/K-na/W					
XII		na/K-naw/W	XI	314-325	321-333	322-334	
XIII		nan/W-hpu./W	XII	326-351	334-361	334-362	
XIV		hpu/K-hpa:/W	XIII	352-358	362-369	363-370	
XV		ba./K-ba/W	XIV	359-376	369-388	370-389	
XVI		bhi./K-me/W					

[Revised version of Okudaira 2000b: 189]
Table 6: Corresponding Chapters between 1782 MS & Richardson's Texts

Firewood, (4)Water [*ibid.*].

In regard to List 8, (1)Strength of the royal family, (2)Physical prowess, (3) Wisdom, (4)Able counselors (or Officers) for the kings, (5)Economic strength such as Properties (*Ossa*) [*ibid.*].

On List 9, these enable the state to develop prosperity: the king should: (1)Hold meetings and consult with his royal counselors three times a day, (2) Tackle affairs with the application of consistent rules, (3)Collect only those taxes and impose only those punishments which tradition allows, (4)Respect and cherish the elderly, (5)Not reign over his subjects oppressively, (6)Make the usual offerings to the Nats who watch over the capital city and the rest of the kingdom, (7) Patronize the Sangha (Buddhist Order) [I- pt.2: hki/W; see also (T) ROBIV: 139/140: 510-511]].

Regarding List 10, these are: To be a man: (1)who offers respectful obedience to the Buddha, since he received the Law, (2)who offers respectful obedience to the Law (Dhamma) that he receives, (3)who offers respectful obedience to the Sangha (Monastic Order) from whom he receives (the Law), (4)who strive not to break those precepts that should be observed, (5)who should be steadfast and full of integrity (*Thamadhi shi.*), (6)who try to speak good words, (7)who has good companions [I- pt.2: hki/W].

Regarding List 11, these are: the king should practice the Four *Thingaha Wuthtu* principles.[71] These are (1)To give alms, (2)To speak words that are loving and kind, (3)To work for the benefits of the people, (4)To be considerate and fair in punishment [I- pt.3: hki/K].

The Buddhas revealed to the World showing the Four *Thingaha Wuthtu* Principles which should be practiced by all the kings. The kings who found the kingdoms and practice the Four *Thingaha Wuthtu* Principles should administer in accordance with the law of Dhammathat in order to admonish the people who live in their own kingdoms. King Mahathamada who was the founder of the kingdom possessed the law, the world, and royal authority. No other person possesses the royal authority. All the kings should be prudent in deciding judicial matters all the time, dispence justice either in the day or at night [I-pt3 *ibid.*].

3. Duties of Judges

In regard to List 12, Four persons who would pass judgments (on behalf of the king) are: (1)a Brahmin who is well versed in astrology, (2)a respectable official who is well versed in *Nimi-kyan*[72], (3)A high ranking administrative official who is compassionate and works for the benefit of others, who cherishes *Thintaya*[73], and who is full of wisdom and (4)who is rich and is well versed in the *Pitaka* or Pāli canons [I -pt.2: hki/ kyaw:].

As for List 13, Four Kinds of People mentioned in the above would be the five judges together with the king. There are five principles to make judgments: these are the principles: (1)that the judgment has to be made in accordance with the previous ones made by the king, (2)that the judgement of the four other judges has to be made in accordance with the Dhammathat, (3)that to make a judgment in accordance with the Dhammathat decides whether one goes to hell, (4)that to be judged just as if a blind person with a stick is led by an ordinary person so that the former can reach a good place, (5)that a judge who should pass judgments straightly like the tongue of the beam of a balance. Let them pass judgments only when these five conditions are present [I- pt.2: hku./W].

In regard to List 14, six people who should not be allowed by the king to pass judgments. These are: (1)one who decides in favour of the noble class, (2)one who gives favour to the person from whom he accepted a bribe, (3)one who gives favour to clans, (4)one who is inclined to give favour to his enemies, and (5)one who passes judgments not knowing right from wrong. In addition, one more is described. That is (6) one who passes judgments in order to threaten another by his authority, though we know which is right and which is wrong. Thus, a person who passes judgments with desire (*Hsanda*), anger *(Dawtha)*, fear (*Baya*) or ignorance (*Mawha*) should not be appointed as a judge [I- pt.2: hku./W-hku/K].[74]

In regard to List 15, there are seven people who should practice like a stone obelisk: those are: (1)the king, (2)the judge, (3)the witness, (4)the commander-in-chief (*Sit-thugyi:*) who arrive at the battle field, (5)the envoy whom the king sends, (6)the clerical staff (*Sachi-sama*), the country land officer (*Mye-daing*) and the forest chief (*Taw: kè*) and (7)the man who apportions food and drinks for all the other persons [I- pt.2: hku/K].[75&76]

In regard to List 16, the judges will be swallowed by the earth and will suffer great infliction in the hell of the four nether world (*Apay-ngayè*). When such judges die, they will be tortured in *Apay Le-ba:* which are: (1)hell (*Nga. ye:*), (2)beast (*Ta.reikhsan*), (3)a being in limbo state (*Peikta*) such as ghost, and (4)inferior deities (*Athurakay*). They shall be tortured in the Eight Dangers (*Be Shit-Pa:*) [I-pt.2: hke/W], mentioned in List 17as below.[77]

As to List 17, the Eight Dangers are of (1)Being swallowed by the earth (hell), (2)Being dragged away by crocodiles, (3)Being caught by ogres (*balu:= bilu:*), (4)Boat Overturning, (5)Lighting strike, (6)Being eaten by a tiger, (7) Vomiting blood and (8) Becoming insane [I- pt.2: hke/K].

In regard to List 18, the ten penal retributions are: (1)agonizing and pathetic suffering, (2)going mad, (3)serious disease, (4)mental dissociation, (5)suffering at the hand of the king (*be:-dan*), (6)being accused falsely by the people, (7) being bankrupt for seven generations, (8)Tending to loose wealth and property in fire burning house with property in it, (9)Tending one's body to deteriorate, and (10)To be less educated and go to hell [I- pt.2: hke/K:-hke:/W;hke:/K:-hkaw:/W].

Thus, the judges should not consider the law by enjoying power and bribe. They should, therefore, observe the duties in accordance with the five pledges (*Badein-nin Apya: Nga-ba:*). In other words, any judge speaks to both the parties of a case : (1)Speak only the words which he should speak. The judge should observe the pledges by saying "Although I should say these words, I will use them only when the time is appropriate. I will not speak when the time is not appropriate.", (2) Speak only the words which should be spoken and speak only the right words. "I will only speak the time is appropriate. I speak only the right words and never speak the wrong words.", (3)Speak only the right words in accordance with the Dhammathat. This means that any judges should observe their duties, saying "I will speak only the words related to the benefit and do not speak the words not related to the benefit", (4) Speak only pleasant and gentle words. This means that any judges should observe their duties, saying "I do not speak cruel words.", (5)Speak pleasant and gentle words but with benevolence (*myitta*) and compassion (*gayuna*). The judges should observe their duties, saying "I do not speak with innate desire to those who have deep-seated anger." [I-pt.2 : hko:/W].

Thus, the judges should observe their duties in accordance with the four classes of words (*Zaga: Aya Inga Le:-dan*); [the judges] should: (1)Speak good words, (2)Speak in accordance with the Dhammathat, (3)Speak gentle words, (4)Speak right words [I- pt.2: hkaw:/W-hko/W].

4. Witnesses

Regarding List 19, on eleven kinds of witnesses in a case: "Oh, King Mahathamada! a man of wisdom (*pinnya-shi.*) is like the ears of paddy and a man who lacks wisdom also like the ear of paddy. A man of wisdom is excessive and a man who lacks wisdom is also excessive. Both a man of wisdom and a man who lacks wisdom are like the ears of rice: the paddy which includes substance droops like a man of wisdom and the paddy which does not include [substance] like a man who lacks wisdom juts out. Both a man of wisdom and a man who lacks wisdom is like a cow in that the former is like a cow which produces a milk full of taste and that the latter is like a castrated ox (*Nwa: Paik*) who does not produce milk. Both a man of wisdom and a man who lacks wisdom are excessive. The former is excessive in virtuous actions (*Kudho kaung:-hmu.*) and the latter is excessive in evil conducts (*Akudho kaung:-hmu.*). In the view of the same people: (1)A care is serious; (2)If a care is serious, it seems serious; (3)If a care seems shallow, it is serious; (4)If a care seems shallow, it is shallow. As people reason in such four manners, Judges should decide cases in accordance with the Dhammathat after considering wisely on their investigations by correctly asking witnesses who are credible [I-pt.2: hkaw/W].

In the time of Brahmas who were born of high social clan, hermits and *Zawgyi* who had attained supernatural power by mean of alchemy, [Pre-

Manu Age and Pre-Buddha Era], witness had to take oath swearing by these holy men in their testimony in what they know, what they had seen and heard. They could also take oath or their testimonies swearing by the weapons of ancient kings and their descendants but not by [the present] King, the king's son and brothers. Alternatively, eleven witnesses must take oath, swearing by Buddhas [*ibid.*].[78]

The witnesses who are credible are those persons who (1)Reveres the three Gems (*Yadana. Thoun:-ba:*), (2)Has attained mindfulness (*thati=dhadi.*) and concentration of the mind (*thamadi*), (3)Is upright because of wealth (*ossa-mya:*), (4) Is respected by people or has many friends (in all social circles), (5) Speak the truth because he is virtuous person (*Thu-taw*), (6) Knows good consequences (*kaung:-jyo:*) and bad consequences (*ma.kaung:jyo:*), (7)Enjoys meritorious deeds (*kaung:-hmu.*), (8)Is well known for his good reputation, (9)Enjoys meritorious deeds and is complete with all the five required parts of a perfect body (*inga-nga:-ba:pye.-son thaw thu*), (10)Does not covet other's possession (*alo yan min ma. shi.*) and (11)Does not give favour [to others] due to social and economic status (*myet-hna kyi:-nge ma kyi.*) [*ibid.*].

In regard to List 20, there are five people who should not be in the place of witnesses. They are: (1)a king, (2)a crown prince, (3)a queen, (4)a holy monk who becomes Ariyas (*Ariya-Thanga Myat-taw*) and is morally upright (*theikhka*) and (5) a genuine princess [I-pt.2: hkaw/K].[79]

Regarding List 20, there are sixteen types of people who should be excluded as witnesses: these are: (1)a convict, (2)a thief, (3)a person susceptible to bribery, (4)a person who does not know what is right and what is not right: a person who has fear, (5)a person who is not ashamed to do (criminal or immoral) conduct, (6)a person who is not trusted by anyone, (7)an enemy of either the plaintiff or defendant, (8)a person who is malicious, (9)a man who frequently commits adultery, (10)a hermaphrodite, (11)a person who makes fun of three gems, parents and elders, (12)an idiot or a stupid person irrespective of his or her age, (13)a minor who has not yet reached the one-tenth of the normal life expectancy, (14)a dumb person, (15)a man who has been driven out of the family because he did not accept chastisement, and (16) a lunatic [I- pt.2: hkaw /W: - hkan/W].

As to List 21, there are also twenty-eight people who would be temporally disqualified to appear as witnesses. These are: (1) a man while he is sick, (2) a beggar, (3) a prisoner of war, (4) a man while he is being tortured, (5)a person who indulges in excessive sexual pleasure, (6)a gambler while engaged in bet (a man who loves to bet on cock fights and dices), (7)a pregnant woman or a woman in labour, (8)an alcoholic man or woman (while he or she is under the influence of intoxicant), (9)a hot tempered man, (10)an exhausted traveler, (11) a sea voyager, (12) a toddy palm juice collector while he is collecting juice, (13)a man who owes debt to either to the plaintiff or defendant, (14)a man who has connection with either the plaintiff or defendant, (15)a slave of the plaintiff or defendant, (16) a very poor person, (17)a laundry-man while washing clothes, (18)a dependent of either plaintiff or defendant, (19)a close relative of either plaintiff or defendant, (20)a musician while playing music, (21)a dancer while dancing, (22)a painter while painting, (23)a blacksmith at work, (24) a malevolent person(?), (25)a disabled person, (26) a blind person, (27)a leper and (28) a deaf person [I-pt.2: hkan/W: - hkan/ K-hka/W].[80, 81, 82 & 83]

Relating to List 22, there are five kinds of witness: these are: (1)an eye witness, (2) an ear witness, (3)one who wants to give without being asked, (4) one who speaks only when asked as he does not wish to say voluntarily and (5) one who says before being asked [I- pt.2: hka: K]. Among these five kinds of witnesses, /the judges/ should not ask one in (3) mentioned above, because the person spoke before being asked. /On the other hand/, the judges should trust the words of the aforementioned (4)who has honest eyes and faces and who speaks only after the judges asked the person to do so. The judge who punished like that would not go to hell [I-pt.2: hka:/K-nga./W].

In regard to List 23, a litigant (contestant) who repeatedly disregarding the court proceedings conducted by the judge and either physically or with facial expression insolently fidget in his seat or repeatedly standing up or sitting down should be sentenced to five lashes.

A litigant who after confessing that there was no other witness and after the said witness was interrogated by the judge, the litigant declares that he wishes to have another witness, the litigant should be punished and have him paraded through the village.

If a witness is engaged by two contesting litigants and by his truthful testament one of them wins the case, the winner should reward the witness with one tenth of the property involved. Why the witness should receive one tenth of the property is because if he was not good, the litigant is liable to be punished. On the other hand if the witness professed as truth what he could not know or see or notice he is liable to be sentenced with eightfold ten serious punishment and also to suffer in the four hells. Therefore, he is entitled to one tenth of the property [I-pt.2: nga./W].[84]

Regarding List 24, the Dhammathat is like: (1) the hand of *Sakka* (=*Indra*) or *Thikya* (=*Dhaja*) (Lord of the first and second levels of existence of the *Nat devas*), (2)the *Manizota* gem of the Universal Monarch (*Sekkya-wade min:/*

Chapter IX— 'Duties of Kings and Judges' of MD (1782MS)

Cakkavattin) which has the power to fulfil all the wishes, (3) the weapon of the king (*Min*:), the minister (*Amat*), the rulers (*Pyi-so*:) and the judges (*[Taya:]* thugyi) who carry out their duties for the great country, (4) the ruling cord (*tamyi-hkyi*.) of the carpenter, (5) the introductory book for the physician, (6) the lamp which can be held to give light inside an extremely dark building in which are different varieties of precious gems, (7) the eye that can discern a good appearance from a bad one, (8) the ear that can hear /both/ the pleasant sound and unpleasant sound, (9) the moon that makes the four islands be bright at night, (11) the tusks of a full-grown male elephant that is fully endowed with ability and strength and (12) the milk of a mother [I- pt.2: ga./W -ga./K; ga/W- ga/K].[85 & 86]

"Oh, Noble King Mahathamada!, the four pronouncements handed down from the person who was destined to be a good king, the first ruler in the world are these: (1) A law that was enacted and passed by the monarch (*Egayit=Eigarit*), (2) A decision made after (both parties of the litigants) had been tested at the depth of water ordeal [See Okudaira *ibid.*: 73-74]), (3) A judgment based upon the strong evidence of one party and (4) a solution made based on the belief in the words of one party. If these four pronouncements are overturned, the country would be destroyed, there would be drought, and there would be serious of calamities (*be:dan*), which there would be followed by death and injuries. The country and the villages of the people who /observe the Dhammathat/ would be prosperous [I- pt.2: gi/K-gi/W].

In regard to 'Duties of Kingship and Judges' prescribed in the above Ch. IX of 1782MS, the framework of these duties are also included in the *MD* (1760MS= Richardson's text; 1903 Burmese version). [Aung Than Tun 2003: 115] Aung Than Tun pointed out as follows: the *MD* "not only includes customary rules and tradition but the framework of Myanmar social life and cultures. It gave direction how to build cities, town and villages and now to build pagodas and monasteries also." [Aung Tha Tun *ibid.*; see also *ibid.*: 113-120]. This apparently shows that the MD (1782 MS) is a revised version of 1760MS (=Richardson's Myanmar text).

Chapter X
Commentary on 'Duties of Kings and Judges'

1. Interpretation of the preamble to the *MD*

a. Legitimacy of Kingship and Political Thought

When the capital city of Ava was under threat, there arose an ardent expectation among the people that a kind of "Saviour" would make a miraculous appearance. U Aung Zeya (later King Alaunghpaya) was seen as the man who could rescue the country from collapse. According to the Myanmar genealogies, U Aung Zeya was born in 1076M.E.(=1714 A.D.), the fifth child of Min Nyo Zan (Thiri Maha Dhamma Yaza), the headman of Mouk-hso-bo village, and Min Saw U [HSTH 1976: 32-33]. Apart from the fact that U Aung Zeya's father was an established local administrative officer, there are other factors supporting his royal lineage. A chronicle tells us that Min Shwe Pa Chouk, who came six generations earlier, was a grandchild of Shinbyushin Thihathu, the fifth king of Ava (Inwa), who was enthroned in 783 M.E.(=1422 A.D.). The mother and father of Min Shwe Pa chouk were Shwe Pyi May, a daughter of King Shinbyushin Thihathu and Min Gyi Byu, a nephew of the king [YKM: 232]. It also refers to the fact that forty-seven successive kings from Pyu Saw Di (=Hti) [168-243 A.D.] in Bagan to Alaunghpaya, who belonged to the solar dynasty continued without any interruption, and that the ancestors of King Alaunghpaya migrated to Shwebo under the rule of Mo Hnin, the eight King of Ava in the early half of the fifteenth century [*ibid*.: 25-26]. The chronicle also says that Alaunghpaya, who belonged to the lineage of the solar dynasty, ascended the throne in April 1752 [KBZ I: 10] [Okudaira 2003a: 52; 1994: 63].

The chronicle portrays King Alaunghpaya as a descendant of the royal family. Myanmar scholars, however, have pointed out that Yazawins (the chronicles) were compiled after Alaunghpaya ascended the throne as that the accounts of royal families are rather exaggerated and that sometimes they lack reliable sources. No doubt the compilers of the Yazawins wrote in an exaggerated manner [Maung Thaw 1976: 93]. Even if Alaunghpaya descended from a royal family, it seems to have been not from the direct line. The compilers of the Yazawins exaggerated his ancestry to give extra support to King Alaunghpaya's legitimacy as a king. Incidentally, it may be worthwhile to study the accounts on the founders of the Myanmar dynasties before the Konbaung period. Yazawin tells us that King Anawrahta [1044-1077], the restorer of Bagan and the founder of the unified Bagan dynasty, is said to be the forty-second king of the Thamudari, who was the founder of the Ngadaba dynasty. Dabinshwedi (=Tapinshwehti)[1531-1550A.D.], the founder of the Taungu dynasty, was the Prince of Min Kyi Nyo, the lord of Taungu, and the thirty-third King Yenandameik [1597-1605A.D.] was the lord of Nyaungyan. All of these kings were from powerful families [HMY III: 121]. Because Alaunghpaya was not a hereditary king, but was chosen as the awaited "Saviour", who would rescue the country from chaos, he could be compared to Mahathamada, the first legendary Buddhist king. The royal legitimacy of the Konbaung dynasty had to reply on Alaunghpaya's inherent qualities, personality and charisma, in short his personal accumulation of *Karma* (*kudho-kan*). His law status as descended from village headmen[87] may have caused the compiler of the *MD* added to elaborate on the detailed mythological story [Okudaira 2003a: 52-53/ 1994: 63-64].

b. Elaboration of the Myth of Kingship

The problems and the tasks faced by the new King Alaunghpaya were gigantic. Reconstruction of the Myanmar kingdom largely depended upon his personal quality. "The temper of the time", as Koenig asserted, "provided early Konbaung kingship with an undeniable element of Messiah, which popular lore adapted from Theravāda Buddhist eschatology" [Koenig 1990: 65]. King Alaunghpaya urgently needed to provide credentials for his own royal legitimacy and that of the Konbaung dynasty. To this end the compilation of a new law book containing a Buddhist derived theory of state, was a very convenient tactic. King Mahathamada and King Alaunghpaya were similar in that they both became kings because the circumstances demanded it. Mahathamada lent his weight in support of Alaunghpaya's royal legitimacy.

c. Meaning of 'Myth'

The *MD* has the most elaborate preamble[88] of all the Dhammathats. The first half of the preamble is not the original one. It just seems to have been cited from Chapter I of *Maha- yazawin-gyi* by U Kala, the early eighteenth century chronicle, which reminds us of *Aggañña* Suttanta[89]. By adding a second half comprised of cleverly adapted judgement tales[90], the author presented a unified 'Myth' which we can call his 'Myth on Kingship' [Okudaira ibid.: 54].

What is the meaning and function of 'Myth' ? Cassirer says there were conflicting and controversial views on this. Anthropologists, according to him, saw myth was, as a very simple phenomenon for which scarcely any complicated psychological or philosophical explanation were needed. It was neither the outcome of reflection or thought, nor a mere product of human imagination. There is also an element of "primeval stupidity" that is an absurd and contradictory element [See Cassirer 1966: 4]. Indeed, the preamble to the *MD* is said to be a tale that is "childish" [Lingat 1949: 296], "curious" [*ibid*. 1950: 15] and "colourful" [Maung Maung 1963: 2]. Cassirer goes on to say that the historians could never accept the views. They looked for a better and more adequate explanation, though their answers were mostly divergent in accordance with their own special scientific interests [*ibid*.: 5]. Lingat, a French legal historian, described the author of the preamble to the *MD* as a "good psychologist" [Lingat 1949: 296]. He called it "an attractive addition" [*ibid*.]. We can also view *Manugye*'s author as a good political theorist. He illustrates not only the nature of Myanmar law, but also the whole structure of the "Theravāda Buddhist State" [Okudaira *ibid*.: 55-56].

d. Structural Features of the Preamble

The framework of Chapter one's preamble to the *MD* is elaborate and skillfully constructed. The thirteenth century Pāli Dhammasattham which is known as King Wagaru's *Manu Dhammasatthan* and as the *Wagaru Dhammathat*[91] has already been presented briefly as a legendary tale on Kingship, and it has also given a whole framework to the preamble [*Wagaru* 1892: 1]. The other Dhammathats, such as *Dhammawilatha*[92], *Manotheikka* (*Manussika*), *Manu Kyetyo*, and others, which are regarded as legal works in the Bagan period from the eleventh to thirteenth centuries, also describe the legendary tale, including the story of the seven decisions by Manu [Okudaira *ibid*.: 57].

Andrew Huxley, an English jurist, divided the preamble of the *MD* into three sections: the first section is the one which deals with the story from the beginning of the present world to the Great Elect of King Mahathamada, obviously borrowing the framework from the *Agañña Sutta* (*Suttanta*) in the *Dīgha-nikāya* of Pāli Canon; the second section is the one which recounts the twelve wise decisions by the cowherd (*nwa:-kyaun:dha:*) in his village; the third section is the story of Manu, a counsellor to the king, after his resignation from his post due to misjudgement: his becoming a hermit and traveling to the boundary wall of the universe and his finding the Dhammathat and his final presentation of it to King Mahathamada [Huxley 1997: 22-23]. Huxley notes that the author of the preamble of the *MD* "has inserted his own contribution between his version of the *Agañña Sutta* and the thirteenth century account of Manu's seven judgments popularized in medieval Bagan" [*ibid*.]. Huxley asserts that the introduction of the cowherd into the preamble to the *MD* represents one stage in Myanmar's adaptation of Theravāda texts to its own purposes [Huxley 1997: 38]. In his view, Kyone-wun Bhumma Zeya, who is regarded as the compiler of the *MD* thought of law as a social science, as something which traced its origin from human relationships [*ibid*.]. He argues that the twelve decisions in the village represent such a shift that the positions were reversed from the capital to the village by 1750 and that it was the villagers who knew best in matters of adaptation of the law [*ibid*. 38-39; Okudaira *ibid*.: 55].

e. Essential Factors of the Legitimacy of Kingship

The myth of Alaunghpaya's *Manugye* gives the account of a person named Manu who was elected as Mahathamada, the first king of mankind in the Theravāda Buddhist context. It mentions the five factors that affect royal legitimacy.

(1) Hpaya-laung (=Bodhisatta)

The person named Manu, who was erected unanimously as the first king in this world, emerged at first as a *Hpaya-laung* (corresponding to Bodhisatta inPāli, one striving to attain Buddhahood). This tradition was taken over by the Myanmar kings, because *Hpaya-laung* qualifies a person to become a king. King Alaunghpaya, the founder of the Konbaung Dynasty regarded himself as '*Hpaya-laung*' in a royal edict issued on 2nd January, 1755, when he was leaving his capital city of Shwebo on a campaign to crush the Mons in lower Myanmar [ROB (2, January, 1755) (T) ROB III 1985: 90]. The concept that the king is *Hpaya-laung* firstly gives the people a divine image, secondly tacitly legalizes his seizure of political power and thirdly, summons the feeling of respect and administration of all through self-sacrifice as his postponement to *Neibban* (=*Nibbana* in Pāli) or "ultimate reality" to save his subjects in this life [See Aye Kyaw 1979: 163; also see Okudaira *ibid*.: 56].

(2) Mahathamada(=Mahāsammata)

The preamble of the *MD* narrates that "having gone to this man *[Manu]*, *[*the original inhabitants of the world*]* proffered their request and conferred upon him the three kinds of beiktheik [Beiktheik]"(or consecration). It also stated that "Because he was thought worthy to be chosen by many, he was called Maha Thamada [Mahathamada]and because he had dominion over the land, he was called Hkattiya and because he was capable of instructing men *[*rational beings (*Thattava= Dhadawa*) in accordance with*]* the law he was called Yaza *[Raja]"* [RMD 1847: 7] "Conferring upon him the three kinds of beiktheik *[Beiktheik]* (*thoun ba:thaw beiktheik thun:-chin*:) means to bless him by the pouring of water for enthronement. This ceremony implies that Manu named Mahathamada, promised the original inhabitants to restore law and order from a chaotic situation and to establish a peaceful and prosperous society. Reciprocally, they promised to reward one tenth of their good rice yield (*thale zaba: go hse-hpo tit-hpo*) to King Mahathamada [Okudaira *ibid.*: 7]. These three kinds of consecration ceremonies were introduced in the successive dynasties of Myanmar and other Theravāda Buddhist countries in the mainland Southeast Asia. These ceremonial rites meant that the king became a lawful (*de jure*) ruler instead of a factual (*de facto*) ruler [See Aye Kyaw *ibid.*: 149: Okudaira *ibid.*: 56].

(3) Hkattiya

Hkattiya, which is a Pāli loan-word corresponding to Kśatríya in Sanskrit, originally meant the second class in the Hindu caste system. Gautama Buddha belonged to this class before he renounced the world. Myanmar people accepted the idea that their kings belonged to the direct line of King Mahathamada, as well as the *Sakya* Family, who belonged to the Kśatríya class. In Myanmar, the concept of Hkattiya was "Lord of Paddy Field"(*lemye-do i. adhibadi*). This phrase implies that the ownership of land was one of the indispensable factors for securing legitimacy of kingship in an agricultural society like pre-modern Myanmar or Thailand [See Aye Kyaw *ibid.*: 150; also see Okudaira *ibid.*56-57].

(4) Yaza

As we have seen, the person named Manu was called Yaza by the original inhabitants. The king who was endowed with Taya (corresponding to Dhamma in Pāli, meaning 'law') such as 'Ten Royal Duties', etc, for his good administration. The successive Myanmar kings, called Mintaya or Dhammayaza, were obliged not only to maintain law and order, but also to secure the moral order in their kingdoms. The concept of Dhammayaza, as Michael Aung-Thwin, a pre-modern Myanmar historian, defined that it "was to justify the creation of new dynasties, particularly at times of disorder" and "it was used when the king's duties as defender of the faith were needed to control the powerful Sangha" [Aung-Thwin 1985: 57]. As Than Tun asserted, "King Alaunghpaya was one of the typical Defenders of the Buddhist religion" [Than Tun 1985: 23] and he was regarded as *Min-Taya-gyi*: or the Great King of Law [KBZ: 69-71; (T)ROB(1 January, 1760 (T) ROB: 231-233]. [See also

Okudaira *ibid.*: 57].

(5) Ne-min i. Ahset-anwe(=The Descendant of the Sun)

The preamble of the *MD* described that King Mahathamada was a direct line of the sun (*Ne-min: i. Ahset-anwe*) as well as the founder of the solar dynasty and that he was a second sun (*hnit-hku-myauk thaw Ne-min:*). The concept that the king was identified with the sun was widespread in successive dynasties of Myanmar, particularly in the Konbaung Dynasty, and was most frequently used for King Alaunghpaya [(ROB (20 June,1755)(T)ROB III: 100; ROB (8 May, 1756)(T)ROB: 150, etc.]. For King Alaunghpaya declared himself the descendant of the solar race in his letter of reply to the monks of all nationalities dated 19th October, 1756, as the descendant of the solar race [ROB (19 October, 1756(T)ROB III: 169]. He also stated in his message dated 8th May, 1756 to His Majesty the King of England George II that he was "descended from the nation of the sun" [AMA (8-4-1756: 50)] [Okudaira *ibid.*: 57; 1994: 65-68; 1989: 61-65]

In the preamble of the *MD*, the compiler can be seen enhancing King Alaunghpaya's legitimacy by identifying him with King Mahathamada [KBZ I: 21]. In addition to the tradition since the Bagan period that the successive dynasties of the kings of Myanmar regarded themselves as *Hpaya-laung*, the compiler of the the *MD* stressed the legitimacy of the Konbaung Dynasty by emphasizing the fact that King Alaunghpaya was in direct lineage of the solar dynasty. The rhetoric of this opening passage serves to increase King Alaunghpaya's dignity in comparison with other kings [See (T) ROB I-X, etc.]. Its peculiar feature is the use of King Mahathamada as a model for King Alaunghpaya. In the background can be seen his extraordinary determination of King Alaunghpaya to re-establish a strong Theravāda Buddhist State by restoring law and order to Myanmar.

2. Implication of the New Chapters of *the MD* (1782MS)

The *MD* (1782 MS) states probably for the first time in the Myanmar's Dhammathat literature that the king is the supporter and propagator of Buddhism. Than Tun says that "the king is the defender of faith, and under good kings the religion prospered. In this respect, the king helps in two ways. He supports any programme in the propagation of the religion and on the other hand he is expected to protect the religion by suppressing heresy" [Than Tun *ibid.*: 213]. In the clauses described in Volume I (pt.2), the seventh Factor among 'The Seven Factors Observed to Keep Prosperity (of the State from)

Deterioration' (*Apareikha Niya Taya: Hkunit-pa*:) is as follows: "*[for the king]* to patronize the Sangha [1782MS: pt.2:hki/ wun:] and *[the Sangha]*, relying on the support of the king, are to propagate religion" [1782MS *ibid.*: gi./K]. These passages place the relationship between kingship and Sangha at the centre of the Theravāda Buddhist State [Okudaira ibid.: 59].

Why then were the new important chapters added? We shall say later more. Let us note that King Badon, who became one of the most powerful leaders among neighboring countries in mainland Southeast Asia, was eager to give a realistic account of "Theravāda Buddhist State". In short, the king, as the supreme defender of Buddhism, support the Sangha. The Sangha, through correct observance of the precepts, transmitted the Dhamma; and when the Dhamma flourishes, the king is legitimate [See Ishii 1986: 46]. This triangular system [See again Table 2] of the state structure was the essence of the Theravāda Buddhist Polity. It was institutionalised as a royal directive by the *Manugye* written at the start of King Badon's long reign.

3. Changes in the Role of the Myanmar Dhammathat in the early Konbaung Period

In the most general terms, the preamble to the Myanmar Dhammathats suggests that "the law is found, it is not made" [Hooker 1978: 18]. This source of laws is transcendent, immutable and universal. This "law is qualified as an absolute ethic"[*ibid.*]. However, the contents of the rules prescribed in the Dhammathats to a large extent reflect changing times and conditions. The Dhammathats aimed at supporting the notion of a law which was superior to the customary rules and the orders of kings as well. At the same time they directed attention to the eternal order of the world in accordance with Buddhist ideas. During the reign of King Alaunghpaya, there was a revival of intensive scholarly activities in Buddhism, which had a profound effect on Dhammasatthan literature. In addition, the rule prescribed in the *MD* gradually became more prolix and complex as a consequence of bringing together numerous sources in an unsystematic manner. As a result, these Dhammathats lost most of the authority and sanctity which the old Pāli Dhammasatthans had maintained [See Lingat *ibid.*: 21; Okudaira 1999: 480-481].

The role which the Dhammathat played in the administration of justice became more Buddhicised and popularized during the reign of King Alaunghpaya. As the Sanskrit-Pāli prototype factor of the Dhammathat gradually diminished, it began to function as the provider of secular laws based on Buddhist morality and ethics, which were familiar and understandable to the public. Under the reign of King Badon the Dhammathats were incorporated into the structure of the 'Theravāda Buddhist State'. The extra chapters of the *MD* (1782MS) Chapter V, as "(for the king) to follow the traditions such as Dhammathat" [I pt.2: hki/kyaw:]; "the king who found the kingdoms should administer them in accordance with the law of Dhammathat in order to admonish the people who live in their own kingdom" [I pt.2: hki/K] and "All the judgments should be made in accordance, not with the Papathat ("Law of Vice"), but with the Dhammathat ("Law of Virtue")"[III: has:/K]. These clauses evidently show the high value King Badon placed on the Dhammathat. Probably King Badon was trying to restore the Dhammathats to the centre of Myanmar life, where he was powerful and long-lived enough to achieve partial success in this [Okudaira *ibid.*: 1999: 481].

4. Authorship of the 1782 MS

The 1782 MS is a revised edition of the original *MD* which was said to have been compiled during the reign of King Alaunghpaya by a minister Kyone-wun Bumma Zeya. We do not know who revised the former, because we do not find either the name of the author(s) nor the date when it was revised both in the introduction nor colophon. We can not deny that a number of authors were involved for writing between the reigns of King Alaunghpaya and King Badon. "Many authors had added more explanations in the text at various times and it is not improbable that an expert on Myanmar law who went to serve the new king at his new capital city would have been asked to edit it and he would probably add his own contributions wherever he deemed necessary" [Than Tun 1985: 28-29]. While the authors and the scribes are probably not always the same persons, it seems likely, judging from the script of the palm-leaf manuscript, a single scribe copied all of it from the beginning to the end probably immediately after the enthronement of King Badon and completed it within two months. It is conjectured that the original authors wrote on parabaik first, then the scribes copied it on the palm-leaf manuscripts (Pe). It is not improbable that King Badon himself compiled the revised version of the 1782MS. But, if it was written by a single author, he is more likely to be one of the monks or ministers resident at the court of Ava in 1782. It is possible that eight authors, though we can not define who the true author is among them. The eight authors are as follows: the Manle Hsyadaw (1714-1805), the Sonda Hsyadaw (1718-84), the Chaung-kauk Hsayadaw (1736-93), the first Bagaya Hsayadaw (1783-1800), Tun Nyo (better known as the Twinthintaik-wun Maha sithu, 1726-92), the first Maung Htaung Hsyadaw (1755-1832) and Shin Sandalinka who compiled the *Maniyadonabon* in 1781 [See in detail Okudaira & Huxley 2001: 252-254].

5. The Sources of the Eleven Lists

The palm-leaf manuscripts are usually directly copied from the original palm-leaf and recopied again and again before crumbled into pieces. Even if a new Dhammathat was compiled, the author would have copied some of his text word for word from some sources. Other texts he re-wrote, or revised, or paraphrased from other sources.

In case of Pt.2 of the Chapter I of the *MD* (1782MS), it is apparent that some portions were based largely on 1757and n.d. (copy-date unknown) versions of the *Dhammawilatha Dhammathat* and the 1762 version of the *Manu Kyetyo Dhammathat.*, just as the Chapter III owed much to these versions of the Dhammathats. Pt.2 of the Chapter I of the 1782MS consists of four parts: (1) kingship (No.1-10), (2) Judges (No.11-17), (3) Witnesses (No.18-22&24) and (4) Qualities of the Dhammathat. Among these, it is very likely that the portions of No.1-2, 13, 15-17, 18-22, 23, 24? were re-written basing on the 1757 and the date unknown versions of the *Dhammavilatha* Dhammathat and the 1762 version of the *Manu Kyet-yo Dhammathat* which are closely related each other. We have not found yet the rest of the portion, such as No.2-9, 11, 12, &14 not only in these versions of the Dhammathats, but also in other Dhammathats before King Badon.

From No.1 to 11, we had already shown that eighteenth century Myanmar political theory could be found in such genres as royal orders, descriptions on inscription, Pāli canons, chronicles, Niti (ethical proverbs), Myittasa (epistle for royal family from monks), *Rajovada* (special works on kingship). Among these genres, Nīti literature [See PNTB 1981 s.266-287: 22-24; James Gray 2000 reprint], most of which were originally written in Pāli verse during the Ava period (1368-1555) and translated into vernacular in late eighteenth century, includes traditional Myanmar political science. One of the earliest and surviving examples is *Dhamma-niti* whose chapter on kingship begins with verse enumerating two of the lists [*ibid.*: 37-118]. But the rest of eight lists are found in *Lawkathara-pyo* (=*Lokasara-pyo*) [See Okudaira & Huxley *ibid.*: 253-254]. Out of these lists, relating to No.1, we have not traced the

Dhammawilatha Dhammathat

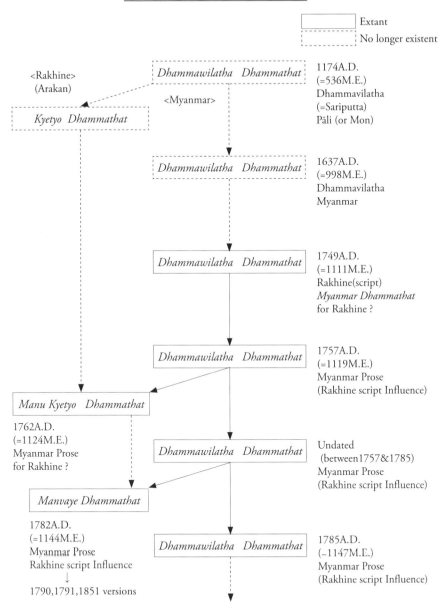

Table 7: Origin and Copies of the *Dhammawilatha Dhammathat*

original source in any earlier source of Myanmar and India. We have only come across the description referring to the Twelve Royal Duties [(T)ROB IV(21-8-1785): 124; 468; also see *Cakkavatti-sutta* 35-351; Thukha 1970: 230]

It seems likely that the author of the 1782MS had studied and extracted the portions of ten lists, out of eleven from *Lokathara-pyo*, out of which only List 2 is also included in aforementioned versions of the *Dhammawilatha Dhammathat* and the *Kyetyo Dhammathat*. Judging from the attitude of the author of the 1782MS who largely referred to these two Dhammathats in the Chapter III, he compiled 1782MS, basically using 1760MS, referring to the two Dhammathats:*Dhammawilatha* and *Manu Kyet-yo* and supplying information from aforementioned Niti literature.

Chapter XI
'Early Konbaung Thirty Rulings' and Some Additional Information in the *MD* (1782 MS)

1. Thirty rules added to the 1782 MS of the *MD* (1782 MS)

Thirty rules on various subjects which are newly inserted into Chapter III are as follows: [III: hse/K:- zaw:/W].

(1) The law in regard to whether an elephant, horse, buffalo, bovine animal (bull), goat or duck should be returned (to the sellers) after the transaction has been made [III: hse:/K:-hsaw:/W].

(2) The law in regard to (the transactions) of prisoners of wars [*ibid.*].

(3) The law in regard to the price drop? in the transactions of animals, such as buffalo, bovine animal (bull) bull, elephant or horse after it was bought [III: hsaw: /W:-hsaw:/ W:-hsaw:/K].

(4) The law in regard to the sale and purchase (*yaun:-way*) of inanimate properties, such as gold, silver or gems [III: hsaw:/K:-hsaw/W].

(5) The law in regard to the dispute over the ownership of the offspring of pregnant slaves, pregnant buffaloes, and pregnant cows that are being traded [III: hsaw/ K:].

(6) The law in regard to the sale and purchase of fruits, plants, roots (*Amyit*) or bulbs (*A-u.*) in a garden (or plantation) or cultivated land [III: hsan/ W:-hsan/K].

(7) The law in regard to the damage of fruits and plants in the farms at the high level and in the farms at the low level due to inundation [III: has:/W].

(8) The law in regard to the entitlement to the water supply and the decision whether to close (the floodgate) of the water supply [III: has:/K].

(9) The law in regard to the decision made by the king in accordance with the law of virtue (Dhammathat), but not with the law of vice (Papathat) [III hsa:/K].

(10) The law in regard to boundary dispute between two villages over [III: za./W].

(11) The law in regard to the demarcation of religious land (*hpaya:-kyaun:*

Mye) and those belonging to warriors (*thu-ye*:)[III za./W].

(12) The law in regard to the destruction of a wooden embankment (*kanthin =gadhin*) which is a demarcation of land between towns, villages or districts [III: sa/W].

(13) The law in regard to the demarcation of divisions and districts [III: sa/W - gi./W].

(14) The law in regard to the dispute over land, open space?, pond (*ain*), natural lake (*in:*), well, man made pond (*kan*), garden, plantation and trees belonging to another person [III: gi./ W:-gi./K].

(15) The law in regard to the confiscation of the land belonging to warrior (*Sit-thi Thu-yè*) and commoners (*athi-ala*) and the confiscation of donated land for religious purposes (=sacred land) (*Wuthtu- kan-mye*) by the king [III: gi./K-gi./W].

(16) The law in regard to accusation whether it is suitable to use a certain piece of land as a farm which is extending from the land marked for the construction of a house or a monastery or ordination hall [III: gi./W].

(17) The law in regard to accusation [III: gi./K].

(18) The law in regard to the division of the four categories of slaves by the king [III: gi. /wun:-bu./W].

(19) The law in regard to a son defying the authority of his parents and pupil against the authority of his teacher [III: bu./W].

(20) The law in regard to (the rulers) or travelers to make way to others on route during their journey [III: zu./W].

(21) The law in regard to the bullying of the poor by the rich and nobles [III: zu/w].

(22) The law in regard to misconduct of defecating (*kyingyi:*) and urinating (*kyin-nge*) *[*improperly*]* [III: zu./K] at improper places .

(23) The law in regard to the discourse which monks or Brahmins should not make to the audience [III: zu./W].

(24) The law in regard to words which should not be uttered such as insulting someone who can see and hear by calling-----as the blind or the deaf [III: zu./ K].

(25) The law in regard to rude remarks which should not be made about the blind or the lame [III: ze/W].

(26) The law in regard to wrong accusation of someone as a witch [III: ze/W].

(27) The law in regard to the use of the word 'slave' to insult or slander someone who is not a slave [III: ze/K].

(28) The law in regard to the wrong accusation of someone who is not an adulterer or a murderer as an adulterer or murderer and-----verbal attack

on him [III:ze/wun:-ze:/W].

(29) The law in regard to the wrong accusation of someone that he sold unlawfully something) [III: ze:/W].

(30) The law in regard to four types of accusation (=impeachment) [III: ze:-ze/W -ze:/K].

The contents included in the Chapter III of the *MD* (1782MS) which are listed above, presents some interesting matters on Myanmar customary law at that time. We will examine each of them more in detail.

The thirty rules included in the Chapter III of 1782 MS is roughly divided into three categories: (1) to (6) are related to Sale and Purchase; (7) to (16) are related to Land and Demarcation of Boundaries; and (17) to (30) are concerned with accusation, defamation, verbal assault, abusive language, etc.

Concerning (1), one of the most important principles of a business transaction was that it is subject to change within ten days in case previously undisclosed defects arose after the transaction: the *MD* says as follows:

> "If the transaction of properties such as elephant, horse, buffalo, bovine animal (bull), goat, pig, chicken and duck, has been made by fixing the price at such public places as in the market, on the way side, at the foot of trees and bamboos groves, in the wayside public rest-house (*zayat*) with roof, and cave and monastery[93] and if previously undisclosed childhood injuries (*nge-jyo: nge-na*) appeared *[after that]* and *[the buyer]* disliked the goods, he can return *[it to the original seller]* within ten days, but *[the buyer]* cannot return it after a lapse of ten days." [III: hse:/K].[94]

However, regarding (2), in the case if transaction of a prisoner of war or a slave, the buyer could not return him if he discovered the defects within ten days and should not get the refund, because he or she could not have known the defects during the transaction. The *MD* continues as follows:

> "On returning a slave within ten days of purchase for his any defects, such as insanity or leprosy or lameness, *[the seller]* should not refund the price, as the buyer should have noticed the true conditions during the transaction. If a non-master slave runs away on the day he was sold, *[the buyer will not lose*, but

rather/ he will be refunded." [III: hse:/K].⁽⁹⁵⁾

"If the seller and the buyer know about that a person who is a foreigner, such as, a prisoner of war (*Thoun;-ya./Hpan:-ya./ Let-ya.*)⁽⁹⁶⁾,Talaing, Kala, Brahma, Shan, Yun, Yodaya, Danu, Kayin, Chin, Kachin, Linzen, Kathe, etc.was sold fixing the price either at market, residence, the rest house during the traveling, or the compound of a temple, the seller is not liable if the person runs away on the very day when he was sold." [III: hse:/K-hsaw/W].

In regard to (3), it deals with the purchase of the animate beings.

"In case of all the animate beings, such as elephant, horse, slave, buffalo, cow, etc. /the buyers/ shall pay the remaining price in accordance with the estimate considering days, months, or years, if fixed price has been remained'. Regarding the animate beings, they shall decide in accordance with the monthly installment, if they died or fled within seven days. If in a case of human beings, the remainder of the price should not be paid. They shall pay half of it. The man who fled shall pay the other half." [III: hsaw:/W-hsaw:/K].

Relating to (4), it deals with the sale and purchase of the inanimate things.

"Any [seller and buyer] will decide the price of the inanimate property, such as gold, silver, gem, iron, ruby and will give the date for payment within a certain date. If /the latter/ was not able to pay the amount within the days decided upon, he shall have to pay double /of the amount/ calculating in accordance with the exceeded days or months". "If any inanimate thing, such as gold, silver, gem, iron, is sold, and it is not genuine, let the article be returned to the seller and the buyer refund for the amount received." "In case of inanimate things, the buyer should return them to /seller/ not changing their /texture and/ appearance. The former should not change/ the appearance as he likes without notice of the latter" "--- the buyer who has damaged the original appearance shall be responsible for it and the seller shall be exempted from the responsibility." [III: hsaw: / K-hsaw /W].

In regard to (5), it says that when the appearance or condition of animate things changes, the seller shall be liable for it and the buyer

shall be exempted from the responsibility. It says as follows:
"If the appearance of animate thing has been changed and when the original owner appeared, he should not say that he sold buffalo, cow, horse with the condition of not being castrated, blind, horn broken, tail cut when he sold them. Also he should not say that it was true that I sold the animate things, but alas!, the appearances have changed. If the owner appeared, he shall be liable and the buyer shall be exempted from the responsibility." [III: hsaw/W][97]

This item also includes a unique law perhaps not dealt with in all the other Dhammathats. It says as follows:
"If the price for any pregnant human being, buffalo, cow, horse, elephant, goat, or pig was fixed, the offspring shall be considered as the half of the adult. If the buyer has not paid and the child was born, he shall pay half of the price. He shall take all the [being]s]. [But] if [the mother] gave birth to a dead child, he should not say 'is it good to die?' If the child was born and has grown up, the seller shall get the half of the suitable amount. He should fix the price with a person who knows the childhood (*mwe:-si nge-si*) of the animal and shall give the half of the price. [But] he should not say that he would get it after the child had grown up because the child was still young."[III: hsaw/K-hsaw/W].

Concerning (6), it deals with the sale and purchase of the cultivated land. The rule is as follows:
"To buy or sell cultivated land, on which was planted the fruits bearing trees, roots and bulbs are planted. The seller evaluates the land and the fruits, vegetables and roots grown on it this year is valued such. The buyer limited the number that much, settled the price and bought them. If he got as he said, he shall pay as much as he could. If the rain is little and he will not be able to get as much as he mentioned in the year, he shall keep them until the next year and pay and settle the account. If he cannot get them pleasantly even though he got and quantity is not enough and it has not reached the number mentioned above yet, he shall get the amount mentioned above." "If the sky and the land are normal and [the cultivators] has gotten vegetable, fruits, bulbs and roots, etc., the buyers shall receive if they

requested. If they sell secretly, the buyers shall take with the double price. If the sellers do not give /the products/ over the year, even though was decided as such, they shall have to value the price for buying. They should not say they will do next time. If the weather is not normal and could not get /the products/ they shall keep half of them take back the rest in future." [III: hsaw/W-hsan/K].

In relation to (7) and (8) above, concerning disputes over the water in irrigation systems, all /cultivators/ should have access to the water supply unless they inflict damage to the plantations of their neighbours. The *MD* says as follows: "On the use of irrigation system water by cultivators on low farm lands and those who draw water on high farm lands. /During the dry season/ cultivators who fill high farm lands have good harvests. /Unlike them/ cultivators who fill low farmlands could not have good harvest; so /the cultivators who fill high lands/ should allow water /from the irrigation system/ to flow downwards to the low farm lands." [III: has:/W-has:/K].

In relation to (9), in disputes over the distribution of water in irrigated areas, no judgements should be based on the law of the Papathat ('the law of vice'), but should be made in accordance with the Dhammathat ('the law of virtue'). The *MD* says as follows:
"If a case has been brought to the king's court, it is a case for the king to decide. Judgments should be made in accordance with the Dhammathat or 'the law of virtue.' The Dhammathat is the customs, usages and collections of decisions (*hton:*) of the first King Mahathamada who claims to be the father of successive kings in the world. When kings, monks and people who do not observe religious and moral laws treat a case which is doubtful and reasonable as a serious case and make judgments, then such ruling is called Papathat. During the time when Papathat is being practiced by the people and monks, there would be drought, destruction of the Kingdom, rampant theft and burglaries, unlawfulness, the eight kinds of dangers (*Be Shit-pa:*) and the ten kinds of retributions (*Dan Hse-ba:*). The Dhammathat is the title given to all the decisions made by the kings, the monks and the people who have cleansed themselves of /the consequences/ of their misdeeds by observing the four factors of

Four Solidarities (*Thingaha-wuthtu Le-ba:*)[98], the Seven Factors for the Property of the Country (*Apareitha Niya Taya: Hkunit-pa:*)[99] and another seven factors for the prosperity of the country and another seven *Apareikha Niya*. *[*Through this the people) could enter the Nirvana (*Neibban*)." [III: has:/K-za./W].

The *MD* also refers to the Yazathat which is a collection of decisions by the king. It says as follows:

"Yazathat is the rulings which are exclusive to the king by saying that "Yazathat is mine and I *[*rulers*]* observe in accordance with the Dhammathat", only kings should admonish the high and low and those who should be admonished by exploiting the king for the benefits of both the Yazathat and the Dhammathat in accordance with the preaching of Buddha- to-be (*Alaun:-Arya*) in all successive worlds from the beginning." [III: hsa:/K].

The *MD* explains the relationship between the king and the Sangha as follows:

"*[*The Sangha*]*, relying on the support of the king, are to propagate religion' (*min:ko hmi ywe.thathana-taw ko pyu.su.-kyin:=min: go hmi ywe. thathana-daw go pyu.zu.-gyin:*). This has been preached by different Buddhas in successive worlds." [III: za./W].[100]

(Another way of putting is that the king supports the propagation of Buddhism by supporting the Sangha or the Buddhist Order. In this clause we find conclusive proof that the reciprocal relationship between the king and the Sangha is at the centre of the Theravāda Buddhist polity.)[101]

In connection with (10), "in order to settle the dispute over the demarcation of the boundary between villages large and small, land marks (*ahmat-ahta:*) between them should be studied and referred to' [III: has:/W]. It is essential for the owners of land to mark their boundaries distinctly by burying such things as, logs, bamboo groves planting, bushes, wells, permanent land marks, pebbles, ash of paddy husks, charcoal, bones, etc., in twenty-seven places, such as pagoda, shrine (*nat-ein*), well, pool (*ye-kan=ye gan*), pond (*ye-ain*), cave/ monastery/ appendage to a pagoda (*ku:=gu: kyaun:dazaun*), etc. and with (11), in order to settle the dispute over the demarcation of the boundary between villages large and small."

"Landmarks should be set up to demarcate the boundaries between towns and the villages as well as to mark the land given to warriors and the land donated to the pagodas. Certain lands are not parts of a hamlet or a village or a town but they have been exclusively donated to a pagoda or a monastery or donated for /the construction/ of the ordination hall. When the dispute arises, or when these lands become guarded by a headman (*Thugyi:* (=*Dhagyi:*)), the land officer (*mye-dain*), chief of the forest (*Taw-kè*), a clerk (*Sachi-sama*) or an assistant clerk (*Samin*) from the /nearest/ town, village or the forest, investigation should be made on respective landmarks, stone inscriptions to extract clues to reveal the division marks. The king, the minister and the judge should visit the disputed area between the two territories involved to reveal /the truth/. If /the land marks/ are destroyed, those who did it shall have to commutate and also such a punishment as his being buried upto his neck in the ground and keep him for seven days or half a month, or being expelled from the country, or making him a slave, etc." [III: ga./K].[102]

In relation to (12), "if all the objects, such as wooden fences, trees, bamboos, brooks, canals, rivers, ponds, stones, mountains, etc., which demarcates between the town, village, or township are destroyed, those who destroyed them shall be punished by the state. Let them substitute or compensate with the sum of thirty kyats, etc. If they happened to have broken a log (*thit-si wa-si*) or bamboo, or stone, or brick carelessly, let them compensate, but not be punished by the state." [III: Za./W].

Concerning to (13), "among towns, divisions, districts, countries, and villages, if they plundered each other due to lack of mark /or identification/ in altogether sixteen places /of which are not mentioned in detail/, the town and village headmen, the judges should inquire both the parties. If they cannot show any evidence for demarcation, let them be immersed in water. If one party who could stay longer in the water, /he or she/ shall win and the other party who could not stay long in the water, /he or she/ shall be defeated." [III: Za./W-Za/K].

Regarding (14), "If any person, knowing that /this/ is another land, or other's pond (*ain*), or lake (*in:*), well, tank (*kan*), guarden, or land for cultivation, tree, have taken by force and destroyed, the judges should inquire the truth and decide accordingly. If the destruction is true, the persons who did it are liable to the state punishment by being hit with six hundred strokes. If any landmark or similar evidence can not be shown to demarcate the boundary between districts, towns and villages, the king, the ministers and the judges should divide the land and lead both parties to divide and to possess, just as the parents divide and give tasty food and settle the quarrel when their children are scrambling at and jostling each other." [III: gi./W].

In regard to (15), it deals with the case which the lands of soldiers, warriors, commoners, or religious lands, were taken by force, the king should examine the truth. By examining, if it is found to be true, the party concerned shall be given thirty lashes at the crowded places and shall be requested to pay tax for year or month. In relation to the religious land,

"If the slaves of a king or the commoners with bad character destroyed the religious land which was donated by the ancient kings, saying that there are no inscriptions to provide evidence for this, they shall go to the four nether worlds or undesirable rebirth (*Apay Le:-ba:*)[103]. They would lose their material possessions and be impoverished in this life. Nobody should claim even two inches, six inches or eighteen inches of the land belonging to the religious establishment." [III: gi./K].

Concerning (16),

"If there is no list which is engraved on an inscription, it will be suitable to become the religious land. If it is the land donated by the king, it is suitable to become the royal land. If the king and the ministers donated it, the king should possess it. It is suitable for the king to acquire it because the king is the lord of all land and water." [III: gi./K-g.W].

In regard to (17), *MD* describes cases of libel in various examples as follows:

"If a man accused monks and Brahmin or persons who practice religious works, learned persons, honourable persons, socially high class persons, saying that they did a wrongful act though they actually did not or that they told wrongful words though they never told, the man shall publicly pay respect to them for half a month or a month." [III: gi./K].

"If anyone told such non beneficial words carelessly that monks and Brahmin did not preach in accordance with the religious words, after hearing the words which monks told each other. He is liable to such a criminal punishment as his lip to be cut off or compensation by paying twenty to thirty kyats." [III: gi./K].

"If anyone happened to accuse with untruthful words regarding the royal family or warriors (*thayè*), deputy commander (*sit-kè*), rulers of the country (*pyi-so:-do.*), he shall become slave for life because misdeed of the man who accused is uncountable." [III: gi./K].

"Any town or village fief *[myo.-ywasa:* (=*za:*)*]* struck, torture and reviled the villagers, he shall be expelled from that village. If the villagers accused the */*town or*/* village fief wrongly, their property shall be confiscated and driven out from the village." [III: gi./K].

"If any bad man happened to be oppressive towards a good man and also told disrespectful words, he shall have to cut fodder for elephants and horses." [III: gi./K].[104]

Concerning (18), it says as follows:[105]

"Any Brahmin, wealthy people and poor people are included in one of the four slaves (*Kyun-le:-ba:*) of the king of the country. That is why all the treasures like gold, silver, gem, ruby; elephant, horse, slave, buffalo, cow, sheep, pig, *pareikhkaya* (prescribed articles to use by Buddhist monks) are named as the king's properties." [III: gi./K].

Relating to (19), it says as follows:
"Any son who defies the parental authority and acts disrespectfully toward them should not receive their inheritance and return the same. /If he had already received them/ showing this to him, let him be expelled from the society." [bu./W].[106]

"Any monk who oppose the authority of the presiding monks, should be expelled from the Buddhist Order. If the pupils speak disrespectfully of their teachers, monks, or Brahmins, or sons, grandchildren, and family slaves show disrespect, they shall be punished." [III: bu./W].

As regards (20), it describes as follows:
"Any person riding on an elephant or a horse came, the horse's rider should give way to /him/. If /a horse's rider/ does not give way to /the former/ and /the former/ who had to change the track was bitten by a poisonous snake or got scratched by thorns,, /the latter/ who did not give way shall be responsible for his action." [III: Zu./K].[107]

Regarding (21), it says as follows:
"Any older monks should not use harsh words toward the younger novices. /On the other hand/, the young novices should not use harsh words toward older monks'. Let the man respectfully kowtow to them. Any wealthy person happened to speak haughtily with disrespectful words toward a poor person, the educated judges should examine the case well." [III: Zu. / W-Zu./K].[108]

In regard to (22), it refers to as follows:
"If anyone go to defecate or urinate at a place where he should not go, he shall be punished. If /anyone/ spit at person whom he should not spit is also punished' [III: Zu./K]. 'If /anyone/ cut down a tree which is beneficial /to everyone/ and broke the branches, he shall be punished so that the curse of the trees would come to an end." [III: Zu./K].[109]

"/A stupid or foolish man/ mistakenly destroyed a tree which is beneficial /to everyone/ because he thought it was unbeneficial. Really he wanted to cut the three down. The stupid and foolish man shall be punished and be exiled from the village." [III: zu./K-zu.-W].

In relation to (23), it says as follows:
"If any monk or Brahmin publicly preach which is sub-standard or unsuitable, if he preached the "law of misdeed (*akudho taya:*)" instead of "law of virtuous action" (*kudho taya:*), if he happened to say that the law which a good man is practicing is not the law

which good men shall practice, he shall be punished and made to worship the law with whole heart." [III: zu./K-zu/W].

"No one should say that those who are well versed in Pitakat are not well versed or that those who are respectful are not respectful. Whoever spoke thus should be beaten by cane with many strokes. After that, let him be paraded around without any chance of recompense." [III: Zu/W].

"Anyone happened to accuse his teacher and parents, he shall be punished. After that, let him publicly pay respects to the teachers and parents." [III: Zu /W].

"Any persons who are from the poor class, but his behavior is good and his fighting ability is remarkable, he should be raised to a higher status. If /anyone/ happened to describe them that they were of low class, he shall be seriously punished." [III: Zu/K-Zu/W].[110]

In regard to (24), it says as follows:
"If anyone said, '/you/ are a blind', though he is not blind, and also said '/you/are lame', though he is not, let him be immersed in water. He happened to call person '/you/ are a slave' and it is not true and apologized. He is considered to be free from guilt. He should approach the accuser (*tayashin*)." [III: Zu/K].

"Even if someone is blind or lame or a slave, a person should not say so to embarrass him. The person who said thus shall be considered as guilty." [III: Zu/K].

"If /anyone/ say something, revealing about being blind or deaf or lame and these are true, he shall not be blamed. The person who said so shall have to compensate for his action." [III: Zu/K].

Regarding (25), "If anyone insults or is rude towards a blind, deaf, or a lame person, he shall be responsible for saying so and be considered to be guilty." [III: Zu /K]. [111]

In regard to (26), "If anyone accuses a woman falsely as a witch, it shall be regarded as a serious offence, because she is liable to be driven out from the village." [III: Ze/W].[112]

Concerning (27), "If anyone used the word 'slave' to slander someone, he shall be considered guilty. If anyone says that he is a thief though he is actually not a thief, he shall not be guilty. If a person is falsely accused of theft, mentioning the amount and quantity, if it is not true, he shall be compensated. If it is true, he shall have the right to do so. If he said half in joke, he shall not be guilty." [III: Ze/K].

As regards to (28), which is wrong accusation of someone as an adulterer or a murderer, it says as follows:

> "If anyone happened to accuse someone as an adulterer, though he is actually not, he shall not be considered guilty." [III: Ze/K].
> "Where a man is accused of having had an affair with a woman and was caught by someone, if it is true he should have the right to do so. If it is not true, and is falsely accused at the risk of life, he should be made to pay thirty ticals (=pieces of silver)."
> "If someone is being falsely accused of murder, he should not be liable to punishment. If the murder is actually being committed, all reference regarding the victim should be provided." [III: Ze/K].[113]

In regard to (29), of wrongly saying that one had sold some one as follows:

> "If anyone said that he sold some one into slavery, though he did not actually do so, he shall not be considered guilty. /However/ mentioning the exact amount either in cash or in kind. Then he shall be considered guilty." [III: Ze:/W].

Then, in (30), it concludes that the traditional law should be adapted to the suspicion of accusing as follows:

> "Verbal accusation and oppression by a villain which is sharper than a knife and spear will cause destruction of person and property belonging to him and others. Therefore, all people who are noble and holy should only consider the prosperity of others." [III: Ze:/W-Ze:/K].

> "Those villains who accused and oppressed finally came to the court saying;

"Hey, villains, do not make such a malicious accusation or oppression." [III: Ze:/K].[114]

Finally, the *MD* describes four types of accusation. These are: (i) accusation of similarity /of object/; (ii) accusation without similarity, (iii) accusation because it is true /just accusation/ and (iv) accusation although it is not true /unjust accusation/. "In case of false accusation, /the object concerned/ should be returned. /Should it be damaged/ compensate according to the object be given." "If it is a just accusation, the person concerned should be considered as innocent. If it is falsely accused, an equal amount (?) should be compensated." [III: ze:/ K:-zaw:/W].

Thus, the law of the Dhammathat purports in Chapter III, as Than Tun asserted, that "frauds and fraudulent accusations could be mitigated through compromise" [Than Tun 1985: 40] and that "the Buddhist religion can be propagated with the support of the king." [III: za./W:].

2. Some additional Information described in the Chapter XVI

In Chapter XVI, after having summarised the contents of fifteen chapters, it describes briefly as follows:

a. From the various documents collected, it is observed that the total number of verdicts numbered six hundred and ten. [mi./K - 4th l.].[115]

Among the terminology and expressions repeatedly mentioned, the major ones are ten, ditto fifteen, ditto twenty, ditto one hundred and twenty and ditto three hundred and fifty. Avoiding the use of four categories i.e., falsehood, abusive language, *Thanphapalapa Wasa* (=*Samphapalāpa Wasa*) (frivolous talk) [*ibid*.: 5th l.], good kings and those who aspire for kingship should use two of the above and pass judgments accordingly. From eighteen roots, over hundred twigs and leaves will sprout. [*ibid*.: 6th l.] But they are still attached to the root. "Oh noble and great Thamada! As it is mentioned in this Code of Law using your majesty's discretion what is likely to be punished in hell and what is not [*ibid*.: 7th l.] and judge accordingly". [*ibid*.: 8th l.]

"Among the kinds of love, there is none comparable to Self love. Among the property there is nothing comparable to paddy (rice). Among the words there none comparable [*ibid*.: 8th l.] to Truth. [*ibid*.: 9th l.] There are five types of heroes. Among the cows (bovines), horses, elephants and lions, lions are the best. Besides Lions are the noblest of all, even surpassing men." [*ibid*.: 9th l.]

b. "Among the five types of human beings it should be remembered that there are superior, ordinary and inferior. Also among the inanimate (objects) it is the same. Among the [*mi./W*1st l.] Nine types of Rubies, the name is the same. But there are four types/ Out of which *Zartigu* is the best. Among the four species of diamonds, *Mincho ?* is the best. Among the five kinds of *Nilar* (Sapphire), *Eindanilar* (Amethist) is the best [*ibid*.: 2nd l.]. Among the five kinds of Emerald, *Mawraya* is the best. Among the three types of Pearl, the one known as *Bhrama* is the best. Among the seven types of Cats' Eye (moonstone), *Heindalaka* is the best [*ibid*.3rd l.]. Among the five kinds of Coral, the red one is the best. Among the three kinds of Zircon, *Ambala* is the best. As it has been mentioned above, the jewel known as *Manawmaya* [*ibid*.: 4th l.] should be used by the powerful *Sekkya-wade-min* who uses the wish fulfilling the *Padamya Ashin* is the best. That is [*ibid*.: 5th l.] the best among the inanimate objects. Even among them there are ordinary categories such as Superior and Inferior."

"Oh Noble King-the gold which is considered as the Ornament of the World also has four types such as *Aramat* [*ibid*.6th l.], *Anyamat, Insamat, Niramat*. These four types of gold are obtained from Silver. These four types of gold, *Narani, Naraka, Narmuka and Naraye* is obtained from the *Nagar* (dragon) [*ibid*.: 7th l.]. *Battarani, Urani, Uragote, Uttawatani* these four types of gold is obtained from *Hlaw Myay. Thuwannayathi, Thuwannamani* and *Thuwannayin*-These four [*ibid*.8th l.] types of gold is originated from *Zawgyi* (Alchemist). *Zamabanada, Zakarupa, Diganika* and *Wimanaka*, the four types of gold is obtained from *Kabamye* (Mother Earth)." [*ibid*.: 9th l.].[116]

c. "It should be considered as gold from Twenty places. Noble King- the name of the these gold are *Nipalan, Narani, Narawaw, Nalika, Narimotta, Inzani, Inzani Motta, Azatawanizatayupa, Uranita, Thinhka* [III: mi/kyaw:1st l.]-*neik* and *Zabuyit*, all together, ten types of gold. Why is it that there are twelve types is because only when 80 ticals of *Nipalan* gold is tempered till it is reduced to 60 ticals [*ibid*.: 2nd l.] *Narani* gold is obtained. When 60 ticals of *Narani* gold is tempered till 45ticals of *Narawaw* gold is obtained. When 45 ticals of *Narawaw* gold is tempered [3rd P.R.] till 33 ticals, 7 mu, 1 pe and 2 yway of *Nalika* gold is tempered till it is reduced till you get 25 ticals 3 mu [*ibid*.:4th l.] 2 yway of *Nilamutta* gold is obtained. When 25 ticals, 3 mu and

2 yway of *Nilamutta* is tempered till 19 ticals, 1 yway, 2 hsan is left, [*ibid.*: 5th l.] you get *Inzani* gold. When 19 ticals, 1 yway and 2 hsan is tempered till 14 ticals, 2 mu, 1 pe, 2 hsan is left you get *Inzanimotta* gold is obtained. When *Inzanimotta* [*ibid.*: 6th l.] gold 14 ticals, 2 mu, 1 pe, 2 hsan is tempered till 10 ticals, 6 mu, 1 pe, 4yway, 1hsan, 1 hnan, 3 monyin, 2 than uhkaung is left *Azatawani* gold is obtained [*ibid.*: 7th l.] When 12? Ticals, 6 mu, 1 pe, 4 yway, 1hsan, 1 hnan, 3 monnyin (mustard seed), 2 thanuhkaung (head of a louse) is tempered till 8 ticals, 3 yway, 3 hnan, 2 monnyin, 2 than uhkaung, 3 kanyit [*ibid.*: 8th l.] che is left (Za) *Tayupa* gold is obtained. When 8 ticals, 3 yway, 3 hnan, 2 monyin, 1 (than) uhkaung, 1 nyit che Is tempered till 6 ticals, 3 hsan (a grain of rice), 3hnan (grains of sesame), 4 than ukhaung., 4 kanyitche of *Uranita* gold [mu./wun:1st l.] is tempered till 4 ticals, 2 mat, 2 hsan, 3 hnan, 1 monyin, 6 than uhkaung, 2 kanyitche is left, *Theingineit* gold is obtained. When *Theingineit* gold 4 ticlas [*ibid.*: 2nd l.] 2 mat, 2 hsan, 3 hnan, 1 monnyin, 6 than uhkaung, 2 kanyitche is tempered till 3 ticlas, 3 mu, 1 pe, 4 yway, 2 hsan, 2 hnan, 1 monnyin, 3 than uhkaung, 2 kanyitche is left, *Zabuyit* gold is obtained." [*ibid.*: 3rd l.].[117]

"Since that is unlikely to be possible, when you think carefully, this would mean that it is beyond the power of human beings. It could be possibly to be done by the Nats. [*ibid.*: 4th l.] Therefore gold created by the Nats is superior. Better than *Zabuyit* is *Zamikara* gold. Better than *Zamika (ra)* gold is *Gambi* gold. Beter than *Gambit* gold is *Sampuna* gold. Better than *Sampuna* gold is *Theinganeik* gold [*ibid.*: 5th l.]. As mentioned above, among gold, among animals among one hundred and one human beings (races?) among the Nat (and) Brahma, and among the monks there is inferior, ordinary and superior [*ibid.*: 6th l.] Similarly among the kings (ruling class) *Padeitharit* (chieftain),[118] *Egarit* (monarch),[119] *Dipayit* (lord of an island)[120] *Sekkyawade* (Lord 0f Universe, Universal king)[121] [*ibid.*: 7th l.] and *Mandat* just like there classes just as there is class distinction as in gold. Among what has been mentioned, *Aseindeya Hpaya Thakhin* there is no one incompatible. He alone is unique. Therefore beginning with what is termed as *Shwekodaw* [*ibid.*: 8th l.] it is *Aseindeya* [*ibid.*: 9th l.]. Bearing this in mind that all things are classified into three categories, in order to pass fair judgements (for compensations) for high and low (status) [*ibid.*], all judges beginning with Mahathamada all good kings and those who aspire to be should follow what is laid down in the Dhammathat, in order not to be free from the sixteen kinds of contemplation [*tahse-chauk yat thaw: auk-me kyin:*][122], abstaining from four courses (*Agadi-Le-ba:*)[123] and according to law with love and compassion, and should endeavour for peace and prosperity of the people, to be free from suffering in [mu./K-1ˢᵗ l.] hell. Not following *A] gati Le:-ba:* [*ibid.*: 2ⁿᵈ l.] judgement should be passed in consultation with the learned. Judgments should be passed in accordance with Dhammathat, using your intellect and discretion choosing from the two what could cause suffering in hell (bad *Karma*) and what is not (good *Karma*) [*ibid.*: 3ʳᵈ l.] and pass judgment accordingly. Major sentences should be minimized and minor cases should be eliminated. Thus, spoke the Hermit Manu, son of King Brahma." [*ibid.*: 4ᵗʰ l.].

Chapter XII
Commentary on 'Early Konbaung Thirty Rulings' and Some Additional Information in the *MD* (1782MS)

1. Insertion of 'the Thirty New Rules' in Chapter III of the *MD* (1782MS)

a. What are these rules?

The thirty rules which are contained in Chapter III of the *MD* (1782MS) were inserted between Chapters III and IV of the *MD* (the Richardson's Burmese text, 1760MS), while Chapter III of the 1760 MS was moved to Chapter II of the 1782MS. From where, then were these thirty rules introduced? No doubt they represent the prevailing customary rules at the early period of King Badon's reign. From Myanmar legal tradition and a common-sense standpoint, the author(s) of the *MD* (1782MS) would have consulted some former existing Dhammathats at least in-between 1756 and 1782, such as *Dhammawilatha* copied in 1757& n.d.(date unknown) including the earlier one in 1749. *Manu kyetyo* (copied in 1762) *Manuthaya Shwemyin* (*Wannadhamma Shwemyin*) (1763); *Manuyin* (1767); *Wineikhsaya Pakathani* (=*Vinicchaya-pakasani*) (1771); *Mohawishsedani* (=*Mohavicchedani*) (1771); Manuwunnana (=*Manuvanna*) (1772); *Yazabala* (=*Rājabala*) (1780)which were compiled or copied during the first half of the Konbaung period [See Table 7].

We have surveyed all the major Dhammathats in our possession either newly compiled or copied since the period of the founding of Konbaung Dynasty by King Alaunghpaya to the beginning of the reign of King Badon (1752-1782). We presume that the authors of the *MD* (1782MS) drew principally based on the *Dhammawilatha Dhammathat* (1757) and particularly the date unknown version of it or *Manu Kyetyo Dhammathat* (1762) which is said to be a Rakhine version of the *Dhammawilatha Dhammathat* when they described aforementioned thirty customary rules[124] for 1782 MS. It seems very likely that the authors traced or followed or paraphrased from the Rakhine version into Myanmar or even copied large portions of the *Dhammawilatha* or *Manu Kyetyo*. They still include a great number of words with Rakhine spelling of vocabularies. More than half the rules (No.1, 2, 3, 4, 7, 10, 15, 18, 19, 20, 21, 22, 23, 24, 25, 28, 29, 30), owe much to these two Dhammathats. The other 12 rules (No.5, 6, 8, 9, 11, 12, 13, 14, 16, 17, 26, 27)[125] are written in a different style of Myanmar language. They appear to have been written by the authors taking account of the prevailing customary rules or court decisions at the time of enthronement of King Badon. As yet we have found no parallels from other Dhammathats or from any court decisions or royal edicts or Hluttaw decisions.[126] These facts at least indicate that the newly inserted portions are not always the new ones, but originated in the early Konbaung period and the contents are not all court decisions, but not impossibly the authors' desk works.

b. Influence of the Rakhine Dhammathat upon Myanmar Dhammathat ? or Myanmar Dhammathat introduced to Rakhine people?

Lawka Byuha Kyan (LBK) comments on the destruction of Myanmar historical records[127] when the Mon rebels attacked the capital city of Ava in 1752 and destroyed the Second Taungu dynasty. [See LBK 1968: preface: hka.]. Quoting this, Furnivall assumed that "Many copies of old dhammathats /Dhammathat*s*/ must, however, have survived in monasteries scattered all over the country, and it is probable that these formed the basis for many of the works now produced by apparently undistinguished people", who compiled several versions of the *Viniccayarasi* [*Wineikhsaya yathi*] by monks in versification which seem to be mere reproduction of old lost materials [Furnivall 1940: 370] Thus we can say that the Dhammathats and other legal works were reduced to ashes with the annihilation of Ava during the Mon rebellions. We can also surmise that many legal works left in rural areas, including Rakhine, were collected and gathered and brought to the new capital city of Shwebo under the reign of King Alaunghpaya for compilation of a new law book or re-production of the lost ones.

A revised edition of the *MD* was compiled at the beginning of King Badon's reign in 1782, still exists in Myanmar with later versions of 1790, 1791 and 1851 in complete sets. As it has been mentioned earlier, the new chapters which were added in this revised edition seems to have been largely influenced by the *Dhammawilatha Dhammathat* [DWD] and its Rakhine version. Regarding them, we have at least five versions chronologically arranged as 1111M.E. (=1749A.D.), 1119M.E. (=1757A.D.), 1124M.E. (=1762A. D.*Rakhine* version named *Manu-kyetyo*), 1147 M.E. (=1785A.D.) and dateless incomplete one which lacks the final chapter on Gambling and Betting. The 1749 version which is preserved at the British Library[128] is all written in Yakhine script which largely differs from others. The rest of the four are written in pure prose with plain expressions, while the 1749 is more literary and rigid. All of these versions are very much influenced by Rakhine language and culture. Even the 1782 version of the *MD* is still largely influenced by Rakhine script and culture.[129]

Thus, as we have discussed through some Rakhine script used in the *MD* (1782 MS) that the eighteenth century Myanmar Dhammathat seems to have been influenced by the Rakhine Dhammathat. However, it is also conjectured that the legal texts of the indigenous minority groups such as the Mons, Shans, Rakhines, etc. who accepted Buddhism were more influenced by the Myanmar Dhammathat. The Myanmar Dhammathat which had been compiled since Bagan period seems to have possibly been distributed to the said Buddhist minority groups, particularly under the reign of Kings of Taungu Dynasty, such as Bayinnaung, Thalun, etc. [See MMOS IV s.425: 12-14/ s 475: 102-108/s 476: 108-115]. Although we have no proof to show this by historical records, it is very much possible that some of the Myanmar Dhammathats had been brought under their command, to the said minority groups and even to foreign countries like Chiengmai, Ayutaya, Vienchang, etc. In addition, it is very likely that these Dhammathats were translated into their native languages. In this respect, it is worthwhile tracing the Dhammathats of the Mons, the Shans, and the Rakhines, etc. and comparing them with the Myanmar Dhammathats. If this speculation is correct, the 1749 version of the *Dhammawilatha Dhammathat* which was totally written in Rakhine script may have been compiled for the Rakhine people. What does it imply that *List of the Mon Palm-leaf Manuscript*s [1913: 130] which had existed in Mawlamyine (Moulmein) and Kyaikkami (Amherst) at that time contains the Mon version of the *MD* ? We have not traced this Dhammathat yet. We have no information whether this is still extant or not. It is not impossible that this is a translation of a version of the *MD*.

c. Glimpses of the customary rules during the early Konbaung period of Myanmar?

The thirty rules contained in the *MD* (1782MS) are, as has been stated, divided into three categories: (1)Sale and purchase; (2)Boundary and land issues; (3)Defamation, imputation, abuse, insulting, accusation, etc.

Regarding (1) mentioned above, as Shwe Baw explained, the Dhammathats include comparatively very few rules on buying and selling and this is probably because these transactions which commonly form the barter system, take place mostly in villages in olden days of Myanmar. There is, therefore, no need to observe elaborate rules [Shwe Baw *ibid.*: 193]. However, the 1782 MS deals with six new types of cases shown in the previous chapter on buying and selling which are not seen in any earlier legal works, such as *Wagaru, Dhammawilatha, Manugye (*Richardson of the Myanma text,*1760 MD), Manu Kyetyo*, or *Maha Yazathat,* etc. It means these rules seem to be quite new ones prevalent during the early reign of King Badon.

As regards (2) mentioned above, the idea and definition of the ownership of land in Myanmar is traditionally that the ownership of land is "the ownership of the source of all property and all life and as such is regarded as the highest and /the/ most valuable form of property. Offences connected with land are, thus, regarded with particular gravity by the Dhammathats which safeguard the rights of the owners to land and condemn any acts which infringe upon rights by unlawful or unauthorized encroachments and trespasses.--- Dishonest transactions in land are considered punishable in hell. This being so, the king should try to save his subjects from suffering in hell by preventing them from committing acts of dishonesty regarding land. Just as the father looks after the interests of his children, all kings since the time of the first king who was called Mahāsammata ruled the world have striven for the welfare of their people. Those kings took possession of all the lands in the kingdom and distributed them among his subjects, thus obviating strife and discord" [Shwe Baw *ibid.* 250; DWD1757: ga /W].

The Dhammathats do not lay down any rules as to how transfer of ownership in land should be effective. From the fact that in land disputes, importance is attached to the evidence of witnesses who live in the neighbourhood, it may be assumed that, as a rule, transfers of land were informed to the neighbours, or headman of the village. No rules are laid down either that the execution of a written document is necessary for a valid transfer [Shwe Baw *ibid.*: 252]. As to boundary dispute, it is decided on the evidence of witnesses, inscriptions or written records. continuous possession is an important factor in the case, failing which the testimony of old residents of the locality may be taken [Shwe Baw *ibid.*: 261; DWD 1757gan/W].

With regard to written evidence, it is described not in the *Dhammawilatha Dhammathat,* but in the *Wagaru Dhammathat.* It provides that "in a suit regarding the ownership of land and water, the parties shall be required to produce witnesses and stone-inscriptions or other written materials in support of their respective claims; judgment shall be given in favour of the party who can do so. If both the parties can produce such witnesses and inscriptions, then the party who has been found in continual possession of the property in dispute shall receive it" [*Wagaru* s.169: 37/43]. *Kaingza Manuyaza* also attaches importance to the rolls given by the king's Treasury (*Shwe-daik*) as documentary evidence in land disputes [*Mahayazathatkyi* 1860: 171]. This seems to show that as to documentary evidence, the *MD* (1782MS) was influenced by the *Wagaru Dhammathat* and also the seventeenth century Kaingza's legal work.

Regarding the landmarks, the *MD* (1782MS) (No.10) seems to have been influenced by both *Dhammawilatha* and *Wagaru*. "Landmarks are necessary for the identification of land /as/ proof of ownership. They are the sentinels of property in land and are regarded as having a kind of sanctity. In the absence of landmarks a person is liable to lose his claim to the land. Permanent objects such as banyan trees, demarcation wall, lakes, rivers, hills, drains, and articles such as bones of cattle, charcoal, pieces of pottery, rock (pot shard?), sand, etc. are used as landmarks" [DWD 1757: gan/K, we also cite *Wagaru* Chap. XVII s.171: 38/ 43-44].[130]

On offences against landmarks (No.11), several penalties (*min-dan*) are prescribed. For destroying them the offender is liable to be sold and the proceeds of the sale forfeited to the owner of the landmark [DWD1757: gan/K]. A man who commits offences, such as removing sign-posts, filling up of boundary ditches, destroying a river, cutting a rope used for demarcating boundaries, etc. shall pay compensation [*Wagaru*, XVII s172: 38/44]. If a man removed or destroyed the marks inadvertently, he must bear all fell at the time when the marks were originally set up [DWD1757: ga /W; *Mawhawishsedani* (*Mohaviccedani*): hku/K]. The fine for removing a landmark to a different place is heavier than for destroying and a person who accuses another falsely of an offences against a landmark is liable to criminal punishment (*pahso-awut hcut-shin:ywe. pouk-hka*) [*Mawhawishsedani*:hku/K].

On No.11, disputes relating to the ownership of secular lands are decided on the evidence of such objects as boundary marks, stone inscription of title, documents, etc. "One important point in these disputes is that any resort to violence is prejudicial to the party guilty of violence" [Shwe Baw *ibid*.: 254; see DWD 1757: gan/K]. In most disputes, headmen, elders, and even monks are made available as witnesses. "Boundaries of lands should be marked correctly, and the person who marks them should use trees, well, ditches, --- sand, charcoal, ---etc. If he fails to do this, the head man, Brahmin, or monk should note the boundaries and mark correctly with above mentioned objects" [Shwe Baw *ibid.*: 254 from *Kaingza Shwemyin*]. On the other hand, disputes over religious lands shall be settled by verbal or documentary evidence. Title and deed are also determined on the strength of verbal or documentary evidence. "In a suit regarding the ownership of pagodas and monasteries, or lands (dedicated to Buddha)---if both parties can (produce stone inscriptions or grants in support of their respective claims)---. Preference shall be given to the party which has the priority of alms-giving or founding endowments. If both parties have founded endowments at the same time, and if they be the king and his ministers, the king's claim shall get the preference as he is the lord of the land---" [Shwe Baw *ibid.* 255; *Wagaru*, XVII, 170s: 43/47].

"Where the land in dispute is a remote area and is difficult to find any mark, such person as snake charmer, cowherd, hunter and wood cutter, who are likely to know the fact of dispute may be examined as a witness" [DWD 1757: gan/K]. "The judge who decided wrongfully based on what witness told truth shall go to hell (*ngayè tho. la: le ya i*) [*Manuwunnana* 467s.: 286]. If a dispute cannot be decided, the judges should settle nicely (*kaun:zwa hsin pe ak i.*) the land dispute for both the parties" [DWD *ibid.*: gan/K].

The range of words used in the Myanmar legal vocabulary to describe speech offences include *jou:sut /sutswe:*(accuse), *chopche* (oppress), *ma.you ma. the thaw zaga:/ ma. le: ma.za: thaw zaga:*(un-respectful speech), *hnoutlun* (abusive language), *lethlwe:*(swing one's arm), etc. Richardson's text uses altogether twenty-eight principal terms for abuse [VIIs.6].[131] The Myanmar legal term "for 'defamation' was 'to go beyond one's rights by words' and so it concerned malicious prosecution and abuse" [Htin Aung 1962: 13]. An authentic English Dictionary explains Defamation and other related vocabularies as follows. Defamation is "the injuring of a person's good name or reputation'. Imputation is 'to attribute or ascribe something dishonest or dishonourable to a person". Abuse is "to use incorrectly or improperly or to misuse; to maltreat physically or sexually; to speak insultingly or cruelly to (a person) or to revile. Blasphemy is "blasphemous behaviour or language". Accusation is "an allegation that a person is guilty of some fault, offence, or crime; similar to imputation". Imprecation is "the act of imprecating; malediction or curse" [CED].[132] This last meaning corresponds to No.17- No.30 in the 30 customary rules added to the *MD* (1782MS).

'The Dhammathats regarded defamation as a serious offence. "In this world the point of the sharpest spear kept ready for use in the house is not sharp enough. Passing sharp, indeed, are the words of evil-minded persons. Such persons destroy other's happiness as well as their own happiness. Therefore, those who have their own and other's welfare in their hearts shall renounce the evil habit of talking ill of others---." [Shwe Baw *ibid.* 481-482; see DWD1757: gi./W] (No.24/30)

"When a member of the lower classes defamed, a man of high status like a monk or a Brahmin by a member of the lower classes, he is liable for corporal punishment. On the other hand, if a man of high status commits an offence against another high status man, he shall be liable to pay compensation. For defamation against ruling class, if it relate to a plot to overthrow the throne, the offender is liable for capital punishment." [Shwe Baw *ibid.* 480-483; Okudaira 1986: 111]. No. 17 deals with these cases.

Regarding 'abuse', under Myanmar law, it means to address words to another person directly with the intention of insulting or annoying him. [See Okudaira *ibid.*: 111] For mere using indefinite terms that a person is a thief, no liability arises. But when a person says "you are a thief", a robber committed robbery in the house of specific name of a person or stolen goods and were caught while committing robbery and given a beating, he shall be fined if what he says is false----. If what he says is true, he shall not be liable." [See DWD 1757: ghi./W]].

"The law regarding the abuse is extended to cases of mere mispronunciation of another name. A case is reported where a person is prosecuted for calling another 'Nga Pa Theit' when his real name is 'Nga Pathi'. The court hold this to be an insult and directed payment of compensation [Nga Pa Thi Vs. Nga Pyu (18 06) [YKHP1965: 32-34].[133] For this Shwe Baw commented that "in fact the words in question carry no meaning, but the courts held that to pronounce a name wrongly was itself an offence" [Shwe Baw *ibid.*: 485-486] It is also abuse to ridicule a person for his bodily defects. "A person who makes fun of those who have squint eyes, who is blind in one or both eyes, who have defective limbs, who are hunchbacks, with intention to insult or annoy, shall be criminally punished" [DWD1757 ghi./W-K]. "A person who says 'you blind man' to a man who is blind and 'You lame man' to a man who is lame with intent to insult or annoy shall be fined., whether he belongs to a caste higher than the man whom he has offended" [DWD, 1757: ghi. /W-K]. (No.24/25)

In regard to slandering women, "there are three kinds of imputation looked on with special disfavour. These are accusing a man of having had an affair with a woman, accusing a woman of having brought about her abortion, or accusing a woman of being a witch. On accusation for having had an affair with a woman, the Dhammathats takes the view that the reputation of a man of high class suffers no detriment if the woman alleged to have been involved in the affair belongs to his own class or to the middle class. On the other hand, due to the fact that he has had an intrigue with a woman of low class or a slave, the offender is liable to pay compensation or be sold as a slave" [Shwe Baw *ibid.*: 484 from DWD, 1757: ghi./W-K](No.24/25).

Out of the accusations mentioned above, accusing a woman falsely of being a witch is regarded as a serious offence, because, if the accusation prevails, she is liable to be expelled from her native place. The common method of proof is to throw the suspected woman into the water, and her floating or sinking determines the verdict. (No.26)[134]

As regards the distinction between 'Abuse' and 'Defamation', it is rather difficult to make a clear distinction, but the general rule is that to amount to defamation, it is necessary that the words used must have references to specific facts. If they are vague or in any way indefinite, there is no liability. The distinction between both, the former must be committed in the presence of the other party, whereas defamation may be committed behind his back, but particulars must be given, and bonafide belief in the truth of imputation is a defense. This rule that only specific or definite words amount to defamation is enforced by the court strictly [Mi Pyu V. Mi Hlaing 1789, *Yezagyo Hkondaw Hpyathton* p.6-7./ Shwe Baw *ibid.*: 486- 487] (No.27-29). *Dhammawilatha Dhammathat* says: "Although a man is not a thief or murder, or if someone may call him, "Thief, Murderer", to speak in general terms is not defamation. But should he say "You pierced him with a spear, you cut him with knife, killed him, flung his body from the hillside, strangled him, caused him to be drowned. Thus if a man call him by name, he shall be punished." [See Shwe Baw *ibid.*: 487; DWD1757: ghi./W].

Finally, regarding (No.30), as has been mentioned in the previous chapter, the *MD* (1782MS) added in the last portion, four types of accusation which are not included in such versions as 1749, 1757, the date unknown version. (and 1785) of the *Dhammawilatha* and *the Manu Kyetyo Dhammathat* (1762). The Dhammathat generally urged men who accuse others falsely not to do so, for the good of the country and for their own good.

d. Inclusion of miscellaneous customary rules into the *MD* (1782 MS)

It is noteworthy to mention the content of the *Mawhaweishsedani* Dhammathat. There are only two Dhammathats which attach importance to the 18 original titles from Hindu Dharmaśāstras, such as *Manu-smṛti* [Shwe Baw *ibid.*: 35), and follow to some extent in their texts. These are *Dhammawilatha* and *Wagaru* which belong to the earlier works in 12-13th centuries of Myanmar. On the other hand, most Dhammathats which were compiled in the later period, particularly during the Konbaung Dynasty attach less importance to them and do not follow their order in their texts [See Shwe Baw 1955: 34] with the sole exception of the *Mohawishsedani Dhammathat*. It includes the full 18 titles or roots and follows their order scrupulously in the text. These 18 titles or roots stemmed from Hindu law and became the eighteen radical laws of the Dhammathat : these are (1)Debt; (2)Deposit; (3)Sale without ownership; (4)Gift; (5)Carpenter's wages; (6)Hire; (7)

Breach of promise; (8); Sale and Purchase; (9)Cowherd; (10)Boundary; (11)Imputation; (12)Theft; (13)Assault; (14)Homicide; (15)Husband and wife; (16)Slaves; (17)Inheritance and (18)Wager [See *ibid.*43]. On the other hand, the *Manugye Dhammathat* refers to the 18 titles which were translated from Pāli verse into Myanmar as the radical laws of the *Dhammathat*. These are: (1)Borrowing money; (2)Depositing of property; (3)Stealing and altering the appearance of property and selling it again; (4)When a gift shall be returned on demanding; (5)Dividing the wages of carpenters; (6) Dividing the wages of labourers; (7)The law of decision in case of breach of promise made in presence of respectable men; (8)The law deciding disputes between the owner of cattle and the herdsmen; (9)The law whether property that has been sold(bought?); (10)The law for settling disputed boundaries; (11)The law when an accusation has been lodged; (12)The law of theft or concealment (of property); (13)The law of assault; (14)The law of murder; (15)The law for deciding the proper conduct of husband and wife; (16)The law determining whether a person be a slave or not; (17)The law for deciding if cock fighting, or betting, or gambling debts shall be paid; (18)The law for the partition of inherited property [(R)MD1896: 69].

Thus unlike *Mawhawishsedani* (=*Mohaviccedani*) *Dhammathat* and like most Konbaung Dhammathats, the *MD* does not follow the afore-mentioned order, even though these 18 rules are described in the text itself. With the exceptions of both Chapter III which deals with Debt and Chapter X which explains Inheritance and Partition, other Chapters include conglomeration of rules under various titles. In addition, it is noticeable that following the 18 Radical Rules, the Four Unchangeable Matters[135] and the Five Original Laws[136] are described and that these contents together with detailed customary rules on debt moved to Part III of Chapter I which was newly arranged in the *MD* (1782MS) which was probably revised under King Badon. It is very probable that the author(s) of the 1782MS intentionally constructed the new Chapter I which consists of Part I: The Preamble on Myth of Kingship and Part II: The Duties of King and Judges newly inserted and Part III: The Eighteen Radical Rules with the Unchangeable Matters and Original Rules.

As is mentioned above, the *MD* largely departed from the order and the contents of the 18 Radical Rules which were maintained in ancient Dhammathats. It seems that the newly collected thirty customary rules inserted into new Chapter III in the *Manugye* (1782MS) not as a specific title, but as a selection from various titles which had been dealt with in the Richardson's text. The new customary rules which were included in the *MD* (1782MS) seem not to be systematically categorized. The editor, it seems, moved Chapter III of 1760MS (=the Richardson's text) were moved into the Chapter I (pt.3) of 1782 MS so as to present such basic principles of Myanmar customary laws as the 18 Radical Rules of Myanmar Dhammathat, Four Unchangeable Matters and the Five Originals [See RMD III: 68-70].

2. Addition of Some Information

The colophon of the Chapter XVI mentioned that the chapter was copied on the 14th day of waxing of the moon for the month of Wazo in 1144 M.E.(=1782A.D.).

It suggests that the whole chapter has possibly been copied either from any former Dhammathat or any other legal sources or otherwise newly described. We have, however, not found such chapter in any other Dhammathat yet. This chapter consists of four parts: the first being the summary of the whole chapters from I to XV; the second being the explanation on various kinds and qualities (inferior, ordinary and superior) of love, property, animal, language, gem and gold; the third being qualities of animals; commoners; Nats (spirits) and Brahma, and persons of Royal lineage in comparison with gold and the forth being presentation of Pāli verse with its Myanmar interpretation on qualities of gold. In regard to the first part which uses three fourth of the whole pages [bhi.2-mi.2] roughly summarizing what is described in each chapter there is nothing particular to present. Regarding the second part [mi.1-mu.1], nine kinds of gem[137], four kinds of gold come out from silver, four kinds of gold originated from mythical serpent or dragon, four kinds of gold produced from paddy field, four kinds of gold made from the hands of *Zawgyi*[138], four kinds of gold produced from world earth, and all gold from twenty places.[139] Regarding the twelve kinds of gold, see also *Yazawwada* (=Rajovada) (n.d.:16-18). As regards to the third part, this is the main subject upon which the author would like to emphasize. There are three grades (inferior, ordinary and superior) in animals, commoners, monks including hermits and royal lineage like those of gold.

The purpose of classification into three grades is to encourage all judges to pass fair judgments. Beginning with King Mahathamada, the first legendary king in the world, they should follow what is laid down in the Dhammathat, being free from sixteen contemplation, abstaining from Four Corruptions (*Agati. Le:-ba:*), and act according to law with love and compassion, endeavour for peace and prosperity of the people in order to be free from suffering in hell. Thus judgments should be passed in consultation with the learned and in accordance with law of the Dhammathat using intellect and discretion choosing the alternative: what could cause suffering in hell and what would not. Major sentences should be minimized and minor cases should be eliminated [mu.1].

To add to that, in the fourth part [mu.1-mu.2-me 1], a Pāli verse on gold with Myanmar interpretation on gold, which was found in consultation with the learned monk, are again presented in this Dhammathat so that misleading for judgment should be eliminated. In the end of this part, it is said that this Pāli verse and Myanmar interpretation is quoted from *Hayapakaik*(?) *Kyan* and *Lawka Dipani Kyan*.[140]

Part III
Kingship and Law in the Early Konbaung Period

Chapter XIII
Kingship and Constitution in the Eighteenth Century Myanmar

Theravāda Buddhism was introduced to Myanmar mainly on three separate occasions. Firstly, in the latter part of the eleventh century[141] King Anawyahta (=Anawrahta) brought Buddhism from Thaton, the then capital city of Mon, and then dispatched a Buddhist mission directly to Sri Lanka to bring back the Pāli canonical books so as to comparing to those from Thaton. Secondly, in the late twelfth century under King Narapatisithu of Bagan when Chapata (=Sappata) with four Sri Lankan monks came back from Sri Lanka and established the Sīhala Bikkhu Sangha. Thirdly in the late fifteenth century under Dhammazedi of Hanthawaddy Bago (=Pegu) a Buddhist Mission was dispatched to Sri Lanka by him. Dhammazedi built the Kalyāni Thein (=Sīmā) on the western outskirts of the city. It became a Centre of learning for Theravāda Buddhists. The cumulative effect of these three events was the introduction of the Theravāda Buddhism from Sri Lanka. This helped unify Myanmar people and helped them construct their 'Theravāda Buddhist State'.

At the same time, Theravāda Buddhism gradually infiltrated into the law and custom of Myanmar people. By the eighteenth century it had particularly influenced upon the books of law, firstly the *Mahayazathat* by Kaingza Manuyaza in early Seventeenth century and then through it upon, especially *MD*. The preamble to the *MD* (Chapter I of '1760 MS'=Richardson's Text and Pt.1 of the Chapter of the 1782 MS) elaborately illustrates the structure of the Theravāda Buddhist polity during the first half of the Konbaung dynasty. It presents the basic idea of kingship and law and between the period of reigns from King Alaunghpaya and King Badon.

1. Framework of the Early Konbaung Polity

The preamble to the *MD* describes how Manu, later King Mahathamada was born *Hpaya-laung*, corresponding to *Boddhisatta* in Pāli, or Buddha-to be.

Chapter XIII— Kingship and Constitution

During this worldly existence before attaining Buddhahood, he was born with a high intellectual faculty of moral wisdom. He was both a reformer and a regulator of human society. It was King Mahathamada's responsibility to maintain law, a task that only a man of superior morality could achive. Under King Mahathamada, the purpose of the state was firstly to improve people's morality, and secondly to regulate human society by law and order. How then, did King Mahathamada maintain law and order? [Okudaira 2003 a: 60].

According to the Hindu idea, the Brahmadēva, the chief god as well as the creator of the world who made the king and the law based on the Veda or one of the oldest Hindu philosophical works asked Manu, a semi-divine being and law-giver, to promulgate to the four saints the law named *Manu-smṛti*, one of the most influential of the legal treatises called Dharmaśāstras [Lingat (Trl.by Derett) Lingat 1973: 12]. Dharma, which originally meant 'eternal laws which maintain the world' [*ibid.*: 3] and 'rules of conduct'. The Hindu kings could justify their actions for maintaining law and order, based on Dharma which is in a sense more legalistic than ethical. On the other hand, King Mahathamada, who was usually identified with Manu, is no longer a semi-divine being, but a human Buddhist born into the solar dynasty. The Buddhist 'concept of *Dharma*', the universal moral law, which means-'righteousness' or 'virtue', exists in and of itself a 'revealed' to humans. The law of the Dhammathat through secular attributes itself to Buddha's Dharma. King Mahathamada's function was not to be a maker of law, but its upholder, the interpreter of law, and the arbitrator who settles and decide legal disputes. The Dhamma was upheld in human society through the agent of rulers. As Koenig put it, Dhamma became the standard rule by which the king conducted himself [Koenig *ibid*. 67-68]; also see Okudaira *ibid.*: 61].

'King Mahathamada appointed a village cowherd as the judge and entitled him the name of 'Manu'. Why did King Mahathamada give the cowherd that specific name-the name he himself had held before being elected as King? What does it imply? Is Judge Manu identified with King Mahathamada ? Did King Mahathamada create the story of Manu who discovered the Dhammathat and presented it to him? Was he then the original compiler of the Dhammathat? Richardson translated twenty-three lines of Pāli in the *Manugye Dhammathat* '[*ibid.*], according to which:

> "King Maha Thamada [Mahathamada]; who is to men as their eyes, and by his qualities enlightens all as a second sun-the rules he lays down none dare infringe. Among all rulers, the first is called Menoo

[Manu]. In this world of men the wonderful Para-loung [*Hpaya-laung*] was the first" [(R) MD I 1847: 8].

This hints that King Mahathamada is the solar law-giver whose original name was Manu. What then, is the relationship between Manu (=King Mahathamada) and the other, born a cowherd, who was appointed a judge given the name of Manu, resigned the judge, and became a hermit? Are they two separate people? Huxley suggested that the identification of Manu and Mahathamada was part of the Buddhist reform movement of the 18th and 19th century [1996: 606.]. The last line of every rule laid down in the *MD* (1760MS=thr Richardson's text) reads: 'Thus, Menoo, the sage recluse, hath said' (*Manu myi thaw shin yathe.hso taw mu i.*). Evidently the hermit Manu is a transmitter of the law, but not a law-giver. The law-giver could be King Mahathamada if we think of him as the Buddhist form of the Hindu Manu. Though Buddhist knew he was elected king by the people, they regarded him more as an interpreter than a lawgiver [See also Lingat 1973: 267; also see Okudaira *ibid.*: 61-62].

In sum, it can be assumed that the rules of the Dhammathats were thought to have originated in the precepts of Buddhist canon. Huxley asserts in his conclusion that "MS [Mahathamada] shares equal billing with Manu. The legitimation of law is such a heavy task that it requires the combination of two cultural heroes" [Huxley *ibid*: 613]. Brahma Min died in the previous world and was reborn in this world as a lineage of King Mahathamada and his two sons were named Thubadya and Manu (or Manuthara or Manothara). They brought up and the former brought a book of Astrology and the latter a book of Law [*Manothaya, Manuthaya, Pyumin, Manuyin*, etc.]. In any case, it is apparent that King Mahathamada and Judge Manu instructed, decided and admonished in accordance with natural law before discovery of the Dhammathat. The discovery of the Dhammathat by Hermit Manu on the boundary wall of the Universe indicates that law is given, but not made, and that Myanmar law is transcendent, immutable, and universal [Okudaira *ibid.*: 61-62].

2. Characteristics of the Early Konbaung Kingship

A new law book entitled *MD* was compiled under the reign of King Alaunghpaya, who 'appeared' as the 'saviour' at the critical moment of the Second Taungu dynasty and crushed the rebels restoring law and order in the kingdom. It is apparent that the compiler renewed the preamble with some additions and elaborations considering the fact that the political situation faced by King Alaunghpaya was similar to that of King Mahathamada, legendary first king of the world, who emerged to restore law and order in the society [See KBZ: 10, 20-21; also Okudaira *ibid.*: 62]. King Mahathamada was the particular model used by King Alaunghpaya, the founder of the Konbaung Dynasty. According to the preamble to the *MD*, to be a *Hpaya-laung* (=*Bodhisatta*) was one of essential attributes of a king. Myanmar kings like King Mahathamada, claimed to be *Hpaya-laung.* The preamble did not refer to *Sekkya-wate-min* (=*Cakkavattin*) or a Universal monarch, though King Mahathamada was believed to be *Sekkya-wade-min*. He was described in the preamble as a Buddhist king who was a *Hpaya-laung.* On the other hand, according to the Konbaung chronicles or the Royal orders, King Alaunghpaya was described as both *Sekkya-wate-min* [KBZ I: 17]or *Let-net Sekkya Thakin* [KBZ I: 102/ROB III: 96] and *Hpaya-laung* [KBZ I: 21]. In short, we may say that the compiler of the *MD* identified King Alaunghpaya as King Mahathamada [Okudaira *ibid.*: 62-63].

In this aspect, King Alaunghpaya was an embodiment of the first ideal King Mahathamada. Taking account of the crucial time when the capital city of Inwa (=Ava) was crumbling, King Alaunghpaya faced more critical task than those of King Mahathamada, if comparing are possible. The early Konbaung writers projected him as *Sekkya-wate-min* [*Cakkavattin*]. The concept of *sekkya-wade-min* which is associated with the advent of *Metteya* (=Arimettaya in Myanmar, who is regarded as the "Fifth Buddha" to come after Gotama) evoked political significance. However this special *Sekkya-wade-min* figure, such as King Alaunghpaya was exclusively unique because he can not be a *Hpaya-laung* at the same time, but a *Hpaya-laung* (*Bodhisatta*) may possibly be a *Sekkya-wade-min* during his previous existence [Koenig *ibid.*: 74-75].Thus, the Konbaung writers of the Yazawin (Chronicle), Dhammathat (Law Book), Bayin Ameindaw Pyandan (Royal Order), etc., demonstrated the ideal kingship of Alaunghpaya, identifying him with that of King Mahathamada by renewing the preamble of a newly compiled Dhammathat entitled *Manugye*. [Okudaira *ibid.*: 62-63]

By what factor then was a *Hpaya-laung* and a *Sekkya-wade-min* to be determined? It is *Kan* or *Kudho-kan* (*Kramma/kamma* in Pāli corresponding to *Karma* in Sanskrit) which means 'one's deed, word or thought which pre-determines one's future.' [MED: 12]. Myanmar kingship was, therefore, determined by *Kan*. The Konbaung kings in the first half of the period, particularly King Alaunghpaya, their legitimacy was the most serious problem.

King Alaunghpaya came not from a direct royal lineage, but from a family of a village headman. His father came from the Mu valley area including Mokhso-bo (later called Shwebo) district. King Alaunghpaya, however, took advantage of his *Kudho-kan* and of his distinguished qualities, such as *Hpon* (innate superpower), *Let-yon* (fighting ability), *Ana* (administrative authority). His successors, such as the second King Naungdawgyi, (his first son), the third King Hsinbyushin (his second son), the fourth King Singu (King Hsinbyushin's son) and the fifth King Hpaungga-sa Maung Maung (King Naungdawgyi's son, who ruled only seven days) were legitimised on the basis of *Kudho-kan* and the direct royal lineage. The attempts of the Konbaung writers of Chronicles, Law Books or Royal Orders to legitimize the Konbaung Dynasty were successful, but the issue of legitimacy of the early Konbaung period still remained, at least until the advent of the sixth King Badon (=Bodawhpaya) [See Koenig *ibid*.: 89]. And even during the reign of King Badon literati attempted to strengthen the connection between Konbaung kingship and King Mahathamada[Charney 2006: 85]. Thus the kingship during the first half of the period was characterized by the ascension to the throne by the King Alaunghpaya with the help of *Kudho-kan* and his successors to avoid such controversial legitimacy issue that he did not have a direct royal lineage as the founder of the dynasty. [Okudaira *ibid*.: 63-64]

3. Propagation of the *Yaza Dhamma* or Royal Obligations

Yaza Dhamma, a Pāli concept corresponding to *Min Kyin Taya* [*min:kyin. taya:*]in Myanmar, may be translated as the norm of kingship, the precepts incumbent on a king, or royal duties, or law. It embodies the obligation to be observed by the king in his administration of the kingdom. This principle was established on the role of the rulers as *Sekkya-wate-min* (*Cakkavattin*) or the universal monarch, who was responsible for maintaining the moral order of the universe and whose model most of the Konbaung kings wanted to follow. While King Alaunghpaya exploited the idea of *Sekkya-wate-min* or universal monarch, King Badon instantiated a new concept of Yaza Dhamma by asking his scholars to add the new chapters to the *MD* (1782MS). Here may be found such *Yaza Dhamma* material, such as "The Twelve Royal Duties", "The Ten Royal Duties", "The Seven Factors to be Observed to Keep Prosperity (of the State from) Deteriorations, Four Sanghaha Principles were stipulated in the Pt.2 of Chapter I, as has been stated earlier.

Chapter XIII— Kingship and Constitution

King Badon asked the compilers to add various other subjects on the organization of the state, such as the characteristics of a strong city, the fundamental royal requirements, the components of the armed forces, the subsistence for a city, the royal strengths, qualifications for roles in the legal profession like a judge or a witness, the various characteristics of the Dhammathat, etc. Chapter III of the 1782MS deals with the differences between the Papathat ('Law of Vice'), Dhammathat ('Law of Virtue') and Yazathat (Decisions by the king). It adds that judgements must all be given in accordance with the Dhammathat. Obviously King Badon intended to reset the Dhammathat in its proper position so that it could perform the same function in the structure of the Theravāda Buddhist State as the ancient Pāli Dhammasatthan aimed at. In other words, King Badon attempted to place the Dhammathat in the central position as the nucleus for the royal politics and to revive the authority of the Dhammathat which had been lost in the process of vernacularisation since the reign of King Alaunghpaya [Okudaira *ibid*.: 64-65].

In addition, No.12 of 'The Twelve Royal Duties' (*Min: kyin. Taya: Hse-hnit-pa:*) which seems to be unique in the Dhammathat says:

"*[The king]* administers the people and the monks (*pyithu lu yahan: to. ko ok-chok taw mu thi=pidhu lu yahan: do.go ok-chok daw mu dhi*)" [1782MS- I pt.2: hki/K].

No.7 of "The Seven Factors Observed to Keep Prosperity of the State from Deterioration" stipulates that:

[the king] patronises the Sangha (*yahan: thanga do. hnaik kaun:swa saun.-shauk taw mu thi=yahan thanga do. go kaun:zwa saun.-shauk taw mu dhi*)' [1782MS- I pt.2: hki/K].

Chapter III add that:

"*[The Sangha]*, relying on the support of the king, are to propagate religion." (*min: ko hmi ywe. thathana taw ko pyusu. Kyin.=min: go hmi ywe. thathana daw go pyuzu. gyin.*)[*MD*1782MS III: za. / W].

In other words, the king supports the Buddhist Order so that they may propagate Buddhism. This clause confirms that the relationship between the kingship and the Sangha forms the basic structure of the Theravāda Buddhist State. [Okudaira *ibid*.: 66].

King Alaunghpaya probably asked the compiler of the new Dhammathat entitled *Manugye* to insert a more elaborated myth of kingship in an attempt to assert his royal lineage and thereby legitimize his kingship. Perhaps he might even unify all the existing Buddhist kingdoms in Myanmar as a strong Buddhist king who was recognized as a *Sekkya-wade-min* or universal monarch. However, his untimely death left the second task unfinished. On the other hand, King Badon fulfilled his father's ambitious aims by adding chapters-particularly Part II of Chapter I on the structure of the Theravāda Buddhist State and the administration of the state to the Dhammathat. The process of Myanmar-isation of the Theravāda Buddhist State seems to have worked. Konbaung kings successfully assimilated the majority of the Mon who lived in the Ayeyawaddy (=Irrawaddy) Delta region and Bago (=Pegu), the Rakhine in the West and the Shan in the East. In short the new preamble of the *MD* provided the comprehensive theory of the structure of the Theravāda Buddhist State which had already existed in Myanmar since Bagan period. [*ibid.*: 66].

4. King Badon's Various Reformations

a. A reforming king

King Badon ruled over the country for thirty-seven years. Exclusive of the reign of King Alaungsithu [1112-1167] of Bagan for over fifty-five years, King Badon jointly holds for the longest reign with King Narapatisithu [1173-1210] of Bagan period. King Badon was the first King who conquered Rakhine (Arakan). To have such a long reign until his death was an unusual feat because King Badon tried to rule over the country with benevolence [See Than Tun (ROB IV): vii] and was able to collect thorough information about state affairs and implementation of his politics [*ibid.*]. We can now add to these achievements the fact that he introduced proper and adequate judicial policy. King Badon, while possessing a strong personality and sharing his father, King Alaunghpaya's deep conviction of *Karma* or fate, took further step to establish a strong Buddhist state [See Koenig 1990: 77]. Judging by the Royal Orders promulgated during his reign [Than Tun (ROBIV): vii], he was a man of honesty, of benevolence, of orthodox religious belief, of discipline and at the same time ambitious to extend the boundary of his domain [Okudaira 2005: 82-83]

As soon as King Badon seized power, he started to reform the various fields of state administration so that he could build a stable and prosperous Buddhist state. To this end he corrected and purified the world around him. King Badon was truly a reforming king. He attempted to make reforms in political, administrative, judicial, religious, and social affairs. He underwent

Chapter XIII— Kingship and Constitution 167

the supreme consecration ceremony (*Muddha-beiktheik*) twice in 1783 and 1784 in succession, and asked the compilers to revise or translate the previous law books or to compile new ones.[142] He issued a final decree to approve the orthodox, not of *ekamsika* (*Atin*, An order of monks who cover only one shoulder with robe), but of *Parupana* (*Ayon*, An order of monks who cover both shoulders with robe) in 1784-1785, established the Sangha organisation headed by the *Thathanabaing* or the head of the Buddhist Order and Religious Council in 1788, tried to construct but left incomplete the Mingun Pagoda in 1790, repaired and expanded the Lake Meikhtila in 1795, tried (but failed) to introduce coinage system in 1797 and attempted to reform the Sangha and persuading the leading monks by the king himself to be the Buddha Metteya in 1812, etc. His reforms ran in parallel with all his other efforts [See Mendelson 1975: 58-59; Okudaira *ibid.*: 83].

b. A religious reformation

King Badon inaugurated the religious reforms himself. His first concern, when he usurped the throne on 11 February, 1782, and executed the lord of Hpaungga-sa Maung Maung was to promise solely that he would, like other Myanmar kings, support the Buddha's Religion [Than Tun (ROB VII: viii)]. He always upheld the manual of Buddhist philosophy like *Badon Min Lethswe* [MD-CEACS(B) 1976 RL. No.95-7]. His Buddhist ideas were included in the concept of *Badon Min Ayu Wada* [See LMD-CEACS(B) Rl. No.32-3/ROB(22 March, 1807(T)ROB VI: 19-24/353-392]. His aims were correct and proper, but various factors prevented him from carrying them out. He was confronted by enormous opposition, though it was expressed tacitly. The King wanted to change the religious beliefs and practices of the people, to roll back the later innovations and to regain the Buddhist way of life which had prevailed at the time of Buddha. Finally, he had to concede that people could worship as they thought best [Than Tun(ROB VII): vii-viii; also see MMOS III s. 386-397: 122-129].

From the view point of stable administration for the whole country, King Badon disapproved of unnecessary monastic influence. He, therefore, tried to obtain both the positions of king and primate, so as to be an unchallengeable autocrat and theocrat at the same time [See Desai 1961: 101].During the later years of his reign, he went so far as to announce that he was a Future Buddha, though this was rejected by both the Sangha and laymen [See Htin Aung 1967: 187]. The two important Royal Orders, one of which contains prohibition of intoxicant drinks [ROB IV(20 February, 1782): 220] and another of which includes exile of apostate monks [ROB (10 March, 1783)(T)ROB IV: 233] that the king passed immediately after his ascendancy to the throne show his determination to be a good Buddhist king [(T)ROB VII: viii]. After that, King Badon passed several Royal Orders related to Buddhist religion, which are included in his Royal Order (22 March, 1807) and later summed up in a record dated 23 May, 1818, just before the year of his demise [See Than Tun (ROB VII): xv; See also Okudaira *ibid.*: 84].

Regarding the monks, King Badon attempted to reduce the number of monks so that the Sangha system could be purified.[143] He demanded that the ordained monks should follow the Vinaya or discipline [Than Tun (ROB VII): viii]. No king in Theravāda Buddhist history had ever dared to proclaim a Vinaya rule for the monks [Htin Aung 1967: 187]. A dispute broke out on the style of wearing the robe. One group said that a monk should be allowed to leave the premises of his monastery donning his robe casually covering only his left shoulder (*Atin, Ekamsika*), but another group insisted that he should go in the most proper and formal attire of covering both his shoulders (*Ayon, Parupana*). The two groups met in a debate and *Atin* was defeated. King Badon proclaimed that all monks wear their robes in the orthodox manner, and that the robe controversy should cease forthwith. In short, he claimed that only one form of Buddhism should be practiced in his realm [ROB VII: ix, etc.]. King Badon thought that his religious reforms could be successfully attained by appointing a Supreme Guardian of the Religion (*Thathana-daw-ye: Thathana-hmu*) who was the top of the twelve members committee (*Si: we*:), set up for trial of disputes among monks or trial of monks who did not follow the Vinaya [ROB(27June,1786)(T) ROB IV: 501-502]. [Mendelson *ibid.*58-59; Okudaira *ibid.*: 84-85][144]

Lay men were asked to keep the Five Precepts (*Nga:-ba: Thila.*) and to follow Buddhist way of life strictly during the three months' Buddhist Lent and thereafter [See Than Tun(ROB IV): viii]. While encouraging lay people to build Pagodas and monasteries [Htin Aung *ibid.*: 188][145], King Badon was busy with great works in 1791 (=1153 ME) [KBZ: 69-70] in building Pahto-daw-gyi Pagoda in Mingun which would have been the biggest one in the world if completed. Unfortunately he was not able to complete it due to the prophecy that completion of the Pagoda would be the end of his life [See Desai 1961: 101; Okudaira *ibid.*: 85].

c. Political, Administrative and Social Reformations

To achieve the revival of Buddhist religion in Rakhine (Arakan) [Than Tun ROB (1986): xvii], King Badon conquered the country in 1784-1785. Past successive Myanmar rulers had attempted to do this, but failed. Consequently,

Chapter XIII — Kingship and Constitution

the boundaries of the country were extended to its utmost limit. Next he made an attempt to extend his Kingdom by marching southwards. He himself marched with his troops during the Campaign against the Thai of 1785-1786 in the dry season. He dispatched another army to Thailand in the following year. Both campaigns, however failed [See (T) ROB IV: xxvi].[146] In the administrative aspect, as we saw previously, he introduced a new type of consecration ceremony and himself twice underwent the *Muddhabeiktheik*, the supreme consecration ceremony. This ceremony gave promise to the people that the king would rule with benevolence and justice, and places a curse upon him if he fails to do so. The *Muddha-beiktheik* is the most magnificent of the fourteen consecration rituals [MMOS: 238-248]. King Badon attached great importance to the ceremony and urged Maung Htaung Hsayadaw, who was appointed the Supreme Guardian of the Religion and along with other scholars to collect material on the proper way to conduct it. King Badon asked them to bring non-religious works written in Sanskrit back to the capital city from abroad and to translate them into Myanmar [ROB(30 April 1810) (T)ROB: 237; 732; See also Okudaira *ibid*.: 85-86].[147]

In regard to 'The Ten Royal Duties' King Badon himself proclaimed them in his Royal Order and tried to follow all of them. He also took it as his responsibility to help all ordained Buddhist monks in accordance with the Vinaya. For these meritorious deeds and these performances on his part, "he was rewarded with a rare specimen of white elephant, a variety of powerful weapons and an opportunity to control over quite a relatively extensive territory" [ROB (18, March, 1796 (R) Than Tun ROB V: 113; 624]. Apart from 'Ten Royal Duties', King Badon issued several orders relating to the duties of a king so as to practice them which was prescribed in the Mahāhamsa Jataka (No.534); to learn the lessons from the Jatakas or the Buddha's Previous Life Stories and histories together with such stipulations as Three Qualities of a King[148], Four Samgha Law[149], Five Royal Strength[150], Six Qualities of a Leader[151], Seven Factors to keep Prosperity (of the State from) Deterioration[152], Eight Gratitudes[153], Nine Gems[154], Ten Laws of Universal Monarch[155] and Twelve Means for a Military Success[156]. He also collected about six hundred inscriptions to check the boundaries of ecclesiastical estates in the country, so as to prevent monks from owning more property than donated to them [ROB(24 March, 1783)(T)ROB: 248/also see Desai 1961: 100]. In regard to social affairs, King Badon prohibited making, selling and consuming any kind of intoxicating drink, smoking opium, big game hunting and all kinds of gambling [ROB (20 February,

1782) (T)ROB IV: 5; 220]. As regards economic affairss, King Badon collected revenue inquests (*Sittan*) in 1784 and 1803, which consisted of statistics on land, crops, tax, population, etc for getting an idea on the resources of the country [Desai *ibid.*: 100]. He also carried some public works, such as construction of the Dam of Aung Pin Le Kan (=Gan) in 1788 and Maung Ma Kan (=Gan) (later named Nanda Kan (Gan) in 1789 [KBZ II: 57-63], and repair of the Dam of Meikthila Kan (=Gan) in 1796 [(T) ROB IV: xxviii] [Okudaira *ibid.*86-87].

d. Judicial reformation

King Badon respected the Dhammathats to which his judicial policy owed much. [(T)ROB: V 1986: vii]. He requested scholars to recopy (more precisely to revise) the *MD* which was compiled during the reign of his father King Alaunghpaya which was one of the leading law books used throughout the Konbaung period. As this book has demonstrated, his 1782 MS was significantly different from Richardson's printed version. The 1782 MS seems to be a production of the beginning of King Badon's reign. According to tradition, many Myanmar kings compiled the Dhammathats, when they ascended the throne. Following this, King Badon asked the compilers to revise the *MD* (1760MS) which was compiled under the reign of his father King Alaunghpaya so that it would be compatible with the changing times and conditions. Apart from this project, King Badon may have also asked scholars to compile some new Dhammathats as mentioned in Foot Note No.142.

5. Conclusion

The early Konbaung concept of kingship was created by Buddhist and selective Brahmanic elements. We can see this form the Pt.1 of the Chapter I (pt.1) of the Badon's *MD* (1782MS). It's myth on kingship elaborated out of the *Aggañña Sutta* in the Pāli canon[157] which demonstrates the ideology of the Theravāda Buddhist state in the most elaborate manner. Pt.2 of the Chapter I describes the role of kingship and those functions which had not already been dealt with in the 1760MS. According to Pt.1 of the Chapter I, the first king in the world whose original name was *Manu* was born *Hpaya-laung* (=*Bodhisatta*) to reform the chaotic society and was elected as the King with the people's unanimous consensus to restore the social order and to regulate human affairs by law. Through these two functions of both reformation and regulation, King Mahathamada was also the first *Sekkya-wade-min* (=*Cakkavattin*, a Universal

Chapter XIII— Kingship and Constitution 171

Monarch) who was "a sovereign of the four islands of the universe and possessor of a miraculous chariot and wondrous weapons", though no such a word *Sekkya-wade-min* is mentioned in Pt.1 of the Chapter I. Because King Mahathamada was an ideal king who relieved the people from the chaotic social conditions and restored its order and governed by the universal moral law, he became the model for all the subsequent kings in Myanmar. Relating to the *Sekkya-wade-min*, there are many references in early Konbaung historical and legal literatures on attempting to identify King Alaunghpaya with that of King Mahathamada in the chaotic situation of Myanmar kingdom. Hsinbyushin, the third king, who defended the country from several invasions from China and destroyed Ayutaya also strongly associated with the attributes of a *Sekkya-wade-min*. Then, the sixth king, King Badon who was a man of deep and orthodox Buddhist belief, took further step to establish the Theravāda Buddhist state which his father King Alaung hpaya founded its basis.

Concerning the moral law mentioned above which is called Dhamma has been revealing itself to the human society from the beginning of the world and King Mahathamada was just the upholder of the law. 'The law is given, but not made' in the Buddhist concept of law. Thus, the dhamma was made the standard or criteria or basis for all the conducts of the king and Myanmar people as well. Pt.3 of the Chapter I in No.9 of the 1782MS warns the judges including the king of making decisions not upon Papathat ('the law of vice'), but in accordance with the Dhammathat (the law of virtue).[158] The Chapter I (pt.3) of the 1782MS describes the king's role in the moral order of the Universe which was essential to the welfare of both his subject and himself, a norm of kingship known as *Yaza-dhamma* ("King's Law") was established. This norm are very often seen in the texts of Pāli canon and is common in Myanmar historical and legal works both as subject and explanation. The standard Myanmar formulation of this norm was expressed in *Min:-kyin.-Taya:-Hse-ba:* (Ten Royal Duties). A second sets of often cited principles was *Samgaha-Taya-Le-ba:* ("The law of Four Assistances") and *Apareikha Niya Taya: Hkunit-pa:* ("Seven Factors to keep Prosperity") was the third important set of *Yaza-dhamma*.

The Brahmanic element may be found in the *Nīti-śāstra*s which are 'science of political ethics' or 'treatise on politics' and these books of guidance for political science were introduced to ancient Myanmar and served to compile *Nīti* literature in Pāli. Among these works *Yaza-niti* (=*Rāja-nīti*) in the fifteenth century work stressed the importance of wealth to kingship. However, the most important ceremonies of Brahmanic origin for the rulers were the several kinds of consecration culminating in the *Muddha-beiktheik*. Though kings regarded themselves as omnipotent, they were limited by the Buddhist sanctions on kingship and his ability to control the administrative machinery of state. The good examples of this are King Badon's attempts and failure to introduce a coinage in 1797 and to destroy the monkhood in 1812.

The chaotic and tumultuous circumstances of the 1740s provided the early Konbaung kingship with a sort of 'messianism' derived from the Theravāda Buddhist eschatology. The strength of royal *kudo-kan* or *kyamma* (which implies 'fate by action') was manifested by physically in the *hpon*, *let-yon* and *āna* of the king. King Alaunghpaya, for example, was regarded as a man of physical and administrative strength and power parallel with *Sekkya-wademin, Boddhisatta, Dhammayaza* ("king of Law" or "King of Righteousness). He was seen as a descendant of the solar dynasty and the Sakyan family (Hkattiya) and as king of kings (*Yaza-di-yaza / yaza-dirit*). King Alaunghpaya's portrayal of kingship was taken over and developed by King Badon.

Chapter XIV
Dhammathats and Law in the Eighteenth Century Myanmar

1. Principles of the Judicial Policy

In regard to administration of justice, King Alaunghpaya directed all the judges to study various law texts, decisions, cases, witnesses, nature and characteristics, not to make a hasty or biased decision, and also to take time for a month, a month and a half or seven days, according to the needs of the occasion [ROB (19 August, 1758) (T)ROB III: 214]. Thus he respected the Dhammathats and other old practices. King Badon followed his father, King Alaunghpaya's manner of the judicial policy.

King Badon's judicial policy was based on the principle that 'minimise the serious words and ignore the trifles (*kyi thi. zaga: go nge aung, nge thi, zaga: go pa-byauk aung*) [ROB (3 March, 1782) (T)ROB IV: ix & 229; ROB (18 August, 1783) (T)ROB IV: x & 275].[159] A second principle of King Badon's policy was that judges should refer to Dhammathats, Yazathats [ROB IV(3 March, 1782): 229/(18 August, 1783): 275/ (12 November, 1783): 292, etc.] or Sit-tans [ROB (19 April, 1785)(T)ROB IV: 443]. A third principle was that the judges should reach unanimous among judges. In other words, *ex-parte*[160] decisions should not be made [ROB(18 August 1783) (T)ROB: 28; 275/ ROB (12 November 1783) (T)ROB IV: x; 292]. He regulated the lawyers, ordering that only licensed one should represent a client and defend him within the limits of the Dhammathats [ROB (29 August, 1783) (T) ROB: 30&278]. And he warned the judges not to accept bribes or to become corrupt [ROB (18 August, 1783) (T)ROB IV: 29, 275]. Regarding officers, it was only in King Badon's orders, as mentioned in the next section, that "we find references to officers of the Court, whose functions were to summon the defendant to attend and to answer the claim." [E Maung 1951: 20].

2. Legal Procedure

King Badon prohibited high ranking officers (*wun-zu. wun-shin, mu:daw mat-taw*) to represent one of the parties in lawsuit, because it would most probably influence judge's decision [ROB IV(29 August, 1783) (T)ROB: 29-30, 278/(7 January, 1784: 41, 310, etc.]. He also ordered members of the royal families (*min:-nyi min:tha:*), high ranking officers (*mu:-daw mat-taw*), etc. not to become judges unless they were talented or wise [ROB IV (3 March, 1782): 229]. He instructed judges not to hand down judgment in writing if both the contending parties did not meet each other in court [ROB(14 August, 1783) (T)ROB IV: 271; ROB (18 August, 1783) (T)ROB IV: 275].

The *MD* (Richardson's Burmese text; 1760 MS) gives a short account of the Four Trials by Ordeal (*Kaba le:-yat*) as given as short account: The first one is "trial by fire": each of the parties takes one tical's weight(=one *kyat*) of water in their mouth and light candles of equal length; let one party whose light first goes out be the loser; second is "trial by water": both the parties go under water and let the party who first comes up lose; third is "trial by chewing rice": each of the parties shall chew one tical's weight of rice; one be all swallowed and one not be swallowed all, let the one whose rice is not swallowed all lose; fourth is "trial by lead": each of the parties shall dip the pointing finger into molten lead, let the party who is burned lose [See (R)MD I s.16 1896: 261-262]. All four Ordeals are described in more detail in the criminal procedure of the East Court (She-yon) or the Criminal Court [ROB (12, February, 1785) (T)ROB IV: xi& 425-430]. Apart from these, "trial by water of a witch" is also recognized in Myanmar law books [See *Wagaru:* s162: 42/36; also Kyin Swi 1965: 410]. According to E Maung, however, "Trials by Ordeal" were not encouraged because of its baneful effect upon public tranquility [E Maung 1951: 18].[161]

Written guide to criminal procedure known as the *She-yon Sadan* ("East Court Manual") contained altogether 40 items about, Ordeal, appointment of an Officer of the Golden Capital City (*Shwe Myo-daw Wun*), allocation of duty, on port management, duty of a City Gate Keeper, executers' duty, jail register, men in subordinate service; executions of a person, such as prince, an ex-officer, barber, Brahmin, Faked Fakir (=Muslim religious mendicant), etc,; punishing a Brahmin (Ponna); declaring the nature of crime by beating a Gong before execution and before giving lashes; officers who is to attend Hluttaw (Council of Ministers) daily; various ways of execution, such as

Chapter XIV— Dhammathats and Law

being drowned in water, burnt to death in a burning house, cutting the body with saw, display the head, burnt in fire by bellows, opening the chest, floating on raft the remains of an executed prisoner, cutting the head, cutting the hip and head, hanged by the neck, death punishment, put under a log and leave in the Sun, postponement of execution due to the king's birthday, the Sabbath day (*U Bout ne.*) or too late in the evening, cutting the edges of mouth, quarrelling between "No Hesitation" Executors (*Let-ma.Yun*) and Executor (*Ana-zo*), quarrelling among common folks (*Athi= Athe*), eunuchs in charge of women, etc. [ROB (12February, 1785) (T)ROB IV: 91-108; 416- 437; Okudaira 2005.: 90].

East Court Manual gives detailed methods of execution for various kinds of criminal offences. King Badon obviously permitted criminal punishment, though the *MD* lays down the rule that "--- it is not proper to put a man who has killed another to death in return and a king who in this [*manner*] does not put a murderer to death, will be praised by the gods (*Nat*s) and all good men and supported and adhered to by them" [(R)*MD* V 1896: 130]. Although King Badon agreed that punishment might vary in accordance with the status of a man who committed the crime, he insisted that punishment should be in right proportion to the damage caused by a criminal act. In the case of murder, he held that henceforth it should lead to a death sentence, even though compensation was allowed by the law of Dhammathat [See ROB (5 December, 1789) (T)ROB V: viii; 447-448]. The ambit of criminal law varied with each King, but it was never extensive. Normally, the offences against the State were murder, rape, abduction, robbery, theft and libel.[162] Penalties varied from whipping, confinement in irons, maiming or banishment to death, with or without forfeiture of the offender's possessions [E Maung *ibid.*: 12]. King Badon proclaimed a Royal Order as punishing adultery [See ROB (28 January, 1795: 190) (T)ROB V: 467-468]. Thus, he diverged from the rule of the Dhammathats on capital punishment.

On the other hand, King Badon expected Hluttaw to deal with general administration on affairs of the king, provinces, the capital city and the region if any case was not decided in lower courts [See ROB (4 November, 1786) (T)ROB IV: 511]. Hluttaw (where the king or the heir apparent <*Einshe.-minidha:*> presided) was the highest and final court in the realm in relation to the judicial affairs. Cases involving rebellion and conspiracy against the regime were dealt with in Hluttaw [See ROB IV: xi &(4 November, 1786): 140; ROB V: vii-viii]. (See Table 8)

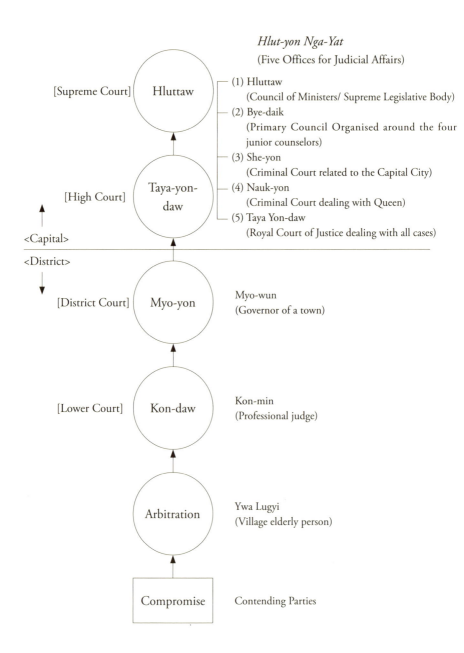

Table 8: The Brief Legal Procedure of the Appealing System in the Kongbaung Period

3. Proper Use of the Dhammathats

The Myanmar kings respected the customs observed since time immemorial. They also respected the precedents of former kings in solving judicial cases with precision and wisdom. The Buddhist religion was the yard-stick by which the kings discerned good from bad. The Dhammathat set rules on crimes to be punished in civil cases. Never in pre-modern period of Myanmar had the whole administrative or political system of the kings been reduced to writing. One or two Royal Orders help one to understand the early approach. Than Tun says that the ROBs of (19 June, 1368) and (28 January, 1795) are the most important among them in this respect [See (T)ROB V: 49-50].

King Badon gave highest respect to the Dhammathats which were basically compiled in accordance with prevailing customs and precedents. Therefore, his attitude towards the Dhammathats are quite precise [See Than Tun 1986: (intro.) vii]. He emphasized that in almost all the law suits, the Dhammathats should be the guide for making decisions [ROB (18 August 1783(T)ROB IV: 28/275; ROB(29 August, 1783)(T)ROB IV: 30/ 278-9; ROB(12 November, 1783) (T)ROB IV: 34/292-3; ROB (5 December 1789) (T) ROB V: 45-46/445-448] with the exception that some Royal Orders were to be taken into consideration before the final decision was made [ROB IV (18 August, 1783)]. He was convinced the law suits should be finished within the minimum at any time, at any law court [ROB (5 December 1789)(T)ROB V: 45, 446-448], because court fees were usually very expensive and many disputes could be settled through arbitration [ROB (23 May 1801)(T)ROB V: 134; 667] except murder [ROB(5 December, 1789)(T)ROB V: 46; 447-448, etc.].

Arbitration was not allowed for a crime where capital punishment should be given. To withdraw such a plaint from the court led to the punishment [ROB (23 July, 1801)(T)ROBV: vii, 180-182; 768-770]. Here King Badon has changed the law not by altering the text but by way of his Royal Orders. The Dhammathats were the transcendent, immutable and inviolable law descended from the age of King Mahathamada, the first legendary king of the world. King Badon used the rules of the Dhammathats in all cases which were possibly settled through arbitration. In civil procedure he followed the old records to verify statements relating to boundary demarcation or ownership of land [(T) ROB V: ix]. In addition, although he respected the Dhammathats (law book), Hpyathtons (court decisions) and Dale-htondan (customs), and urged judges to study them thoroughly for deciding a case.

He also instructed judges to give priority to listening to what both the parties concerned wanted to say when they passed judgment [ROB (28 January, 1795) (T)ROB V: 50(2)&(3), 457; 54(21), 462]. It seems that King Badon followed his father King Alaunghpaya's Order, such as "A judgment should be made only after hearing what each of the contending parties had to say" [ROB (1 January, 1760)(T)ROB III: 64, 232]. (See Table 9)

4. Judicial Policy Incorporated into the New Chapters of *MD* (1782MS)

Several articles have discussed the new chapters added to the *MD* (1782 MS) [See Than Tun 1985; Okudaira 2000; Okudaira & Huxley 2001, etc.]. Therefore, it shall limit ourselves to some comments on how they reflect King Badon's judicial policy. Pt.2 of the Chapter I describes such approaches to the organization of state as The Ten Royal Duties, The Seven Characteristics for a (Strong) City, The Four Components of the Armed Forces, The Five Royal Strengths, The Seven Factors to Keep Prosperity (of the State from) Deterioration, etc. These ideas are not new, and were handed down from ancient times, but the *MD* (1782 ME) was probably the first time that such matters were included in the books of law. As to the king, King Badon issued such Royal orders: (1)Only when descendant kings should bear in mind and practice the law which former good kings had practiced, it will be beneficial to him, to religion and to the people [ROB V(28 January, 1795: 478). Than Tun concisely translated the said Order in such a manner that "Kings hold themselves responsible to rule strictly in accordance with law." [Than Tun 1986: 58]. In another clause, King Badon proclaimed: Bear in mind The Ten Royal Duties and practice in accordance with law [ROB (28 January 1795(T) ROB: 481)]. He himself performed *Muddha-beiktheik* (Supreme Consecration ceremony) five times[163] and tried to observe all the Royal Duties [ROB (18 March, 1796) (T)ROB V: 624]. In relation to the Ten Royal Duties, King Badon's actual practice of 'Mildness', (*maddava= nu:nyan.- thein mwe thaw hna-loun:*), one of the Ten Royal Duties, is proved in such an Order that "Ministers, Minister of Interior and Assistant Ministers shall petition the King when a person is found guilty for committing a crime against the King's property, so that the King could condone his crime and set him free" [ROB V(28 January, 1795): 113-114]. King should not get angry [ROB (28 January, 1795) (T)ROB V(68): 479]. He also ordered that "Princes must rule over the principalities peacefully and not oppressively. There shall be no severe

Chapter XIV— Dhammathats and Law

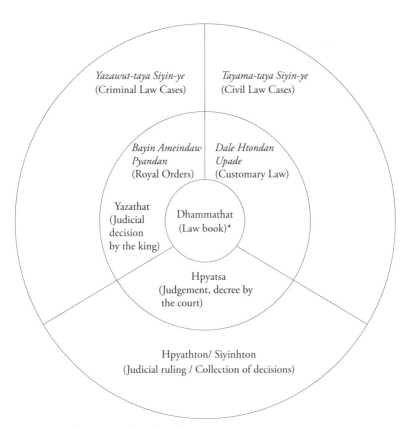

* Collection of Customary rules and precedents

Table 9: Categorisation of Law in the Kongbaung Period

punishments and oppressive taxations in the area they control [ROB (28 January, 1795) (T)ROB V(84): 481]. In accordance with "The Seven Factors to keep Prosperity (of the State) from Deterioration", the king and his councilors have to meet three times a day and he called attention to all his ministers and officers to attend Hluttaw regularly [ROB (4 November, 1786)(T)ROB IV: 139, 510].

Pt.2 of the Chapter I deals with judicial administration listing Five Judges, Four Types of Person Who Should Pass Judgement to Deputize for Kings, Six Types of Person Who Should Not Pass Judgement, Seven Types of Person Who Should Behave Like a Stone Pillar, Ten Types of Chastisement, Eleven Kinds of Person Who Should Be Witness, Sixteen Kinds of Person Who Should Be Totally Dissolved as A Witness, Twenty-eight Types of Witness Who Should Be Removed from the Bunch (Group) of Witnesses and Five Miscellaneous Types of Witness [See also Than Tun 1985: 32-38]. Regarding judges, King Badon issued various kinds of Orders: Judges should always remain free from bribery and corruption [ROB (18 August, 1783) (T)ROB IV: 29, 275]; In a law suit, the winner pays court fee while the loser pay the fine; the king or judge should not take much from either party; he should not take more than one-tenth of the value of a case [ROB (28 January, 1795)(T) ROB: 54, 462]. In regard to Officials, Generals (Thenapati) should not be negligent in capital, provincial and sate affairs, but work for the greater good of the religion, the Monarch, the dynasty and the people [ROB V(28 January, 1795): 65, 478]. Every serviceman must show qualities; good conduct, intelligence and incorruptibility. In addition to these, he must know what is required of him to do in his particular service [*ibid.*: 59, 482].

As regards Judges, Chapter III of the 1782 MD deals with division of work between the judge and the executor, who must be an administrative officer. The East Court Manual describes execution. Judges must decide cases without delay and attend Hluttaw only when they have been ordered to do so. They should conduct judicial affairs only at court, but not at Hluttaw. Only cases which remained unsettled should be appealed [ROB IV (4 November, 1786): 140, 511]. However, the four ministers of Hluttaw should decide the case unanimously after consulting together [ROB IV (12 November, 1783): 292]. As to judgement, Chapter XVI, while comparing different kinds of jewelry and cattle, superiority to inferiority of gold, saying that there are various living beings such as animals (*tarreihsan-myo:*), human beings (*tayatami lu-myo:*), celestial beings (*Nat-byahma-myo:*), monks (*yahan:*) and royal family (*min-myo:*), urges that the judge to decide the case, in accordance with the law of Dhammathat and taking such legal maxim into consideration as

"To mitigate a big matter and nullify a small one" [See *MD (*1782MS): 703-707]

5. How the Judges Used the Dhammathats in Court

a. A Part of King Badon's Legal Reform in Court System

King Badon's Orders show that he attached importance to the Dhammathats in deciding the cases in court. At the same time, he also gave weight to other sources such as precedents, old customs, the teaching of the Pāli Canon, the statements of the parties, testimony of witnesses, etc. It might be said that this attitude of King Badon toward decision making for law suits reflected the practical decisions made by judges in court. Unfortunately all the other collections of decisions (Hpyathton) during the reign of King Badon seems to have been lost or missing. Unless perhaps they were not compiled at all, except for *Yezajyo Hkondaw Hpyathton*.[164] This is a famous collection of decisions of the court of Yezajyo in the present Pahkoukku (=Pakkoku) district. This belongs to the third type which Forcchammer categorized as shown earlier and is a collection of judicial decisions by the Judge (Hkondaw) Maung Hmaing, the first part of which deals with thirty-two law suits of the court from 1151M.E.(=A.D.1789)to 1183M.E. (=A.D.1821) and it gives us much information on judicial cases at the court. The period coincides with the reign of King Badon. Hkon-daw Maung Hmaing was the tutor to Mo Meik Mintha, one of the sons of King Badon and was promoted from this position to the status of a minister under the title of Yandameik Kyaw Htin (=Din). It may be said that Yandameik Kyaw Htin was very close to King Badon. Considering the judicial reforms discussed, we should compare with others before and since. King Badon seems to have requested Hkondaw Maung Hmaing to record his precise decisions as part of the King's legal reform. Perhaps this systematic approach to recording law reports (a summary of the dispute, statements by both parties concerned, remarks by the judge, content of the judgment and brief statement at the end of the dispute with the date) was offered as a model to other judges [YKHP *ibid.*: Preface-hta.]. [Okudaira *2005.*: 99; also see 2003b: 324-325].

b. The Dhammathats is not the only Legal Source

The modern publication of *Yezajyo Hkondaw Hpyathton* mentions that "the process of deducing and deciding the cases was in accordance with the principles of the Dhammathat dealt with in the *Yezajyo Hkondaw Hpyathton*"

[YKHP 1965, (Preface)-hta.]. Shwe Baw, the late Myanmar jurist, writing soon after independence in 1948, stated, "The judgements shows that the courts took great care to follow the rules of Dhammathats. Although they quote the Jatakas and sometimes the Vinaya, it was only to fortify the grounds of decisions which they gave based solely on the rules of the Dhammathats" [Shwe Baw 1955: 122].The impression one also gets is that the guiding principle for the judges at the court of Yezajyo during the reign of King Badon, was to make judgement consulting all the available sources of law aiming at the best one. As we have discussed elsewhere [Okudaira 2003b: 325-326], judges must have sought various other sources of law; such as Buddha's teaching, Pāli Buddhist Canon, precedents, Lawkawut (works on courtesy), Bedin (tales of six branches of knowledge), legal maxims, local customs, words of witnesses, evidence, etc. [Okudaira 2005: 99-100; 2003b: 325- 326]. (See Table 8)

The judge would have probably used several sources for decisions. In fact, the Dhammathats were a major one among many guides to social affairs. Judges were always requested to take consideration of the factors such as the changing times and conditions whenever they make a decision. Early Konbaung rulers, such as King Alaunghpaya and King Badon, encouraged the judges to study the Dhammathats thoroughly and conscientiously and to decide a case in accordance with the law of Dhammathat. They urged judges to listen directly from each of the contending parties what he or she wanted to say. In using the Dhammathats at the court of Yezajyo, both the *Manuthaya* (=*Manusara*) and *Dhammawilatha* (=*Dhammavilasa*) are often cited. the *MD* was also used [YKHP *ibid*.: 9 etc.]. However, the judge relied upon *Mahayazathat* (Hpyathton, actually Shaukhton) and *Kaingza Shwemyin Dhammathat*, both compiled by Kaingza Manu Yaza, to which King Badon gave high priority in his Royal Orders [ROB(21 June,1814) (T)ROB: xvii & 332]. The priority of the Dhammathats to be used was mostly in line with King Badon's several Orders mentioned earlier. Thus, before the judges at the Yezajyo court decided a law suit, he compared, examined and selected source materials from all the available sources of law, while attaching great importance to the Dhammathats, selecting and adapting to the dispute the most applicable rules among various Dhammathats, taking the condition and the region into consideration. It may be said that this process for deciding a case at Yezajyo court would coincide with the legal idea of King Badon as seen in his Orders [Okudaira 2005: 100; 2003b: 326].

In sum, through analysis of the contemporary source materials such as the *MD*, Royal orders, *Yezajyo Kondaw Hpyathton*, we realized that the judicial policy of King Badon was clearly based upon his Buddhist ideas: Dhamma (=Dharma) or Law of Buddha and the Buddhist ethics. He seems to have been benevolent towards his people and country. He tried to rule over the country with proper and adequate regulation projecting a new judicial administrative system. He tried to maintain law and order with precise judicial decisions placing great value on tradition, such as Dhammathat, Yazathat, Hpyathton and old customs validated by Buddhism, while taking account of changing times or conditions and prevailing customs. He himself proclaimed that the king should practise "Ten Royal Duties" with the intention of being a "just and lawful king" by performing the supreme consecration ceremony (*Muddha-beiktheik Ahkan-ana*). This can be seen from the new chapters in the *MD* (1782MS), from the immense numbers of Royal Orders issued during his reign, and from the *Yezajyo Hkondaw Hpyathton* [Okudaira 2005: 101].

6. Conclusion

The Dhammathats which are the collections of customary rules and precedents, form the principal source of Myanmar law. They are secular and not ecclesiastical, but are strongly supported by Buddhism. A number of Buddhist ideas were incorporated into the law of the Dhammathats, but they are the customary law of the Buddhist lay men. They reflect the customs and the rules which were prevalent in Buddhist society. They were accepted in the judicial courts as a binding force only when they reflected the customs and the rules of the society. Thus, the traditional Myanmar law was basically regarded as a moral law. In this aspect, the Dhammathats are often regarded as civil law due to the fact that out of "the Eighteen Branches of Law (=The Eighteen Radical Rules)" contained in them, seventeen come under the civil jurisdiction except the law of theft which comes under criminal law. Actually however, as thirty rules included in Chapter I (pt.3) of *MD* (1782MS) presented, they are, in a strict sense, not pure civil law because they include rules in relation to murder, violence, assault, etc.

Of course, criminal law in its modern conception can be found in the Yazathats. They are collections of judicial decision attributed to the king or the answers by the eminent scholars who were renowned in judicial affairs to the king's questions where the Dhammathats were silent or ambiguous. In other words, they were 'the art of governing' by the king for deciding the case because the right of practical applications of the Dhammathats was bestowed upon the king, though the power to enact the law of the Dhammathats was not endowed to the king. He was the arbitrator and the one who settles the disputes among the people.

The powerful kings in the early Konbaung period, such as Alaunghpaya, Hsinbyushin and Badon, gave importance to the Dhammathats. King Alaunghpaya instructed the Hluttaw to consult the Dhammathats and Yazathats and to take time for consulting them [29 November, 1757 (Yi Yi 1979: 109)]. He also remonstrated the judges not to make haste or a biased decision [ROB(19 August, 1758) (T)ROB III: 53/ 214] and the judges to make judgment only after listening to the words of the contending parties [ROB (1 January, 1760) (T)ROB III: 64/232]. King Hsinbyushin gave order the local authorities to make decision in accordance with the Dhammathat [Yi Yi *ibid.*: 117] He also presented a guiding principle to all the judges in civil cases to use the *Manu Dhammathat* for their guide first and if that proved irrelevant, then to consult the *Manawthaya (Manosara) Manuthara (Manusara) Shwemyin* and if they too proved inadequate, to refer to *Kaingza Manu Dhammathat* [ROB (22 July, 1767) (Yi Yi *ibid.*: 118)]. At the beginning of the reign, King Badon urged the judges to refer to either one or all the Dhammathat, Yazathat or Hpyathton for deciding a case [(T)ROB 3 March 1782, 18 August 1783, 12 November 1783, 25 December & 29 August, 1784] or Dhammathat, Yazathat and Sit-tan [ROB (19 April, 1785 (T)ROB IV: 109-110/443] and also not to make *ex-parte* decision [ROB (18 August 1783)(T)ROB IV: 28/275]. He also remonstrated the judges to remain above bribery and corruption [ROB (18 August, 1783) (T)ROB IV29/275; (7 January, 1784) (T)ROB IV: 41/310] When there is a panel of judges, decision should be unanimous [ROB (12 November, 1783) ROB IV: 34/292-293] and some delicate or difficult point in the interpretation of law shall be discussed among the four ministers of the Hluttaw until an agreement is reached as to its meaning and use [ROB (12 November, 1783) (T)ROB IV: 34/292-293]

The most intriguing characteristic of Myanmar traditional law, however, simply reveals in, as King Badon emphasized the importance, one old legal maxim: "Minimise the tall words and ignore the trifles" (*kyi: thi. zaga: go nge aung; nge thi. zaga: go pa-byauk aung*) [ROB (3 March 1782) (T)ROBIV: 9/229]. This implies that simplicity is, better than complexity, and the best way for settling a dispute is an out-of-court "reconciliation" between the parties concerned. King Badon discouraged suing in the court. When a case was heard at a law court, judges should never let a simple case grow into a complex one [ROB (18 August, 1783) (T)ROB IV: 28-29/275]. The final part of the Chapter XVI of *MD* (1782 ME) also encourages all judges to pass fair judgments in accordance with the law of Dhammathats, refraining from indulging in corruption through desire, prompted by loving kindness and compassion and thus act with the hope of promoting peace and prosperity for the kingdom and its people. The passage ends with the same kind of legal maxim mentioned above: " Minimise a big affairs; let a small fault eliminate" (*kyi thaw aya go nge aung; nge thaw apyit ko pa se ya i.*"). This legal maxim reminds us another one: *mwe ma the douk ma kyo* ("Let the snake stay alive and the stick unbroken". This means 'to live and let live').

Thus, the aim of traditional Myanmar law was to settle a dispute peacefully, benevolently and mercifully.

Concluding remarks and Epilogue

In the first half of the Konbaung Dynasty, the kings were confronted with controversial issues about the legitimacy and lineage of King Alaunghpaya. Although his predestined good fortune was rewarded for meritorious deeds in his previous lives (*kaun: thaw Kudho-kan*) and was believed to have caused him to become King, Konbaung writers also justified King Alaunghpaya's accession by linking his genealogy to a royal family who ruled a kingdom either in legend or in fact, in the past. In these aspects, the Dhammathats tried to convince people to accept the legitimacy of Alaunghpaya's rule. Kyone-wun Bumma Zeya, the minister of King Alaunghpaya, who compiled the *MD* inserted a new preamble to it, intending to legitimize King Alaunghpaya and his dynasty by identifying him with the first legendary ideal king, Mahathamada. The compiler, or more precisely his patron the king, may have intended to illustrate the structure of the Theravāda Buddhist State in such a sufficiently concrete manner that the King or his appointed local rulers could conveniently exploit it to restore law and order and to reunify the splintered kingdom.

Regarding the source materials of the *MD*, we have two different copies: one is the Richardson's text (first printed in 1847), seemingly based on a manuscript of the '1760MS'. The other is the 1782 MS with its extra chapters. A thorough investigation of these enables us to state that they were newly inserted during King Badon's rule. The contents of Pt.2 of Chapter I includes essential constituents such as the kingship, organization of the state, the roles and importance of the Dhammathat and the relationship between the king and the Sangha, etc. These are reflected in the newly-added thirty customary rules which became the new contents of Chapter III, while the old ones were moved to Pt.3 of Chapter I. In other words, Pt.2 of Chapter I provides the essential political theory while Chapter III provides legislative procedure for the Theravāda Buddhist State. Chapter XVI summarises the previous fifteen chapters and emphasizes the importance of precise judgement in accordance with the law of Dhammathat and the legal maxims. All three were probably intentional additions to the *MD* made when it was copied at the beginning of the reign of King Badon.

King Alaunghpaya ordered the insertion of the new preamble to the *MD* so that it could give a more complete version than those of previous Dhammathats. It presents the nature of Myanmar law and the structure of the Myanmar Theravāda Buddhist State in an abstract manner. King Badon added extra chapters which explain the kingship and the state organization in a concrete manner. King Badon also added Chapter III to explain various customary rules in force at that time. It is important to note that King Badon's efforts gave exceedingly high status to the Dhammathat and placed it in the proper legislative position in the Theravāda Buddhist State structure as the original Pāli Dhammasatthan had maintained. The institutionalization of the Theravāda Buddhist State that was inaugurated under King Alaunghpaya was accelerated under King Badon, who wished to reform society and to centralise administration. He ardently desired to establish a stronger and more expanded Theravāda Buddhist State, embracing other Buddhist ethnic groups such as the Mons, the Rakhines and the Shans. Thus, kingship and law during the first half of the Konbaung period, so-called the early Konbaung period in the latter half of the eighteenth and early nineteenth centuries, were characterized by King Alaunghpaya's realization of political theory based on the origin of legislative power by the first legendary ideal King Mahathamada and King Badon's actualization of this political theory to establish the stronger Theravāda Buddhist State in Myanmar. These developments are manifest in the preamble (Chapter I in the 1760 MS or Part I of Chapter I in 1782MS) and Chapters (Part II and Part III of Chapter I, Chapter III and Chapter XVI in 1782MS of the *MD*.

Epilogue

To what extent is the present State structure of Myanmar related to that of the strong "Theravāda Buddhist State" established by King Badon? The present State of Myanmar does not embody the triangular system at all in which the king was the defender and propagator of Buddhism and supported the Sangha, while the Sangha transmitted the Dhamma (Law of Buddha) and the Dhamma legitimated the Ruler. However, the present Regimes are a strong supporters of Theravāda Buddhism. This has been true since May

1980 when the First Congregation of the Sangha of All the Theravāda Buddhist Orders was held under President Ne Win's Socialist State. At present, a new constitution was established in 2008 and has now come into force at the beginning of the Thein Sein' Regime which started in March, 2011 and was succeeded by Daw Aung San Suu Kyi's 'Democratisation Government' since March, 2015. We must pay attention to the relationship between the State and Buddhism under the 2008 constitution, so as to determine what form of state will prevail in Myanmar in future.

Footnotes

[Introduction]
1. (1) In June, 1989, the Government of the Union of Burma proclaimed to change her external official name of the country from "The Union of Burma" to "The Union of Myanmar" corresponding to its original vernacular expression of "Pyi-daung-zu Myanma Nainggan-daw". Throughout this book, "Myanmar" is being used for the country concerned in accordance with the aforementioned proclamation of the Government. The usage, however, does not reflect any political connotation, but just correspond to the traditional vernacular expression of 'Myanma(r)' for the country. Here, it is also used for the language and people for convenience sake. But "Burma" or "Burmese" (Burman as well) are also used when it is cited or quoted from the historical documents and other various source materials, publications such as books, research papers, etc. (2) In regard to translations from English to Myanmar language, this author is responsible for all the works. (3) Regarding citations from the palm-leaf manuscripts of the source material, such as the *Manugye Dhammathat*, every page is shown in the blacket, such as [III: Zu./K-Zu /W], indicating Chapter(III), alphabetical order (Zu. or Zu) and then, the face: W (= Wun:) or the reverse: K (=Kyaw).
2. (1) As to the place names, in principle, priority is given to vernacular expressions which are closer to their pronunciation, in such manner as, "Yangon" for Rangoon, "Pyi" for Prome, "Mawlamyine" for Moulmein, "Bagan" for Pagan, "Taninthayi" for Tenasserim, "Ayeyarwadi" for Irrawaddy, "Rakhaine" for Yakhaine or Arakan, etc., in accordance with the proclamation mentioned above in 1(1). But the old names are also shown in the parenthesis at the sama time, such as Bago (=Pegu), Bagan (=Pagan). (2) In regard to personal name, this book follows such traditional way as Dr. Hla Pe, Dr. Than Tun, U Maung Maung Tin, Daw Yi Yi, etc. (3) As regards specific Myanmar terms or sentences included in this book are mostly described in accordance to four tones (-a., -a, -a:, and -a+(either k, p, t for the double consonant) such as '*Min: Kyin. Taya: Hse-ba:*' for 'The Ten Royal Duties', *Be: Shit-pa:* for The Eight Calamities, etc. (4) In rendering Myanmar historical terms, such as Hluttaw, Dhammathat, Yazathat, Hpyathton, Sit-tan, etc., uses spelling which are familiar to us. In addition, the names of the specific Sanskrit, Pāli or Myanmar are described in the form of Italic form, such as, *Abhiseka, Cakkavattin, Muddha - beiktheik*, etc.
3. Unless otherwise noted, dates are given in the Christian (Gregorian) calendar in such a manner as, Konbaurg period, [1752-1819], (1990), etc. As to Myanmar calendar

corresponding to Christian one, it is shown like 1144ME [1782 A.D.], etc.
4. Dr. David Richardson has been introduced in the name of 'David Lester Richardson' by R.R. Langham-Carter who wrote articles on him [See JBRS 1966: 207-218/AQ 1966: 219-237]. However, we do not find his name, David 'Lester' Richardson in any other historical records [EIRD 1823: 269, etc.]. Professor Andrew Turton also pointed out that 'Lester'was wrong through discussion with us on his article [SEAR 1997: 175-205]. Langham-Carter might have possibly confused with the person named 'David Lester Richardson' [1801-1865] who played active parts in Bengal of India as the contemporary with Dr. David Richardson, at first as an editor of Journals, then Professor of English literature, and later Principal of the Hidu College at Calcutta, also as a poet and a writer after he left India.
5. Dr. Than Tun, who regrettably passed away in November 2004, surveyed 1782 version of the *Manugye Dhammathat* in comparison with that of Richardson's text (1874) and the printed version of the *Manuyin Dhammathat* (1875) in a journal in Japan. See *Tonanajia Rekishi to Bunka* ("The Southeast Asian History and Culture") No.14, pp.28-43.
6. Dr. Nai Pan Hla collected eleven Mon *Dhammasāt*s and published with English translation and synopses under the title of *Eleven Mon Dhammasāts Texts* in Tokyo in 1996. As regards the Shan traditional law, Sai Kham Mong published *Shan Thammasat Manuscripts* with Text and English Translation in Tokyo in 2012.
7. A Japanese Professor Dr. Toru Aoyama has defined Indianization "as a cultural and social change widely extended in the Southeast Asia in the fifth century, through acceptance of the classical Indian culture mainly formed in the Gupta kingdom of India" (explained in Japanese) [Aoyama 2016: 168]

< Part I >
[Chapter I]
8. See *Aggañña Suttanta* in the *Dīgha Nikāya* from Sutta Pitaka. This fact shows one of the manifestation of "Sinhali-zation"or "Pāli-ization" which is a new cultural phenomenon after the thirteenth century in place of that of Indianization [See Ishii 1983: 20]. In Myanmar, "Sinhal-ization" or "Pāli-ization" had already taken place after eleventh century. This story composed of probably *Aggañña Suttanta* mixed with *Spurattadipanītika* and *Visuddhimagga* by Buddhagosa [See Forchhammer 1953: (5)]
9. This was also confirmed by this author through discussion with Dr. H.W. Tambiah, a distinguished Sri Lankan Jurist during the stay in Sri Lanka in 1982. Books of law referred to here means the secular law books of the Sri Lankan version (either in Pāli or Sinhalese language) modified in a Buddhist style, modeled after *Dharmaśāstra*s like *Manusmṛti* (Code of Manu) which had been introduced into Sri Lanka from India. On the other hand, an European writer describes that "A contrary opinion has been

entertained by some writers, who have supposed that the Sinhalese, like Burmese, and Hindoos, posseess the law of *Manu* - - - -They have, indeed, some of these laws, scattered here and there in their works on religion; but they are little known, rarely referred to, and never followed" [Davy 1821: 179]. *Cūlavaṃsa*, one of the major Sri Lankan chronicles in 15C, (hereinafter referred to as C.V., contains many descriptions that indicate the introduction of the Code of *Manu* into Sri Lanka [C.V.80-9, 41, 53; 84-1,2, etc.english translation by C. Marbel Rickmaers from the Geiger's German translation of the original C.V. in Pāli]. *Mahavaṃsa*, another chronicle in 7C prior to C.V., hereinafter referred to M.V. contains descriptions that books of law were compiled during the reign of King Voharika in 3 C. A.D. and King Kalyanavati in 13C [M.V. 36-28; Trl. By Geiger]. From these records of the chronicles, one may conjecture, as Professor M.B. Ariyapala, suggested that there may have been a code of laws, probably modeled upon the Dharmaśāstras [Ariyalpala 1968: 124]. Nevertheless, the facts remain obscure because such a code does not exist today.

In this regard, the Myanmar documents argued as follows: *Pitaka Thamaing Sadan* mentions *Theinko Dhammathat* in the Dhammathat list, where it only says that *Theinko Dhammathat* was compiled by a Theinko King [*Thamaing*1905: 189] who was possibly to be a king before Bagan period. Fuehrer conjectured that "as the Burmans received their religious literature originally through the Thalaings from Ceylon about the fifth century A.D., it seems to be not improbable that some of the secular literature may have reached there from the same source." But inquiry made by him through a Buddhist high priest in Colombo as to the existence of any Pāli works corresponding to the Burmese Dhammathat failed to elicit information on the subject [Fuehrer 1882: 332]. But he gave brief summary in the article, of the Pāli version of the *Manuthara* (*Manusara*) *Shwemyin Dhammathat*, saying that the code was at first kept in the island of Ceylon and was at length brought into the Burmese Empire always called Ramaññadesa [ibid.: 334-335]. Forchhammer made the same kind of explanation [Forchhammer 1885: 2]. Furnivall says in his article that "it seems permissible to suspect that the Dhammathat was introduced from Sri Lanka under King Dhammazedi in the fifteenth century, on the grounds that Pegu, the capital city of Mons, was barbarous and anarchic and an unlikely home for a code of law during the reign of King Wagaru and for the next two hundred years" [Furnivall 1940: 356].

The English summary of the *Manuthara Shwemyin Dhammathat* made by Dr. Tandy from Latin says that "the code, which was at first written in the Pāli tongue, and kept in the Island of Ceylon, was at length brought into the Burmese Empire by certain Budelagosa [Buddhaghosa], and translated into the vulgar language. And such is the origin of the *Dhammasāts* [Dhammathat]" [Sangermano 1966: 23]. However, in the introduction to the *Manuthara Shwemyin Dhammathat* (1220 M.E.=1850A.D. Pāli-Myanmar Nissaya style), which corresponds to that of the Pāli version used by Fuehrer or of English translation by Tandy mentioned above we do not find any word corresponding to 'Ceylon'. Nothing is described to show that the Dhammasatthan

was at first compiled in Sri Lanka and brought to Myanmar afterwards. Thus it seems to be not easy task to show evidence that the Dhammathat came from Sri Lanka. It seems, however, rather an interesting and even romantic exercise to conduct further study as to the earlier contact of legal literature among the Myanmar, Mon, Sri Lankan, for the purpose of a better understanding of and elucidating of the Myanmar legal history. Huxley referred to 'the allusion to Sri Lankan dhammathat which is Sinhalese version of the Dhammasathan' [Huxley 1996: 94] But as far as we surveyed in Sri Lanka in 1983, we learned that such a law book had never been compiled there.
10. Dr. Emil Forchhamer was the Professor of Pāli at Rangoon College and was appointed by the British Government in 1881 to head Archaeologist, but actually however, we have been told by Professor M.B. Hooker that Forchhammer was a Swiss linguist. In addition, we were told by Andrew Huxley that Forchhammer's parents were German and that he was born in Switzerland and was a theologian, doctor and comparative linguist. He was once a Professor of Pāli in the Rangoon College. He was awarded Jardine Prize for his *Essay* in 1885.
11. Lingat asserted in his article that 'no *Dhammasatthan* [Dhammasatthan] had ever been found, not only in India, but even in Ceylon, and that 'all the *Dhammasatthams* [Dhammasatthans] came from Pegu or Burma' [Lingat 1949: 292].
12. Twelve decisions are as follows: (i) Law on the boundaries of land, (ii)Judgment for the destruction of boundaries of land, (iii)Judgment for theft that someone stole the other person's property, (iv)Judgment for taking by force the property of another person, (v)Judgment in accordance with the *Thikya* (*Dhaja* or the king of *Nat*s (celestial beings) when the *Nat*s each other took by force other's possession which the owner of the property is clear, (vi)The case of the squirrel, the gindeik, and the frog, (vii)The case between the owners of the squirrel and the rat, (viii)Of taking a wife by force, (ix)The case that young should pay respect to the elders whether they have reached to legal age or not, (x)Borrowed inanimate grain only to be repaid fourfold, (xi)Borrowed silver to be repaid only double, (xii) The case in which a decision was given by examining the witnesses apart [See RMD 1847: 9-18].
13. The Myanmar expression is: *Dhammathat ko Yazathat chok thi, Yazathat ko Gatipot chok thi.*

[Chapter II]
14. Other legal literatures are: law tales and legal maxim.
15. In relation to the word Dhammathat, an inscription in 1249A.D. includes Dhammathat with which the four judges were ordered to consult by King Kyaswa concerning a land dispute [I.B.pl.174/14]. This was once regarded as the only one word which was appeared in Bagan inscription [Than Tun 1964: 157].
16. We find the word *"Amunwan-ca(sa)"*, which suggests a written penal code in the thirteenth century of Bagan [See Than Tun 1964: 158].

17. According to Andrew Huxley, the 1681's version of *Pitakat Thamaing* is preserved in Berlin, Germany.
18. According to the information by Andrew Huxlry, the Dhammatha*t* list which is included in the Appendix (pp.68-76) is extracted from the *Pitakat Thamaing* (1820) compiled under King Bagyidaw and it deals with altogether 70 Dhammathats.
19. In regard to the story on Tharriputta, Furnivall criticized it, asserting that contemporary inscriptions give it no support and that it remains a legend of doubtful authenticity [See Furnivall 1940: 355].
20. Master degree dissertation by U Kyaw, a Myanmar historian, under the title of *Yaw Thamaing* 1752-1885 ("History of Yaw District-1752-1885") submitted to the Department of History, Arts and Science University, Mandalay in 1977. He used many Hpyat-ca (sa) or local judgments as a primary sources.
21. Some Japanese scholars have been conducting their research works on Konbaung socio-economic history, using Sit-tan. Professor Teruko Saito and her group published the translation of some *Thekkayit* into Japanese. She also contributed to the publication edited by Professor Anthony Reid, using *Thetkayit* [See Saito (in) Reid 1997: 153-184].
22. For example, altogether 52 Myanmar Legal Maxims are included in Aung Than Tun's book [1968: 187-189]
23. For example, altogether 65 Law Tales are included in the book of Maung Htin Aung [1962: 49-157].
24. The six branches of knowledge comprising, phonology, grammar, prosody, glossology, astronomy, and the learning of the rules concerning rites [See p.313, Myanmar-English Dictionary 1992 Yangon: Ministry of Education].

[Chapter III]
25. Pitakat-taik hnit Yinkye-hmu Thutetana Pya-daik ("The Library and Cultural Studies Museum") in Taungdwin-gyi had preserved altogether 24 items of legal manuscripts such *Dhammathat* as *Manuthara Shwemyin Dhammathat, Dhammathat-paun-gyouk, Dhammathat-linga, Dhammathat-hnyun-baun, Daiha-yaza, Dhammathat-linga, Pakeinnaka-kyaw Dhammathat*; such *hpyathton* as *Shin-Kyaw Thu Kauk-yu Hson-hpyat-hcet, Maha Atula Hsayadaw Hpyathton, Maung-htaung Hsayadaw Hpyathton*, etc. as of 1987. But it was reported that the library was suffered from fire and accidentally all these legal documents had been burnt to ashes.
26. The National Commission for the Preservation of Traditional Manuscripts has been established in September, 1994 aiming at collecting and preserving old manuscripts more systematically in cooperation with ministries concerned of the Myanmar Government.
27. These Dhammathats and Hpyathtons are *Manu Wunnana (Vannana), Manuthara (Manusara) Shwemyin, Manuyin (Reng), Wineikhsaya Pakathani (Vinniccaya Pakasani), Wagaru, Yezajyo kondaw Hpyathton, Thudhamma-sayi (Sudhamma Cari)-*

hpyathton, etc.
28. 'The National Commission for the Preservation of Traditional Manuscripts' was established in 1994 [See Teruko Saito & U Thaw Gaung 2006: 16]
29. We had a chance to check the collection in 1987 & 1989 under permission of the Asiatic Society of Bengal and with the help of Professor Guha, the staff of the Oriental Section of the Library.
30. Out of the eleven manuscripts, eight are hand-writing copies preserved at the National Library in Yangon and other three are, according to Nai Pan Hla, the handwriting copies from the palm-leaf manuscripts found in Thailand.
31. Yinkye-hmu Pya-daik (The Cultural Museum in Mawlamyine (Moulmein) possesses the handwriting list of Mon Pe-ca (sa) which was taken notes at the monasteries in Mawlamyaine and Kyaikhkami township in 1913. It contains abundant source materials including a handful Dhammathats including Mon version of *Manugye Dhammathat* (*MD*).
32. The name of the fourteen items of the Thammasat are as follows: (i)*Mang Kyan Tra Muong San Hseang* (1880MS, recopied in 1927), (ii) *Manu Sara Manu Sara* (1842 MS), (iii)*Thammahsat Pyat Tra* (1934 MS), (iv)Thammasat Tai *Khamti* (the copy-date:n.d), (v)*Thammasat Purana Kyam*(the copy-date unknown), (vi)*Thammasat Kyam-gyi* (1943MS), (vii)*Sudhammasari Sung Hpyat Tra* (1942MS), (viii)*Tra Thammasat* (1907MS), (ix)*Tra Taw Sao Thammasat* (the copy-date unknown) and (x)*Thammasat* (the copy-date unknown). (xi)*Lik Sao Thammasat* <Ruling>(the copy-date unknown.), (xii)*Thammasat Tra Taw*<Teaching of *Thammasat*>(the copy date unknown), and (xiii)*Thammasat Tai Khun* (the copy- date unknown) [The information mentioned above has been given by Sai Kham Mong dated on 1st, May, 2008]. Sai Kham Mong, through his research, came to conclusion that 'the Shan Thammasat marked KTM I (*Khun Thammasat*) is purely Shan and devoid of any Myanmar influence. He also pointed out that the Shan Thammasat marked STM I and KTM as the best work to understand the early Shan administrative system, religious belief and values of Shan culture [Sai Kham Mong 2012: 37]

[Chapter IV]
33. Captain George Baker set out with Lieut. John North on 17th July, 1755, as Ambassadors from the Honourable Company under instruction of the Chief of Negrais to accompany the King of Burma.
34. A Baker's account continue as follows: 'I don't remember to have heard any instance of his *Justice---* that deserves to be more remembered for its *impartiality* than *severity*, though the former never fails to meet with encomiums from them about him; for he always causes, and often sees all corporal, or capital punishments to be executed, to the utmost rigour of the Sentence, which generally argues rather a *barbarous* than *humane disposition*'. [DOR *ibid*.: 71].
35. A Chinese diplomatic missions visited Ava under King Bagyidaw via Bamo in

1184M.E. (=1823 A.D.) [See KBZ II: 353-364].
36. There are fourteen types of *Beiktheik* or consecration ceremony: these are: (i)*Hkattiya* and (ii)*Yaza* for making the government over to the king; (iii)*Thakara* for the prosperity of the kingdom; (iv)*Wizaya* and (v)*Zeya* for victory of war; (vi)*Thiripawethana* and (vii)*Maha* for the increase of reputation; (viii)*Mingala* for taking over the elephants and horses; (ix)*Wiwaha* for marrying; (x)*Dwaya* for taking over the palace; (xi)*Ayudiga* for long life; (xii)*Upayaza* for appointing the successor; (xiii) *Maheti* for creating the queen; (xiv)*Muddha* for taking the oaths to govern by laws [See MMOS pt.1s.169: 247-248/Furnivall 1925: 142-143].

Richardson referred to three kinds of *Beiktheik*: *yaza bithik [yaza Beiktheik]*., at the time of ascending the throne; manda bithik *[Manda Beiktheik]*, at the time of marriage with the queen; *Thaga Beiktheik [Thaga Beiktheik]*, after reigning a sort renewal in a more strict way of his engagement to keep all the laws binding on kings [(R)MD1847: 7]. Kyin Swi described as follows: *Yaza Bithik [Yaza Beiktheik]* was performed at the time of throne; *Thaga Bithik [Thaga Beiktheik]* is for the welfare and peace of the country; *Manda Bithik [Manda Beiktheik]* is the most of all the *bithik [Beiktheik]* without which no person would be regarded as a king [Kyin Swi 1965: 14]. *Thaga Bithik* in Richardson and *Manda bithik* in Kyin Swi is regarded as *Muddha Beiktheik* itself referred to in MMOS mentioned above.
37. These views are based on a comment for my draft paper presented at the Collquium on Burmese Studies which was held by the Burma Studies Group in Nothern Illinois University on 25th-27th October, 1996.

[Chapter V]
38. The detailed account of the ceremony observed for the king can be seen in *Vamsatthapakasani* commentary (Tīka) [Jayadekera *ibid*.: 117]
39. After the king ascended the throne, a consecration ceremony was held for opening the upper part of the back of the throne called *U Kin-daw Hpwin Ahkan-ana*.
40. According to *Amedaw Hpye* ("Questions by the king and answers by the monk") which is actually a collection of questions by King Badon and answers by the first Maung Htaung Hsayadaw, King Bagyidaw also practiced the *Muddha Beiktheik* in 1184M.E. (=1822 or 1823A.D.) [AHP:preface (Na.)]. But ROB eidited by Dr. Than Tun says that the date of 'coronation' is 15th March, 1824 [ROB VIII: XII].
41. *Akyo Nga-ba:* or the Five Effects are as follows: (i) To be the true descendant of *Hkattiya* (a Pāli-loan word corresponding to *Kśātriya* in Sankrit), (ii)To observe the royal virtue, (iii)To have desire for the people's progress and prosperity as they are the king's own sons, (iv)Without any discrimination, to love eqally and to share in equal proportion the prosperity and wealth of all living creatures and (v)With loving kindness toward the people, to pray for their safty to protect them[See MMOS I: 239].
42. *Min:-do. Kyin. Ya thaw: Thingaha Taya: Le:-ba* (Four laws for assistance by the king)

are as follows: (i)To collect (not more than) one-tenth of the produce as a source of revenue, (ii)To provide food every six months to soldiers, (iii)To lend money to cultivators, and after three years, collect it without interest, and (iv)To speak sweet words.

43. Suggestions by an unknown scholar for my draft paper (which was actually not submitted) for the *Journal of Burma Studies* for Volume I (1997).

[Chapter VI]

44. Andrew Huxley argues that these chronological accounts by Forchhammer are not reliable due to want of their authenticities.
45. Although the *MD* is newly compiled under King Alaunghpaya, no evidence has been found yet that he instructed to give top priority to it for deciding a case.
46. PTS says that it was written by Letwe-nanda-sithu, the minister, but the date of the compilation is not mentioned.

[Chapter VII]

47. Yandabo is a village, only fifty miles south from the capital city of Ava, where both a Myanmar and a British peace missions met and concluded the peace treaty on 24th February, 1826 under the conditions of (i)the cession of the territories of Rakhine (Arakan), Tanindhayi (Tenasserim) and Assam by the Myanmar king to the British, (ii)Recognition of Manipur, Cachar, and Jaintia as British territories by the Myanmar king, (iii)Payment of an indemnity of one million sterling pounds in four installments by the Myanmar king to the British government, (iv)Reception of a British resident representative at Ava by the Myanmar king and of a Myanmar resident representative at Calcutta, (v)Conclusion of a commercial treaty between the British East Indian Company and the Myanmar king in due course [See Htin Aung 1967: 214].
48. We visited Dr. Richardson's grave in 14th December, 1998 accompanied by the late Dr. Hla Pe and were informed by a person in charge of the Kyaikthanlan Pagoda that it had been buried in the eastern part of the ground inside the compound of the Pagoda because of the landslide which occurred on 16th September, 1945. We confirmed that there was no more grave stone on the ground in the area.
49. Mr. and Mrs. Judson began their missionary life in Amherst on 2nd July, 1826 [See E.Judson 1883: 288].
50. For instance, *thanthaya bawa. ahset-hset neibban ma. yauk ma. chin:* was translated as 'through all ages till he obtains *Neibban*. But 'all ages' may be replaced by 'cycle of birth and re-birth' [RMD1896: 124]. *Hpaya: ma. hpyit mi* was translated into 'before the god (Gautama) appeared. But it may be translated as 'before Gotama attained enlightment.' [*ibid* .: 131]
51. The one from the National Library in Yangon is vol.II (the date of copy: 1222 M.E. (=1860A.D.). Another one which the Universities Central Library in Yangon

possesses is X & XI Vols. (the date of copy: 1223 M.E.=1861A.D.) and 1236 (=1874A.D.). Apart from these, the Mandalay University Library has preserved Vol. I & II of the *Manugye Dhammathat* (date of copy 1236M.E.= 1874A.D.) These volumes seem to have been used for specific subjects at law courts rather than extant in incomplete condition by chance.

52. Apart from the *Wagaru Dhammathat*, these Dhammathats do not describe the copy-date of the palm-leaf manuscripts in the texts published.

< Part II >

[Chapter VIII]

53. It seems that Dr. Forchhammer did not use the palm-leaf manuscript of any *MD* but used 1874 printed version, because he did not listed up it in his reference in *Jardine Prize: An Essay*.
54. We have traced 1760MS in and out of Myanmar. Particularly we have been looking for it so long since 1980s in Yangon, Mandalay, Magwe, Shwebo, Mawlamyine, etc., but in vain.
55. The Digest includes *MD* (1144M.E.) as one of the Dhammathats used in compiling it [See Digest Vol.I 1898: Dates of Original Dhammathat---].
56. We first of all checked the *MD* (1782MS) at the National Library in Yangon, in April, 1981.
57. We do not know why the Chapter XVI was included though it seems to be a new one which does not include in Richardson's text (1760M.S) and any other former Dhammathat.
58. We have not confirmed yet whether it will support our hypothesis that the Chapter I (pt.2 & 3), the Chapter III and the Chapter XVI which are not included in 1760 MS, were inserted at the beginning of the enthronement of King Badon in 1782. But according to the colophons of these chapters, except the Chapter XVI, all seems to be original because they do not mention the copy-dates, just like newly inserted.
59. It is generally accepted that Pāli language is one of the ancient Indian languages which was used in western part of India as one of the major Prākrit (colloquial language) corresponding to Sanskrit (elegant language) and it is different from Magada language, though it contains many factor of the Magada language [See Mizuno 1980; 24 in *Pāli Go Bunpou (A Grammaer of the Pāli Language)*. Intention of the authors of the *Pyumin Dhammathat* and *Manuthara Dhammathat*s who referred to the Magada language is unknown. However, we may dare to say that these authors regarded the Magada language as the Pāli language.
60. It means our earth where alone is inhabited by human being. Buddha appears only in this island and teach them how to escape from the cycle of existences [See Ba Han 1965: 13]

61. For example, *Mahayazawin-gyi* compiled by U Kala in the early eighteenth century narrates the story of Elect of King Mahathamada and of presenting the Dhammathat to him. [MY Vol. I 1960: 7-19]. The author of the *MD* very likely copied the preamble from that of the *Mahayazawingyi*.
62. See *Aggañña Suttanta* in the *Dīgha-nikāya* of Sutta Pitaka. In regard to such description that 'the present world (*Badda Gaba*) came into existence after previously existed worlds had been destroyed seven times by fire and once by water [See RMD 1896: 1], the compiler seems to have wrongly copied from a former source, very likely from U kala's *Mahayazawindaw-gyi*. We do not find any such description in the *Milinda Paññha*. Actually, such description is seen in the *Anagatavaṃsa Aṭṭhakatha* ("Sutta on Future") [See HMY I: 11].
63. The preamble to *MD* says that "the hill of Myint Mo Taun (or Mount Meru), the seven surrounding hill, the four large islands, the two thousand small islands, the Himawunta forest, the great river and lakes, and the pillars of this *Sekya* world, by the force of nature came into existence all at once, on Sunday, the full moon of the Tabaung *[Twelfth and last month of the year]*, came into existence" [RMD I: 5-6] It illustrates that either because of the first living beings' power, or even present law of nature, the sun rose to the top of the center hill of the eastern island, and it became light. After the sun had gone round to the other side, the absolute darkness followed. At the time when all the original inhabitants wished for some kind of light, the moon, shinning with serence radiance, with the twenty- seven constellations, and the other stars surrounding them, made their appearance in the East [See *ibid.*] According to the Buddhist cosmology from which the Myanmar cosmology originated, at the center of the earth is Myint Mo Taun above which is *Tavatimsa*, ruled by *Sakka* (or *Indra*), who heads the thirty-three *Nats* or celestial being. Ba Han explains this more indetail that the universe of Myanmar "cosmology is made up of innumerable worlds or spheres (*Setkyawala*), each of which has its own earth, sun, moon, heaven and hell. These worlds are separated from one another by hells. The center of world is Mount Meru *[Myint Moe Taun]*, where the gods (*deva*) dwell. The sun circles round it. Seven concentric mountain ranges girgle the earth, and seven great river (*Sita*) intervene between these ranges. Beyond them lies the vast ocean with four great islands named after the huge tree *Uttarakura, Zambu- dipa, Pubhavideha* and *Aparagoyana,* in the North, South, East and West respectively" [Ba Han1965: 12-13]
64. The Myanmar word, corresponding to *Abhiseka* in Pāli and *Abhiṣeka* in Sanskrit, means consecration usually accompanied by pouring of lustral water.
65. It tells that a cowherd about seven years of age, who had commencing with his little companions could speak to the satisfaction on men and women, old and young in his village.
66. In regard to the dialogue between King Mahathamada and the Cowherd on whether the latter will accept the King's request to be a judge, the *Dhammavilatha Dhamma-*

that described more in detail [DWDI: 27-28; ke/K].
67. The first day's decision is on a dispute concerning the old and new paddy seed; the second day, on male and female cattle; the third day on a large and small cock; the fourth day, on taking a child away; the fifth day, on woodcutter; the sixth, on the division of a golden pot between the wife of the man who found it and four others and the seventh, a dispute, on the small cucumber case.
68. The seventh day's dispute is as follows: in a small village two men made gardens closely adjoining each others, and separated by a prickly fence. In one garden a small cucumber sprang up and ran into the garden of the other, and bore fruit and he plucked it. The dispute reached Judge Manu. The owner of the cucumber said, "the root is mine". The other said, " Having come to my garden, it is mine'. Then, Manu decided that it had gone into the other garden and borne fruit and that the owner of that garden should have the right to pluck it". Then both *Nat*s and men did not accept Manu's decision. So he tried again and decided that the owner of roots of the cucumber was entitled to receive compensation from the owner of the neighbouring garden for the loss of the small cucumber [See translation in RMD I: 25/ Maung Htin Aung 1962: 149].
69. Judson's Burmese-English Dictionary says; *Zan* means: "a certain attainment or state of mind, which enables the possessor to traverse different worlds, to fly through the air, or go through the earth" [Judson 1966: 431].

[Chapter IX]
70. We do not find any provisions in this *MD* for such four *Thingaha Wuttu* Principle included in Pāli Canon as follows: (i)Collecting only one-tenth of the produce of land as revenue, (ii)Disbursing provisions to soldiers in every half a year, (iii)Granting loans to cultivators and collecting them without interest only after three years and (iv)taking only sweet and pleasant words.
71. The Seven Kinds of Paddy are these: (i)*Thale* (A kind of fragrant rice), (ii)*Kauk-kyi* (Variety of paddy which takes a longer time to ripen), (iii)*Lu* (the common millet), (iv)*Jyon* (wheat), (v)*Pyaung* (millet maize), (vi)*Bali* (Barley) and (vii)*Hsap* (Italian millet). Ten Kinds of Jewel are: (i)*Shwe* (Gold), (ii)*Ngwe* (Silver), (iii)*Pale* (Pearl), (iv) *Paddamya-ni* (Red-ruby), (v)*Paddamya-pyauk* (Spotted-ruby), (vi)*Mya* (Emerald), (vii)*Kyaun-myet-ywe* (Cat's eye), (viii)*Hkayu-dhin* (Conch shell), (ix) *Kyauk - thalin* (Quartz) and (x)*Thandal* (Coral) [See M-E-D:].
72. This seems to be a Sanskrit work originated from the story of names of seven kings.
73. This seems likely a Sanskrit loan word 'Samsāra' (Myanmar pronunciation is *Thanthaya* (which means 'cycles of rebirth').
74. Regarding the four biases (*Gati.-Le:-ba:*), the hermit Manu said: "the people who observe biases stay at the judicial court and observe the Dhammathat that I gave to the king and study the behaviours and original history of both parties and bear in mind weather they are right words and which to say first and which to say later and

see the four bad baises and instruct in accordance with the good four biases. If a judge makes judgment, not in accordance with the four good biases, but with four bad, wealth and reputation would fell as the moon dwindles in size in its waning days. What are four biases?: (i)*Hsanda.-gati.*: [the judge] passes judgment, based on his own desires giving the victory to those who should be defeated and giving defeat to those who should be given the victory; (ii)*Daw:tha-gati.*: [the judge] passes judgement in anger, giving victory to those who should be given defeat and giving defeat to those who should be given victory; (iii)*Baya-gati.*: [the judge] passes judgment for fear of danger, giving victory to those who should be given defeat, giving defeat to those who should be given victory; (iv)*Maw:ha-gati.*: [the judge] passes judgment out of ignorance which can give rise to misdeed, being unable to differentiate those who should be given defeat from those who should be given victory. Thereby, the judge breaks the law. This is as if the full-moon dwindles in size in its waning days. These are the four biases (*Agati.-le:-ba:*)." [I pt.2: hku. /K -hku./W].

"Therefore, any judges who pass judgment to give victory to those who should be given defeat and to give defeat to those who should be given the victory, saying that this man is my relative and this is not my relatives, this is not the person who is acquired with me and this is not the person who is not acquainted with me, are those who follow *Hsanda.gati.*[by the judge].; any judges who pass judgment in anger, giving favour to one party and giving defeat to the other on saying that the man has intended to kill me, and that the man has destroyed my benefit, and that the man has not paid respect to me or that the man is my enemy, are those who follow the *Daw:tha-gati.*[by the judge]. Any judges who pass judgements out of fear, giving favour to one party who should be given defeat and giving defeat to the other, saying that this man is going to make mischief because he is acquainted with the king and that he is going to set fire to the house because he is a thief as well as a destroyer and that he is going to steal and destroy my property, prosperity and welth, are those who follow the *Baya-gati*. Any judges who pass judgemnet not knowing whether the defeat or victory is to be given, are those who follow the *Mawha-gati*.

Therefore, Oh! King, every judge should pass judgments not in accordance with the four biases, but in accordance with the good *gati*. (discretion), irrespective of the social status of the litigants concerned. Judges should not get angry even if loser who could not accept his own defeat which was caused by his luck of justice should not remain slander and exercise judgment of the law at the judicial court. Only the kings (*pyide-shin-mingyi:-do*.) should admonish (*hson:-ma*.) such slanders [I pt.2: hku./K]

Oh, King Mahathamada ! The anger makes one unaware of his own benefits. The anger adheres to king closely. Oh, King! the king's anger which is his license makes him unaware of his own benefits. One can not recognize his own benefits just as the man can not see his own reflection on the bubbling surface of the boiling water. One can recognize his benefits only when he does not get angry or control anger just as the man can see his reflection on the surface of the still water. Therefore, the judges

including the kings should practice like a stone obelisk by not following to the country of anger." [I pt. 2: hku./K].
75. The hermit Manu said: "like the Lion king (*Chinte.-min:*) who ruled the forest of Himalaya, any judge should pass judgments by the book of Dhammathat without trembling. When the person who should win presents a deer while the other who should be defeated presents a lion or the person who should win presents grass, while the person who should be defeated presents a ruby, the judge must pass judgment without being influenced by the presents. *[*The judges*]* should make judgement by the law of Dhammathat in the care of the enemy just in the same way as those of their own children, or the other persons or close friends and relatives. Then the hermit Manu told stories as examples for the judges who will solve and pass judgment, considering in accordance with the four good biases (=discretion *Gati. Le:-ba:*), but not with the four bad biases (*Makaun: thaw: Gati. Le:-ba:*)." [I pt. 2: hke/ W].
76. In this regard, as examples, law tales are inserted as follows: "There was a hunter who filled (smeared) his feather tipped arrow with poison and he himself became the victim of his own poisoned arrow". There is another examples of a man who wrapped a rotten fish in sweet smelling *Neza Thaman Myet* (Saccharum cylind-ricum-Kusa grass). "By doing so, the grass became rotten and smelled like the rotten fish. Yet there is another man who had a score where in its early stage a fly laid its egg, and when he realized it, the wounded had festered and spread to the whole body and he lost his life. Those vicious people (villain) who are not well versed in law are similar to the loathsome poison, rotten fish and flies. Such judges are the same as the loathsome poison, rotten fish and flies. Such judges are the same as the feather (or the arrow)and sweet smelling grass. When they die they will without any doubt, fall into hell. And Your Majesty, during the time of Dāpamkara Buddha and a hermit named Martin contested at a law court. Although Kala, the Brahman warned against the hermit Martin, the king without thoroughly investigating the case passed the judgment in favour of kala, the Brahmin. For letting the Brahman win the case, the king was swallowed up by the earth and he had to suffer in hell." [I. pt.2: hke/wun:-hke/K].
77. Relating to List 16 again, the hermit named Muni showed the four nether worlds. *[*The judges*]* are apt: (i)to go to the big hell which consists of the eight stages (*ngaye:-gyi: shit-htat*) and the small hell which consists of one hundred and eight stages (*ngaye:nge taya hnit shit-htat*); (ii)to become a being in Linbo state (*peitta*); (iii)to become an inferior deities (*athurake*) and (iv)become a beast (*tareik- hsan*)[II pt2: hke:/W]. The eight stages of hell are these: (i)hell(*naraka*), (ii)animals (*tiryañc*), (iii) hungry spirits (*preta=Peitta*), (iv)heaven of long life (*dirghāyur- dēva*), (v)remote places (*pratyata janapala*), (vi)the state of being blind or deal, etc. (*indriya- kalya*), (vii)secular prejudice (*mithyādarśana*), and (viii) the period of absence of the Buddha (*tathāgatā-nām anutpāda*). [See *Japan-English Buddhist Dictionary* 1991 (revised edition): 106, Daitō Shuppansha].

As to what it means to suffer in the hell as *Peitta*, two law tales are described as follows: "My Lords!, at that time, I was residing at the Keissakok mountain. When I descended from that Keissakok mountain, I saw a man traveling through the sky, carrying on his shoulder his own house together with a huge earthen jar (pot). He has to travel, he has to live in the same house, together incessantly followed him and pecked at him and ate his flesh. The man, in great pain, cried aloud. That man was a judge dispensing judgments in villages big and small, in this kingdom of Yezajyo. He used to pass judgments by forging (falsifying) documents. For that reason, he has to cry in pain. The judge who falsified the documents had to carry on his shoulders his own house together with the huge jar while he travels and had to live in the same house with huge jar. He has to cry in pain because cros, vultures, green pigeons and kites pecked at him and he had to cry in pain and suffer in the hell of *Peitta*.

There was a Brahmin who accepted bribe and let the one who should lose, win the case and let the one who should win, lose the case. Once, this Brahmin offered (donated) a ripe mango to a hermit (eremite). Because of this good deed he became an owner of a mango orchard near the Ganges River, with an area of three *yuzana* (*jojana*). Because of his misdeed of accepting bribe and passing the judgment unjustly, in the day time, the actual size of a needle hole. His complexion was as red as Pauk (Butea monosperma) and his finger and toe nails, he scratched at his own flesh and ate them. Because of the repeated scratching and eating his own flesh, his strength waned and his body was carried away by wind and during the day he had to suffer in hell as a *Peitta* and because of the result of his good deed of having offered a ripe mango, at night he was released from the hell of *Peitta* and enjoy the pleasure (luxury) of being entertained by the five musical instruments of nats such as si (drum), saung (harp), *nyin*: (a kind of wind instrument), etc. Such is the existence of a *Peitta*." [I pt.2. hke:/ W-hkaw: /W].

78. In regard to Ordeal by Water: "if the witnesses say that they would tell what they saw and heard, let them do so accordingly. They should not testify by Oath, by Scripture and by Lord Buddha. If the trial takes place during the age of pure breed of Brahmin, ascetic or *Zawgyi*, it is natural that they do not testify by Oath, by Scriptures and Lord Buddha. Such noble beings should testify by holding the object of their pledge and give oath. Sons and brothers of the emperor (king) descendants of former kings, sons and grandsons and lesser prices should be administered the ceremonial water of oath whatever arms they bear." [I pt.2: hkaw:/W-hkaw/W].

79. "Any statement given by them would be taken for granted as being true. Before giving a statement, a witness is required to take an oath according to his religion. Members of the royal family shall drink water from a cup in which weapons are immersed and declare that in the event of telling a lie, they shall be destroyed by the weapons" [Than Tun 1985: 35; also see I pt.2.: hkaw:/K].

80. It continues as follows: "the judges who pass judgments in such manners attain glory, have long life and became wealthy. After death, they would not go to the four nether

worlds. In the care of judges who fail to find the credible witness in deciding /alleged/ sexual crimes (*kama-gon*), physical assaults, murders and robberies which took place in forests, at night, or in secluded places should accept females or males who actually witnessed these /alleged/ witness or witnesses. The judges should consider carefully the credibility of such persons as witnesses just by their report that they had seen /the alleged crime/. /The judges/ should believe the testimony of witnesses of one party if they outnumbered those of the other side when both sides have managed to find witness /to support their claims/." [I pt.2.: hkan/K]

"If a person encountered /alleged/ crime /supposedly/ taken in a place, though he /said/ he had seen or heard such acts two or three times, /the judges/ should trust him only if he is a credible person, when he should be trusted. Even though he is the sole witness, /the judges/ should trust him only if he is a credible person. If it cannot be said that he is the sole witness, he should not be trusted. Even though the person is a male and has been a witness, /the judges/ should not trust him, if he is not credible. /On the other hand/ even a person is a female, /the Judges/ should trust her if she is credible. In their case of a unscrupulous person, let him take an oath in accordance with the requirements for his status. In the case of a Brahmin, let him also take an oath in accordance with the requirements for his status. In the same way, let a relative be a witness and let a comrade be a witness." [I pt. 2 hkan /K-hka/W].

81. "If /the judges/ get a good witness by cumulative result of past meritorious deeds (*hpon-kan a-lyaw-zwa*), it is a blessing. /The judges/ should believe the testimony of witnesses of one party if they outnumbered the witnesses of the other side. When witnesses of both parties have testimonies which have equal weight, /the judges/ should believe the testimony of the witness who has integrity and wisdom. When the testimony of the witnesses of both parties have the same weight and the witnesses among inferior, middle and superior classes [See F-78] have the same level of credibility and wisdom, let them go through /the ordeal of/ the depth of water (*ye net-ya la: jya ze*). If witnesses of one party give false testimonies the person will have bad consequences though both clans and the same level of witnesses from both side seems to have the equal weight, these false witnesses will go through eight calamities (or eight kinds of punishment, *Be Shit-pa*:*) and ten kinds of retribution (*Dan Hse-ba:***). Even after they die, they have to go to *Apay Le:-ba:*.* Even if they were set free from *Apay Le:-ba:* i.e. hell, animal, departed ghost and the host of *asura* demon, they shall die through starvation. When the sun rises, let /them/ face to the east and the east-north and take an oath. If it is not correct or they fail to do so, let /them/ to put the Letter of Oath on their heads and take an oath again. /The judges/ should ask witnesses individually. Only through this, any judges should pass judgment. If it is revealed that a witness of the winning party commits any particular crimes within seven days /after he took oath at the court/, then, let the winner lose and let the loser win because /the judges/ gave victory to due party in front of the statement of the witnesses. /The judges/ should give such witnesses the king's punishment (*Min:-dan*)

(See Footnote 82 as below).

"A large village should provide nine witnesses, a small village five and a hamlet three. Witnesses consist of nine members in a big village, five in a small village and three in a jungle. However, even if there is only one witness who is a man of wisdom and integrity (*Thamadi*), /the judges/ should his head shaven, blacken his face with ink, let him carry broken pots and go to his enemy's house to beg for food." [I pt.2.: hka/W:-hka:/K].

* It consists of calamities (*be:*) of (i)*Mi:* (fire), (ii)*Min:* (King), (iii)*Ye* (water), (iv) *Balu:* (ogre), (v)*Hko:-thu* (thief), (vi)*Yu:thaw-*(insanity), (vii)*Nu-thaw-*(leprosy), (viii)*Wek- yu: na thin. Thaw* - (epilepsy) [See Thein Hlaing 2000: 111; 2016: 127]

** They are these: (i)To be subject to severe pain, (ii)impoverishment, (iii)injury to the body (e.g.), loss of limbs, or (iv)serious illness (e.g. leprosy), or (v)lunacy, or (vi)misfortunes following the wrath of the king, or (vii)wrongful and serious accusations, or (viii)loss of relatives, (ix)destruction of wealth, or (x)the burning down of his houses by fire or by lighting. After the dissolution of his body, the fool will be reborn in the place of continuous suffering (*niraya*) [See *Dhammapada* trl. by Daw Mya Tin 1990: 52; also see TPTS trl. by K.R. Norman 1997: X (Violence: 21-22)

82. *Min:dan* is like this: "those contestants at the trials, who with the intention of tricking the judge and making him confused with changes in behaviour, facial expression, and bodily movement-sitting one moment and standing up the next, should be punished by whipping five lashes with a cane. Those contestants after saying that there were no other witnesses apart from the one whom they had brought into the court, should they bring a new witness after the sentence has passed they should be punished and made to parade through the streets of the villages. Should be the case won because the witness had testified according to what he had heard or seen, the contestant who won the case should give one tenth of the property he had gained to the witness. The reason why the witness should receive the one tenth of the property is because if the witness was not good, /the contestant/ could have been penalized. Therefore, the witness deserves the one tenth of what has been gained. On the other hand, if the witness had made a false statement because he was not able to know or see the truth, or failed to notice it, he is liable to face the eight calamities (or eight kinds of punishment, *Be Shit-pa:*) and receive the penalties (punishments). Besides he would have to suffer in the four hell. Therefore, he deserves to receive the one tenth of property gained by the contestant who won the case." [I pt.2.: hka/W-hka/K].

83. With regards to the false witnesses, should the damage be caused by (to) a small animal, seven houses to the east, seven houses to the west, seven houses to the south and seven houses to the north of the house of the witness should be destroyed. "Should the damage be caused by such animals as cows and buffaloes, ten houses to the east, ten houses to the west, ten houses to the south and ten houses to the north of the house of the witness should be destroyed. Should the damage be caused by a

horse, fifty houses to the east, fifty houses to the west, fifty houses to the south and fifty houses to the north of the house of the witness should be destroyed. Should the damage be caused by an elephant, five hundred houses to the east, five hundred houses to the west, five hundred houses to the south and five hundred houses to the north of the house of the witness should be destroyed. Should false witness uttered for the lay person, or for the sake of land and water (propert) for gold and silver, one thousand houses to the east one thousand houses to the west, one thousand houses to the south and one thousand houses to the north of the house of the false witness should be destroyed." Thus spoke Manu, the hermit. [I pt.2.: hkaw/K- hkan/ W–hkan /K].

84. "Whether any witness, or any judges, they have to be suffered by misfortune if they have mistaken because of fault" [I pt.2.: nga./W].
85. The *Dhammawilatha* (*Dhammavilasa*) *Dhammathat* in prose preserved at the National Library in Yangon (the copy-date of MS is unknown) also describes almost the same contents. The 1749 version of the *Dhammavilatha Dhammathat* in Nissaya style preserved at the British Library also describes the same kind of contents in brief [ki./W-K]. It is very possible that the author of the *MD* (1782 version) copied this part from that of the afore-mentioned either 1757 version or the date unknown *Dhammavilatha* in prose which seems likely to be later version of the *Dhammavilatha* (1749 version).
86. It is said that the Dhammathat is full of grace and great benefit (*goun-kyezu*:). [regarding(1)], the reason why the Dhammathat is like the hand of *Thija*: (*Dhaja:*) is :as *Thijya:-min:* (=*Dajyamin:*) could not be victorious against the *Athura* without using his weapon, the administrators, such as the king, the ministers, the judges and rulers [of territories], cannot settle a quarrel between both parties over a case without the Dhammathat. [In relation to the (2)], the reason why the Dhammathat is a *Manizota* gem, which can fulfill wishes, of the Universal Monarch is: as the Monarch could not fulfill the wishes [of others] without the *Manizota* gem, the king, the ministers, the rulers and the judges who carry their duties and administer the country like the Universal Monarch cannot pass the judgment in accordance with the wishes of both parties without the Dhammathat [I pt.3: ga./K].

[As to (3)], the reason why the Dhammathat is like the weapon of the king, the minster, the rulers and the judges is that [they] cannot carry out the duties of the country without the Dhammathat. [Regarding (4)], the reason why the Dhammathat is like [the carpenter's] ruling cord [planning the wooden surface] is: as any carpenter cannot get a straight line in something the surface of a wood plank without the ruling cord, the king, the ministers, the rulers and the judges who carry out the tasks of the country-just like the carpenter cannot make judgment without the Dhammathat truthfully for both parties of litigants who are like a curved surface. [In regard to (5)], the reason why the Dhammathat is like the introductory book for physician is: as a physician cannot cure various diseases in accordance with three seasons without introductory book, it would be impossible for the judges to pass judgments without the Dhammathat to extinguish the angers of both parties which resemble various diseases [I pt.2.: ga./W].

[As to (6)], the reason why the Dhammathat is the oil lamp which light the extremely dark building which is full of treasure is: as the officers in charge of treasuries cannot take gold, silver, other properties and precious gems to /appropriate/ places without the light of oil lamp, the king, the ministers, the rulers and the judges who carry out the task of the country like the officers in charge of treasuries cannot pass judgments without the Dhammathat to satisfy both parties of the litigants which resemble the inside of the dark building without the Dhammathat. [Relating to (7)], the reason why the Dhammathat is like the eye that can discern a good appearance from bad one is: as the blind man cannot discern a good appearance from bad one, the king, the ministers, the rulers and the judges who do not know law in carrying out their tasks cannot pass judgments without Dhammathat which is like the eye that can discern good appearance from the bad one, for both parties of litigants who resembles a good or bad appearances.

[In regard to (8)], the reason why the Dhammathat is like the ear that can distinguish the plesant sound from the unpleasant one is: as the deaf can not distinguish the pleasant sound from unpleasant one due to the lack of hearing (*thawta-pathada*), the king, the ministers, the rulers and the judges who carry their tasks of the country - like the deaf - can not pass judgments without the Dhammathat which resembles the ear that can discern the pleasant sound from the unpleasant one for both parties of the litigants without the Dhammathat which resembles the ear sense that can discern the pleasant sound from the unpleasant one [I pt.2. ga/K-gi/W].

[Regarding (9)], the reason why the Dhammathatis like the moon that makes the four islands bright at night is: as a very dark /place/ can not be illuminated without the moon light, the king, the ministers, the rulers and the judges in carrying their tasks like the darkness can not pass judgments clearly without the Dhammathat which resembles the moon that can light the four islands for both parties of the litigants who also resembles the darkness. [As to (10)], the reason why the sun that can light the four islands at day time and light going around there without knowing day and night, is: the king, the ministers, the rulers and the judges is carrying out their tasks – like the four islands – can not make judgments without the Dhammathat which is like a thousand rays of the sunlight for both litigants who are like the complete darkness and can not differentiate the day from the night [I pt.2.: gi/W].

[Relating to (11)], the reason why the Dhammathat is like the tusks of a full-grown male elephant that is fully endowed with ability and strength is: a full - grown male elephant that is fully endowed with ability and strength- without its tusks - is not capable of obtaining the victory in battle or of dominating the other /rival/ elephants /in his group/, the king, the ministers, the rulers and the judges in carrying out their tasks - like a full - grown male elephant that is fully endowed with ability and strength – can not pass judgments without the Dhammathat which resembles the tusks of a full – grown male elephant for both parties of the litigants who are like the battle [I pt.2.: gi/K; see also translation of Than Tun 1985: 38-39].

[As to (12)], the reason why the Dhammathat is like the milk of mother is: as any mothers can not stop the baby crying without milkj, the king, the ministers, the rulers and the judges in carrying out their tasks –like the mother's milk – can not pass judgements peacefully without the Dhammathat which resembles the milk of mothers for both parties of the litigants who resemble the baby crying fiercely [I pt.2: gi/K].

[Chapter X]
87. It is said that King Alaunghpaya was a decorous as well as capable man, and he was portrayed as "vengeful exuberantly self-adulatory, shrewd but unsophisticated and direct" He is said to have been a man of inexhaustible energy [See Lieberman 1984: 234].
88. It has been pointed by a scholar that speculation on the origin of the state in the *Mahābhārata,* the great epic poem of the Hindus, and the *Dīigha-nikāya* from the *Sutta-pitaka* showed a marked similarity [See Altekar1984: 26-31]. Kautilia also refers to the process of the origin of the state and to the fact that people themselves elected Manu as their king and agreed to pay him the necessary taxes [R.P. Kangle pt.2: 28].
89. It is included in the *Dīigha-nikāya* of the Sutta Pitaka.
90. Such Pāli Canons as *Vidhurapandita-Jātaka* [No.545] and the *Mahā-Ummaga* (or *Mahosadha)-Jataka* [No.546].
91. It is said that the King Wagaru's *Manu Dhammasattham* in Pāli was translated into Myanmar by the jurist Buddhagotha (Buddhagosa) [See Furnivall 1940: 356].
92. The British Library has preserved a palm-leaf manuscript of *Dhammavilatha Dhammathat* transcribed in 111M.E.(=1749A.D.) which seems to be related to twelfth century work originally by Thalaing monk named Thariputta (=Sariputta) who was given a title of Dhammavilatha. The 1749 version of the *Dhammavilatha* is written in the style of *neiktaya* (=*nissaya*) or Pāli-Myanmar literary translation with Rakhine script. Professor Aye Chan, a Myanmar historian, told us that it was written in Rakhine language. On the other hand, the National Library in Yangon possesses a manuscript of the *Dhammavilatha Dhammathat,* the copy-date of which is not found probably due to incomplete set. This version is almost all written in plain Myanmar prose. In addition, 1757 and 1785 versions of the *Dhammavilatha Dhammathat* which are preserved at UCL (Universities Central Library, Yangon) are also written in Pāli-Myanmar prose. We may conjecture that there was a sort of "Local-ization" movement of Pāli legal literature in the early Konbaung period.

[Chapter XI]
93. "Such places as in a house, near a market, in the far distance, under the root of a tree or bamboo, in a monastery crossing the public rest house and edifice to a pagoda"

94. "If the case is the sale of a slave, the relevant period is not ten days, but seven days. If the slave absconds within seven days the seller must return the price" [Shwe Bo 1955: 192; DWD 1757: gaw/W].
   "If he attempts to return it after ten days without having signified his disapproval during the period he shall be punished. The reason is that he should have made up his mind within ten days whether he would keep or return the object he had purchased" [Shwe Bo *ibid*.: 192; DWD 1757: gaw/W].
95. Explanation on these vocabularies are made in the following (3). Similar cases are seen in the other Dhammathats:
   "An exception is made if the slaves Talaing, Kachin or any other non-Burmese race, the vendor is not liable if such a slave runs away even on the day of the sale transaction" [*Manu Kyet-yo* 1762: hgu/W, see also DWD1757: hgaw/W]
96. Prof. Than Tun explains as follows: "in the sale of a prisoner of war as slave, the former owner would not be held responsible if the slave escaped even on the very day of sale, because it is a known fact that such prisoner of war are always trying to escape" [Than Tun 1985: 40].
97. Under Myanmar law, "he need only to take back the article and return the price paid to the purchaser" [Shwe Bo 1955: 193].
98. These are: (i) to give alms, (ii)to speak words that are loving and sweet, (iii) to work for the benefit, and (iv)to be considerate and fair in punishment.
99. In other words, seven ways not to make things worse which enables the state to develop prosperously. These are: (the king should) (i)hold meetings and consult with his royal counselors three times a day, (ii)tackle affairs with the application of consistent rules, (iii)collect only those taxes and impose only those punishments which tradition allows, (iv)respect and cherish the elderly, (v)govern his subjects paternalistically, without oppression, (vi)make the usual offerings to Nats who watch over the capital city and the rest of the kingdom, and (vii)provide for monastic community.
100. As far as we surveyed, it seems to be the first time that the relationship between the Kingship and Sangha is clearly described in the Dhammathat literature.
101. See Chapter I 4 and Table 2.
102. "Land marks are necessary to the identification of land in proof of ownership. They are the sentinels of property in land and regarded with a kind of sanctity. In the absence of land marks a person is liable to lose his claim to the land. Permanent objects such as Banyan trees, boundary walls, lakes, rivers, hills, drains, and articles not affected by wind and weather, such as bones of cattle, charcoal, pieces of pottery, rock, sand, etc. are used as land marks" [Shwe Bo *ibid*.: 293; DWD 1757: gan/W also see *Wagaru* Chapter XVII s171: 43/38].
103. A state of punishment, of which there are four: (i)*Ngayè* (hell), (ii)*Tareikhsan* (animal), (iii)*Balu:* (departed human or celestial being reincarnated as a ghost, ghoul, goblin, etc, and (iv)*Athurakay* (a fallen Nat who banished from the celestial regions).

104. See also DWD [1757: gha./W.]
105. This clause seems to be incomplete or confused, considering 1757, the unknown dated version, 1785 of the *Dhammavilatha Dhammathat* and *Manu kyeyo Dhamma that*.
106. See DWD [1757: gha/W], *Manu-Kyetyo* [1762: ghaw/W].
107. See also DWD [1757: gha./K], *Manu Kyet-yo* [1762: hke:/W?], *Mawhawishsedani (Mohavicchedani)* [hke:/W].
108. See also DWD [1757: gha. /K] , *Manu Kyetyo*.[1762: ghaw/W].
109. See also DWD [1757: gha /W], *Manu Kyetyo* [1762: ghaw/K]
110. See also DWD [1757: gha/W], *Manu Kyetyo* [1762: ghan/W]
111. DWD [1757 ghi./W], *Manu-Kyetyo* [ghan/K]
112. See also DWD [1757: gha. /K-ghi./W], *Manu Kyetyo* [1762: gha:/W]
113. See also DWD [1757: ghi./K], *Manu Kyetyo* [1762: gha:/K].
114. In this regard, Shwe Baw described as follows referring to the *Dhammavilatha Dhammathat*.: "The Dhammathats take the view that the reputation of a man of high class suffers no detriment if the woman alleged to have been involved in the affair belongs to his own class or to the middle class. On the other hand, if the accusation is that he has had an intrigue with a woman of low class or a slave, the offender is liable to pay compensation or be sold as a slave" [Shwe Baw *ibid.*: 484 DWD [1757: ghi./W]].
115. 'The total number of verdicts (*si-yin*) numbered six hundred and ten', but these are all from the eighteen roots (*Amit Tit-se Shit hkan*:) [See 1782MS: mi./K].
116. The descriptions about various information on "Gold" are included in both the books called "*Yapahtaik Kyan*" and "*Lawka Dipani Kyan*" [See *MD* (1782 MS: me/W]
117. These are Myanmar units of weight [See JBED 1966]: tical - equal to *kyat* which is a weight equal to four *mat*s. [p.210] *Mu* - a weight of which there are two kinds, the great and the small;the big *mu* is equal to two big *pe*s, or one eight of a *kyat*. [p.764] *Pe* is a weight equal to six or eight seeds of the *Abrus precatorius* (*hkyin ywe*) [p.646] *Ywe-kyi*: a kind of tree, of which there are two varieties: the *Adenanthera pavomina*; the seed of said plant used as a weight, one being equal to two of the *Abrus precatorius*: four make a great *pe*, three a small *pe*; there are one hundred and twenty *ywe*'s weight of gold in one rupee's (*kyat*'s) weight. [p.864]. In relation to some Myanmar vocabularies such as *hsan*- husked rice; *hnan*- the sesamum;*than uhkaung*- head of a louse; *kanit*- a Stylus; *kanyit-che* – an iron style.
118, 119, 120, 121. According to JBDE, *Padetharit* is a soverign of a division of one of the four grand islands [p.616]; *Egayit* is a soverign of one of the four grand islands [p.616]; *Dipayit* is the soverign of a continent or great islands [p.545]; *Sekkya-wademin* is a universal monarch [p.616] *Mandat* is a large shed or booth, a building created for a temporary use, as for the performance of a *Zat* (drama) or *Yotthe-pwe* (puppet show) or for a feast [See JBED: 742]
122. The English translation for *tahse-chauk yat thaw: aut-me. kyin:* in Myanmar shall

correspond to " remorse and regret for the loss of sixteen kinds of occurrence".
123. See Footnote 74.

[Chapter XII]
124. Why was the number of the thirty rules selected? Is there any relation between these thirty rules and the thirty major branches mentioned in *Manuyin Dhammathat* [*Manuyin* 1878: 2]
125. Out of these items, No.5 includes such a new case of an pregnant animate that seems not to have been dealt with in any former Dhammathats.
126. It is not probable that such customary rules would not have been discussed at the Hluttaw or Council of Ministers. We should also trace the *Thekkayit* ("Dated documents") and study them [See Chapter II d.].
127. The records which belongs to the crown by tradition or palace chronicles.
128. Furnivall says: "There is also still extant a version known as the *Dhammavilasa* [*Dhammawilatha*], which purports, according to copy in the British Museum, to have been compiled in 1637 by a monk of that name. This *Dhammathat* seems to be the 1749 version of the *Dhammavilatha*" [Furnivall 1940: 355].
129. This is confirmed by Dr. Aye Chan, a Rakhine historian, to whom I owe much for better understanding of the 1749 version of the *Dhammawilatha Dhammathat* written in Rakhine script. It was copied at the end of the Taungu period. It is not impossible that it was kept in the capital city of Danyawaddy Kingdom for Rakhine people and was taken away to the Great Britain under its British colony. It seems unlikely that it was kept in the capital city of Ava due to annihilation by the attack of the Mon rebellions.
130. "If no such marks have been placed, then the head of the village, the priest, and the Brahmins shall settle the limits of such land. Any land whose boundaries are not fixed by the above mentioned marks shall not be deemed to possess any boundary marks" [*Wagaru ibid.*]
131. In regard to abusive language, RMD refers to altogether twenty-eight kinds, such as calling another a witch; a murder;thief; adulterer; degraded; blind; deaf; weak in body; bow-legged, etc. [RMD VII s.6: 1896: 186]
132. P.10, *Collins English Dictionary* (1995, reprint of Third edition in 1994) Harper Collins Publisher.
133. This is not the case of abusive language. It is, therefore, that the accused Nga Pu is not liable to a guilty, but all the court fee should be paid by Nga Pu to Nga Pathi. The rules directed against witches reflect the superstitious belief of the people. The Dhammathats mention as many as sixty-six kinds of witches [*Atthanhkiep-wunnana* s.30].
134. A person who seizes a woman and throws her into the water, believing that she is a witch, shall pay a fine of one hundred ticals, if she sinks and does not float. The reason for this is that although not a witch, she has been publicly put to disgrace. If

she floats, there shall be no fine. Because floating is a proof that she is a witch" [DWD1757: ghi./K]
135. These are: (1)Lands given to pagodas or convent; (2)Slaves given to pagodas, temples; (3)The boundary marks between cities and villages, and (4) A slave who has descended in the family from the fore-fathers of the owner, and whose class is unknown [(R)MD1847: 69-70]
136. These are: (1)An owner of lands, dry or wet, permitting another person to cultivate them for ten years, of which there is evidence; (2)Money lent, and not demanded for ten years, though living in the same village or district with the debtor seeing and knowing that he is there; (3)A salve bought of a known class living for ten years in the same village or district with his master, without being employed; or head-man, which may have been discontinued; (5)The masters connected with inheritance [(R)1847: 70].
137. The nine precious stones ie ruby, pearl, coral, emerald, topaz, diamond, sapphire, garnet and cat's eye [MED 1993: 221].
138. *Zawgyi* is 'a Alchemist who possesses super natural powers' [MED: 150].
139. No such twenty places are described in detail in the *MD* (1782MS).
140. According to PTS (p.60), this is compiled by Pahtugyi Thingayaza during the reign of Tadominbya, the founder of the first Ava dynasty in 1364A.D.. In regard to '*Hayapakaik*? (or *Tayapataik*?), some part of the alphabets are not clear in the original palm-leaf manuscript and even though its spelling is correct, we have not confirmed yet about what kind of literary [Chapter XIII] work is it and who is the author ?

[Chapter XIII]
141. We only rely on the description in *Thathana Lingaya Sadan* ("History of Theravāda Buddhism in Myanmar") [See TLS 1956: 58].
142. These law books are: such Dhammathat as *Balabhodana;, Dhamma-Wineikhsaya (Vinicchaya), Pakinaka, Wineikhsaya (Vinicchaya), Wineikhsaya Pakathani-linga (Vinicchaya-pakasaani-lanka); Thekugaykyin-hsayadaw, Thankeip Wineikhsaya (Sankhepa–vinicchaya)* and such *Hpyathton* as *Zonda-hsayadaw, Talwinpyu, Yezajyo Hkondaw*. [See Forchhammer 1885: 108].
143. King Badon reformed the Sangha Order. He appointed four senior monks and later added other eight junior monks. In other words, he created eight posts to help the first great elders. Thus he newly established the council of the Sangha Order in 1148M.E. (=1786A,D,) [See TLS 1956: 196-198]
144. King Badon wanted the view of U Po U, his learned minister on such King's idea that the Buddhist Canon should be set to fire if monks were not well versed in them [UPUS Vol. I 1968: 262].
145. King Badon also encouraged all the people to study Pāli Canon, particularly Jātakas [See Than Tun (ROB V): 61] and he was doubtful of the authenticity of the so-called Pāli Original Texts which were prevailing at that time and therefore, requested the

educated monks and laymen to rewrite them without failure [AHP: 678].
146. U Po U encouraged King Badon to dispatched his army to Thai [UPUS: 5-6].
147. According to the suggestion of Maung Htaung Hsayadaw, King Badon dispatched a study mission including ten Brahmins to get copies of treatises on worldly affairs from Calcutta [TAS 1976: hka].
148. Three Qualities of a King are: (1)To deliberate everything with wise men, (2)To collect provisions, arms and soldiers, and (3)To punish or reward without favouritism [See Than Tun 1983: 199].
149. In regard to Four Samgha Law, see Footnote 42.
150. Five forms of Strength are: (1)Military strength, (2)Economic strength, (3)Many officers of intelligence, (4)Strength in lineage and (5)Strength in wisdom [See Than Tun *ibid.*: 199].
151. Six qualities of a Leader are: (1)Patience, (2)Vigilance, (3)Energy, (4)Distribution, (5)Compassion and (6)Foresight [Than Tun *ibid.*: 199].
152. In regard to Seven Factors to Maintain Prosperity, see Chapter IX 1.a.5.
153. Eight Gratitude of a King are these: (1)Royal parents, (2)Queen, Concubines and their Children, (3)All members of the Royal families, (4)All warriors, (5)Rural population, (6)Frontier people, (7)Holy men and (8)All animals [See Than Tun *ibid.*: 199].
154. Nine Gems are these: (1) Ministers, (2)Holy men, (3)Astrologers, (4)Spies, (5) Members of the Royal families, (6)Daughters of every household, (7)Rich men, Traders and Farmers, (8)Warriors and (9)Producers of Arms and ammunition [Than Tun *ibid.*: 199].
155. Ten Rules (to be observed by) Universal Monarch *Sekkya-wade-min* (=*Cakkavattin*) are these: (1)To give enough provisions to the retinue, (2)To subsidize vassals who are crowned kings in their own principalities, (3)To give allowance to vassals who have to reside at the capital city of the Universal Monarch, (4)To give provisions to Brahmin, (5)To give loans to farmers, (6)To give provisions to Holy men, (7)To recognize sanctuaries for safety of wild animals, (8)To forbid all misconduct, (9)To give charity to the poor and (10)To seek advice from the Holy men [Than Tun *ibid.*: 200].
156. Twelve Means for Military Success are: (1)Wise strategy, (2)Unity of king and ministers, (3)Regular reinforcement, (4)Absolute control by the Commander—in-chief, (5)Numerous heroes, (6)Good *Yatra* ("a magical contrivance) and Mantra ("Charm"), (7)Good luck, (8)Ample food supply, (9)Free from epidemics, (10)Good spies, (11)Offering to gods and (12)Good horses, elephants, etc. [Than Tun *ibid.*: 200].
157. See HNY I: 11-18.
158. See also *MD* (Richardson's text; 1760MS): 148&154.

[Chapter XIV]
159. It is linked with a legal maxim as '*kyi thaw ahmu. go nge aung, nge thaw ahmu. go pa-*

pyauk aung (or) *pa lat se'* ("Mitigate the big affairs and nullify the small affairs")

160. *ex-parte* = A latin word which means 'from one side (only)'.
161. Symes says: The "Birmans being governed by the same authority, observes nearly similar form; but as knowledge increase, and mankind become more enlightened, these absurd practices lost ground, and have of late years been discountenanced by the judicial courts both of India and Ava" [Symes 1800: 468].
162. E Maung explain in Latin as *Scandalum magunatum* which means 'slander of magnate'.
163. It is generally accepted that the *Muddha-beiktheik* ceremony was performed by King Badon twice during in his reign. It is not unlikely that he performed it five times considering his long reign, but no further information is found yet.
164. *Yezajyo Hkondaw Hpyathton* is included as *Yezajyo Hkondaw Kauk-hcet-su* in 'List of the hand-written and palm-leaf manuscripts from the collection of Kinwun Mingyi' at the National Library in Yangon.

References

A. Bibliographical Guide to Myanmar (in chronological order of publication date)

1. General

Ashton, Stephen R. 1985. *Source for Burma*. London: India Office Records.

Asian Research Trends. No.1 (1991) & No.4 (1994). Tokyo: The Centre for East Asian Cultural Studies for Unesco, Tokyo: The Toyo Bunko.

Aung-Thwin, Michael. 1979. *Burma* (Southeast Asian Tools). Southeast Asian Paper No. 16, Part III, Southeast Asian Studies, Asian Studies Program. Hawaii: University of Hawaii.

Barnett, L.D. 1913. *A Catalogue of the Burmese Books in the British Museum* [BUR PBS 1 & 2]. London.

Bečka, Jan. 1995. *Historical Dictionary of Myanmar* (Asia Historical Dictionaries, No.15), Metuchen, N.J. & London: The Scarecrow Press.

Bechert, Heinz, Daw Khin Khin Su and Daw Tin Tin Myint. 1979. *Burmese Manuscripts* Part I, Stuttgart: Franz Steiner, Verzeichnis der Orientalischen, Handschriften in Deutschland.

Bechert, Heinz, ed. (Assisted by A, Peters). 1996-2000. *Burmese Manuscripts*. Part III-IV, Stuttgart: Franz Steiner, Verzeichnis der Orientalischen, Handschriften in Deutschland.

Bernot, Denise. 1968. *Bibliographie Birmane Annees 1950-60*. Paris: Editions du Centre National de la Recherche Scientifique.

Blackmore, Thaung. 1985. *Catalogue of the Burney Parabaiks in the India Office Library*. London: The British Library.

Biruma Kenkyuu Guruupu. *Biruma Kankei Hogo Bunken no Kaidai oyobi Mokuroku* ("Burmese Studies in Japan 1868-1985 Literary Guide and Bibliography") Edited by the Burma Research Group). 1985. Tokyo: The Burma Research Group.

Cady, John F. 1983. *Contact with Burma 1935-1949*: A Personal Account, Athens (Ohaio): Ohio University Center for International Studies Southeast Asian Program.

Desai, W.S. 1988. *Burmese MSS in the Royal Asiatic Society Library*. Sir WILLIAM JONES-BICENTENARY OF HIS BIRTH Commemoration Volume 1746-1946, Calcutta: Royal Asiatic Society of Bengal.

Frank N. Trager and John N. Musgrave. 1956. *Annotated Bibliography of Burma*. New Haven: Burma Research Project, New York University.

Griffin, Andrew. 1979. *A Brief Guide to Sources for the Study of Burma in the India Office*

Records. London:India Office Library and Records.
Herbert, M. Patricia & Anthoney, C. Milver. *South-East Asia languages and literatures: a selected guide*. 1988. Scotland: Kiscadale/ 1989 Honolulu: University of Hawaii Press.
Herbert, Patricia. 1991. *Burma* (World Bibliographical Series) Vol.132, Oxford: Clio Press.
Hibler, Anita & Tuchrello, William P. 1986, *Burma – A Selecitive Guide to Scholarly Resources*, Washington D. C.: Asia Program. The Wilson Center; Asian Division, The Library of Congress.
Hla Pe. 1985. *Burma*, Singapore: Institute of Southeast Asian Studies.
Hsaya U Hpye. *Yangon Myo Bana (d)Pitakat-taik Let-ye-sa Pe-sa Sa-yin hnit Kin-wun Mingyi htan hma ya shi thi Let-ye-sa Pe-sa Sa-yin* ("The list of the manuscripts of Yangon Barnard Free Library and the lisy of the manuscripts of the collection of Kinwun Mingyi). 1906. Yangon: Pitakat Printing Press.
Kenneth Whitbread. 1969, *Catalogue of Burmese Printed Books in the India Office Library*, London: Her Majesty's Stationary Office.
List of Microfilm deposited in The Centre for East Asian Cultural Studies (Part 8-Burma). 1976. [LMD(B)] Tokyo: The Centre for East Asian Cultural Studies (c/oToyo Bunko). [See also Thu Nandar. *The Catalogue of Materials on Myanmar History in Microfilms*, Vol. I (2004) & Vol.II (2005). Tokyo: The Centre for Documentation & Area-Transcultural Studies, Tokyo University of Foreign Studies.]
Pearson, JD. *A Guide to Manuscripts and Documents in the British Isles relating to South and Southeast Asia*. Vol. I: London (1989); British Isles (excluding London) (1990), London: Mansell Publishing Limited.
Pe Maung Tin. 1924. *Burma Manuscript Catalogue in the British Library* [ORC BUR MSS 1 & 2]. *JBRS*, Vol.14-pt.3: 221-246. School of Oriental and African Studies. 1963 *University of London Library Catalogue*, Vol.22 (Catalogue and Microfilms), Boston.
Pruitt, William & Bischoff, Roger. *Catalogue of the Burmese – Pāli and Burmese Manuscripts*. 1998. London: The William Institute for the History of Medicine.
Pugh, RB. *A Reviewed and Expanded Version of Public Record Office Handbook No.3: Records of the Colonial and Dominions Offices*. (n.d) London: Public Record Office.
Shulman, Frank Joseph. 1986. Burma- *An Annotated Bibliographical Guide to International Research 1878-1985*. Asian Program. The Wilson Center, Lanham: University Press of America.
Tan Sok Joo. 1979. *Survey of Library Resources on Burma in Singapore*. Singapore: Institute of Southeast Asian Studies.
The Bernard Free Library Catalogue. 1903. Rangoon: Office of the Superintendent Government Printing.
Thiri Maha Zeyathu. *Kawi Lekhkana Dipani*. from Kawi Lekhkana Thoun-kyan-twe by U Hsaya Htun 1965 (2nd impression) Mandalay: Kawi Lekhkana Bookshop.
Tin Tin Myint and Heinz Braun. 1985. *Burmese Manuscripts*. Vancouver: Department of Asian Studies, University of British Columbia.
Trager, Frank N. 1973. *Burma – A Selected and Annotated Bibliography*. New Haven:

Human Relations Area Files Press.

Thurston, Anne. (n.d.) *Sources for Colonial Studies in the Public Record Office*. London: Public Record Office.

Wainwright, M.D. & Matthus, Noel. 1965. *A Guide to Western Manuscripts and Documents in the British Isles Relating to South and Southeast Asia*. London: Oxford University Press.

Yi Yi. 1965. Burmese Sources for the History of Konbaung Period 1752-1885. *Journal of the Southeast Asian History*, Vol.6-pt.1, pp.48-66. Deutschland.

2. Law

Aung Than Tun. 2009. *Kinwun Mingyi and Dhammathats*. Yangon: The Tun Foundation Bank Literary Committee.

Gledhill, Alan. 1970. *Burma-Bibriographical Introduction to Legal History and Ethnology E/7* edited by John Gillissen, Bruxelles: Editions de l'institut de Sociologie, Universite Libre de Bruxelles.

Ishii, Yoneo. 1978. *A preliminary Bibliography for the Study of Customary Laws of Southeast Asia and Taiwan*, Osaka: Kokuritsu Minzokugaku Hakubutsukan (Osaka Museum for Ethnology).

Sa-kyi-taik shi. Dhammathat Pe-hmu Sayin ("List of the Dhammathats"). 1983. Yangon: Universities Central Library.

Tin Tin Win, Ma. *Myanmar Dhammathat hnit Hpyathton hsain-ya Sasu Sayin* ("Bibliographical Guide to the Palm-leaf Manuscripts related to the Myanmar Dhammathat and Hpyathton"). 1983. Yangon: Sa-kyi-taik Pinnya-htana, Yangon Tekkado (department of Library Education, Univwersity of Yangon)

Tin Maung Cho. 1989 (December). *Dhammathat Sayin* ("List of the *Dhammathat*") Yangon: Universities Central Library.

B. Myanmar Sources

1. Inscription, Chronicles and other historical documents

Alaung Minthaya Ameindaw-mya [AMA] (eidited by Khin Khin Sein). 1964. Yangon: Myanmar Naing-gan Thamaing Kawmashin (Mynmar Historical Commission).

Alaunghpaya Ayedawbon by Letwe Nawyatha (pp.1-152); by Thwin Thin Taik-wun (pp.153-233) [AAT], edited by U Tin Hla. 1961. Yangon: Yinkye-hmu Wungyi-htana & Shehaung Thutethana Hnyun-kya-ye -wun-youn (Ministry of Culture and the Department of Archaeology.

Ame-daw-hpye [AHP] by the First Maung Htaung Hsayadaw. 1961. Mandalay: Padetha Pitaka Printing Press.

Badon Min Ayu Wada ("King Badon's Idea"). [LMD=CEACS(B), 1976 Reel No.32-3]

Badon Min Let-swè ("King Badon's Manual") [LMD-CEACS(B), 1976 Reel No.95-7]

Bagyidaw Hpaya Beiktheik Hkan Sadan-1185 hku ("Record of King Bagyidaw's Beiktheik

References

Ceremony 1185 M.E.) [LMD-CEACS(B), 1976 Reel No.44-7]

Bama-pyi Hnit-paung Hnit-ya Hmattan-gyi. 1969. eidited by Kanbawza Myint Lwin.

Burmese Sit-tans 1764-1826 Record of Rural Life and Administration, edited by Frank N. Trager and William Koenig. 1979. Tucson: The University of Arizona Press.

Epigraphia Birmanica [Ep.Birm], English translation of Mon Inscription, eidited by the Director. Archaeological Survey of Burma. Vol. I pt.-i & ii (1919) [1960 reprint], Vol.I pt.I & ii (1920) [1961 & 1962 respectively]. Rangoon: Government Printing Office.

Hkithaung Myanmar Thamaing Thutethana Abeikdan by U Thein Hlaing. 2000. Yangon: Universities Historical Research Centre. [See English version 2016]

Hmannan Mahayazawin-gyi [HMY], Vol.I(1963); Vol.II(1954); Vol.III(1955). Mandalay: Mya Zaw Printing Press.

Hman She Tak Hswe-daw Zin [HSTH], photo-copy of the manuscript of 1225M.E. (=1893A.D.), edited by U Maung Maung Tin. 1976. Yangon: Tekkadho Poun-hneik-taik (the University Press).

Hluttaw Hmat-tan ("Records of the Council of Ministers") by Taw Sein Hko. 1960. (reprint). Yangon: Government Printing.

Hsinbyushin Min-taya Abhitheik Sadan ("Record of Hsinbyushin's Consecration Ceremony") (Palm-leaf MS) [LMD-CEACS(B)1976 Reel No.95-2]

Htun Yi (ed.) 2009: *Konbaung-hkit Muddha-beiktheik Hkan-yu-pon* ("Collection of *Muddha-beiktheik* Consecration Ceremonies of Konabug dynasty"), Yangon: Yapyi Saok-hsaing).

Kalyani Inscription (1476). 1892. The Text and Translation. Rangoon: Government Printing.

Konbaungzet Mahayazawin-daw-gyi [KBZ], edited by U Maung Maung Tin. Vol.I/Vol. II(1967); Vol.III(1968). Yangon: Ledi Mandaing Press.

Konbaung Pyi Yazawin. (the copy date of the manuscript is unknown), the typed copy (1966). Yangon.

Konbaung Sha-poun-daw (edited by Nyo Mya). 1997. Yangon: Myawaddy Sape Taik.

Lawka Byuha Kyan (Inyoun Sadan). 1968 (Third edition), edited by U Hpo Lat. Yangon: Baho Printing.

Letwè Nawyatha i Muddha-beiktheik-hkan Ahkan-ana hnit Parabaik-pon-mya [LMBM], (the copy date of the manuscript is unknown), edited by Shehaung Sape Thutethi Tayauk. Yangon: Myanmar-hmu-beikman Sape-ban.

MahaThiri Zeyathu. 1885. *Pitaka Thamaing Sadan* [PTS]. Yangon.

Mahayazawin-gyi by U Kala [MY], edited by Hsaya Pwa. Vol.I (1960); Vol.II (1961); Vol. III (1961). Yangon: Hanthawaddy Pitakat Press.

Mandalay Myo-thi Nan-thi Sadan, edited by Sithu Maung Maung Kyaw. 1959. Mandalay: Yadanadipan Printing House.

Mandalay Yadanaboun Mahayazawin-daw-gyi by Kanni-myo Sit-ke Minhtin Yaza, edited by U Maung Maung Tin. 1969. Mandalay: Tet Ne Lin Printing House.

Myanmar Mingala Minhkan-daw. 1905. Mandalay: The Star of Burma.
Myanmar Maha Mingala Minhkan-daw, eidited by U Ya Kyaw. 1968. Yangon: Pinnya Saouk-taik.
Myanmar Min Okchok-pon Sadan [MMOS], edited by U Tin, pt.I & II (1965), III (1970), IV (n.d.) & V (1983). Yangon: Yinkye-hmu Htana (Ministry of Culture) [Tsl. By Euan Bagshaw under the title of "The Administration by U Tin in 2001", Bangkok: Ava Publishing House]
Myanmar-sa Nyun-baung Kyan [MSHB]. Vol.I (1990), edited by U Myint Kyi, Yangon: Sape-Beikman.
Myanmar Sweson-kyan ("Encyclopaedia of Burma") [MSK] Vol.II (1955), VIII (1963), Yangon: Sape-Beikman.
Myanmar Thu-yè Gaung, edited by U Thein Maung. 1966. Yangon: Zwe Sa Poun- hneiktaik.
Nan-sin Poksa (Alaunghpaya Ame Atula Thathanabaing Ahpye in 1115 M.E.=1753 A.D.), the typed copy of palm-leaf manuscript 1219M.E.. 1967. Yangon: Ministry of Trade.
Shwebo-myo-nay Mahananda-kan Kyauksa-mya [SMKKS] (Handwriting copy) possessed by Dr. Than Tun.
Shwe-nan Thon Wohara Abeikdan ("Dictionary used in the Palace"), edited by U maung Maung Tin. 1975. Yangon: Department of religious Affairs.
Shwebon Nidan by Jeya Thingaya.1963 (Third edition). Yangon: Hanthawaddy Press.
Than Tun. 1983. The Royal Order (Wednesday 28, January 1795) of King Badon, *Journal of Asian and African Studies,* No.26, Tokyo: Institute of Asian and African Studies, Tokyo University of Foreign Studies.
Thathana Lingaya Sadan [TLS] ("History of the Theravāda Buddhism in Myanmar"). 1956. Yangon: Hanthawaddy Pitakat Printing Press.
Thekkata Abhitheka Sadan [TAS], Palm-leaf manuscript, the copy-date unknown (the original in 1144 M.E.(=1782A.D.) included in HSTH. Yangon.
The Royal orders of Burma [ROB], pt.I-IX (1598-1885)+pt.X (Index), eidited by Than Tun. 1983-1990. Kyoto: The Center for Southeast Asian Studies, Kyoto University.
Thwinthin-Myanmar Yazawin-thit ["The New Myanmar Chronicle by Thwinthin"] by Thwinthin-taik Wun Mahasithu"], Vol.(1968), Yangon: Mingala Printing House.
U Po U Shauk-hton [UPUS], Vol.I & II (1968). Mandalay: Pitakat-taw Pyan-pwa-ye Press.
Yadanathihka Konbaung Maha Yazawin Akyin [YKM] by Naga Bo Hteik Tin Htwe. 1967 (2nd edition). Yangon: Pounnya Saouk-taik.
Yadanatheigha Myo Ti Sadan (the copy-date of the manuscript is unknown), hand-writing copy by U Taung (Ye-U).
Yazawwada. (n.d.), printed from a palm-leaf manuscript preserved at Barnard Free Library (present The national Library).
Yi Yi. 1961. Konbaung-hkit Yazawin hsaing-ya Ahtauk-ahta-mya ("Proof relating to the History in Konbaung Period"). *Journal of the Burma Resaerch Society (JBRS)*XLIV(ii): 249-296.

—. 1966. Konbaung-hkit Sittan-mya, *JBRS*, XLIX(i): 71-127.

—. 1979. Additional Burmese Historical Sources 1752-1776. *Nainggan Thamaing Thutethana Sasaung* (Research in Burmese History) No.3: 65-75.

2. Legal sources

Atula Dhammathat Hpyathton [ADP] by Atula Hsayadaw in 1145 ME (=AD1783). Typed copy of the palm-leaf manuscript of 1211ME.= AD1849.). 1966, Yangon.

Dhammathat Kuncha. The manuscript of 1238 ME (=AD1776). Yangon: National Library.

Dhammawilatha (Dhammavilasa) [DWD]. (i)the palm-leaf manuscript of 1111ME. (=AD1749). The British Library in London; (ii)the palm-leaf manuscripts of 1119ME (=AD1757) [UCL No.7490]/1147ME (=AD1785 [UCL No.9926]/ 1212ME (=AD1850). The Universities Central Library in Yangon, (iii)the palm-leaf manuscript (the copy-date is unknown), The National Library in Yangon.

Gandhi Dhammathat. (the copy-date of the palm-leaf manuscript is unknown). Yangon: The national Library.

Gaung, U (ex-Kinwun Mingyi). *Thonze-chauk Saung-dwè Ahme-hmu-gan Dhammathat* (1897) [TCD] and *Thonze-le: Zaung-dwè Ein-hmu-gan Dhamma- that* (1899), Yangon: Government Printing [Translation of these two volumes are: Vol.I *A Digest of the Burmese Buddhist Law concerning Inheritance, being the collection of texts from Thirty-six Dhammathats* (1903) and Vol.II *A Digest of the Burmese Buddhist Law concerning Marriage, being the collection of texts from Thirty-four Dhammathats* (1909) <DIGEST>. Yangon: Government Printing].

—. 1841. *Atthasankhepe Wunna–kyan* [AWD], Yangon: Government Printing (also in 1882. *Atthasankhepa Wunna Dhammathat*, Yangon: Government Printing. Also printed in Mandalay in 1882 and the extract version on Inheritance in 1963).

Kaingza Manuyaza. (i)*Kaingza Manuyaza Hpyathton (=Mahayazathat)* [MYK], Hand-writing copy of the palm-leaf manuscript of 1222ME (=AD1860), Amarapura (U Pinnya Zota), (ii)*Mahayazathat-kyi* (1232M.E.=1870A.D.), Yangon: Maung Bo Ku Press, (iii)The versions of 1900 & 1940 Yangon: Myanmar Thandawshin Printing House.

—. *Kaingza Shwemyin Dhammathat* [KSD]. (n.d.). Yangon: The National Library.

King Wagaru's Manu Dhammasatthan [KWMD]. 1892. Text, translation, and notes, Rangoon: Government Printings (later edition in 1934).

Manothara Dhammathat [MNTD], Palm-leaf manuscript [No.2051]. Yangon: The National Library.

Manugye Dhammathat [MD]. (i)Palm-leaf manuscript of 1144ME. (=AD1782complete set); (ii)Palm-leaf manuscript of 1153ME (=AD1791, complete set), both (i)&(ii) are preserved at the National Library in Yangon; (iii)Palm-leaf manuscript of 1152ME (=AD1790., complete set) & Palm-leaf manuscript of 1213ME. (=1851A.D., complete set with 16 volumes), both (iii) & (iv) are preserved at the Universitites Central Library in Yangon; (v)*The Dhammathat or the Law of Menoo* (Myanmar text and English translation) by David Richardson. 1847 (1st edition, Moulmein: American Baptist Mission Press). 1874 (2nd edition) and 1896 (4th edition) Rangoon: Hanthawaddy Press, (vi)*Manugye Dhammathat* (Myanmar text), 1903 Yangon: Hanthawaddy Press; *MD* (2nd ed.) 2010. Yangon: Seik-ku: ChoCho Anupinnya.

Manu Kyetyo Dhammathat [MKD]. Palm-leaf manuscript of 1124 ME (=AD 1762) Yangon: The National Library.

Manutheikka Dhammathat. Palm-leaf manuscript (incomplete?, the copy-date is unknown). Yangon: The national Library.

Manuthara Shwemyin Dhammathat [MTSD]. (i)the manuscript of 1218ME (=AD1856), Yangon: The National Library; (ii)*Manoo Thara Shwemyin Dhammathat* (1878 A.D.) edited by Maung Tetto, Yangon: Government Printing.

Manu Wunnana Dhammathat [MWD]. (i)Vol.7 of the palm-leaf manuscript of 1205ME. (=AD1843.), (ii)*The Manoo Wunnana Dhammathat or Digest of Burman Law* by Wunna-Dhamma-Kyaw-deng, 1878, edited by Moung Tetto, Rangoon: Government Printing.

Manuyin Dhammathat. (i)Palm-leaf manuscript of 1222 ME (=AD1860), Yangon: The National Library; (ii)*The Manoo-reng Dhammathat* or *The Original Book of Manoo* [MRD=MYD]. 1878, edited by Moung Tet-to, Rangoon: Government Printing.

Mohaweikhsedani Neittaya [MWD]. Palm-leaf manuscript of 1249 ME (=AD 1887), Yangon: The National Library.

Nai Pan Hla (ed.). 1992. *Mon Dhammasāt Texts*. Tokyo: The East Asian Centre, Toyo Bunko.

Pyumin Dhammathat [PD]. (the copy-date of the palm-leaf manuscript is unknown), Yangon: The national Library.

Sai Kham Mong (ed.). 2012. *Shan Thammasat Maanuscripts*. Tokyo: Mekon Publishing Compay.

Yandameik Kyaw Htin. 1965. *Yezagyo Hkoundaw Hpyathton* [YKHP] (3rd edition), Yangon: Hanthawaddy Press.

Yezagyo Hkoun U Hpyu Kauk-hcet ("Judicial Decision by U Hpyu") [LMD= CEACS Reel No.11-7 [LMD-CEACS(B), 1976]

Yazabala Dhammathat [YD]. Palm-leaf manuscript of 1237 ME (=AD1874.). Yangon: The National Library.

3. Secondary Sources (in Myanmar)

Aung Than Tun. 1968. *Myanmar Min-mya Taya Siyin-ye* ("Judicial Decisions of the Burmese kings"). Yangon: Kalaung-byan Book House.

———. 1969. Myanmar *Dhammathat-mya, Ngwetayi,* Yangon. pp.33-36.

———. 1970. *Myanma Yinkye-hmu-Taya-ye hnit Luhmu-ye* ("Myanma Culture-Judicial and Social Affairs"). Yangon.

———. *Myanmar Dhammathat Thamaing* ("History of Myanmar Dhammathats") Vol.I (2005), Vol.II & III (2007). Yangon: Sape-Beikman.

Hpo Lat, U. Thutethana Thayoup-pya Abeikdan. 1955. Yangon: Pinnya-nanda Press.
Kyaw, U. 2011. *Konbaung Hkit Yaw-detha (A.D.1752-1885)* ("Yaw Area of the Konbaung Period") Yangon: Htun Foundation.
Maung Maung Thaik. 1969, Konbaung-hkit-u Lu-ne-hmu Ache-ane (in) *Myanmar Nainggan Pyidaung-zu Sape hnit Luhmu-ye Theippan Jane* ("The Union of Burma Journal of Literary and Social Science") Vol.II-No.I, pp.45-75.
Maung Thaw. 1976. *Konbaung-hkit Sit-tan*, Yangon: Hain-kyi Sape Taik.
Than Tun, Dr. 1964. *Hkit-haung Myanmar Yazawin*. Yangon: Maha-dagon Printing Press.
Than Tun, U. 1980. *Shwebo Nidan*. Yangon: Loka Poun-hneik Taik.
Thukha Hmat-su. 1970. Yangon.
Toe Hla. 2003. *Konbaung-hkit Myanmar Lu-hmu Ahpwe-asi hnit Taya-hmu- hkin-mya* ("The Social Organization and Lawsuits during the Konbaung Period"), Yangon: Universities Research Centre.
Uteikhka Dhamma Lingaya. 1969. *Myanmar Yet-swè Thamaing (Konbaung-zet)*, Edited by Dr. Than Tun, Mandalay: Bama-hkit Sape Hpyan-chi-ye Htana.

C. Pāli & Sanskrit Sources

Agañña Sutthanta ("A Book of Genesis"), *Dīgha Nikāya*. Sacred Books of the Buddhist Vol. I, Oxford: The Pāli Text Society.
Cūlavaṃsa: Being the more Recent Part of the Mahāvaṃsa [CV], 1953, pt 1-2, Transl. by Mrs. C. Mabel Rickmers into English from German translation by Wilhem Geiger, Colombo: The Ceylon Government Information Department.
Kangale, R.P. 1986, *The Kautilia Arthaśāstra* Pt.II, an English translation. Delhi: Motilal Banarsidass.
Mahāvaṃsa [MV]. (i)1934. Trasl. By W. Geiger. Reprint, London: The Pāli Text Society; (ii)1950, English Translation, Colombo: The Ceylon Government Information Department.
Mānāva Dharma Śāstra or Institute of Manu by G.C. Haughhtun. 1982 (Fourth Edition). Edited by Rev. P. Pereival. New Delhi: Asian Educational Services.
Pāli Nīti Texts of Burma [PNTB] (Text Series No.171). 1981. Critical Edition and Study by Heinz Bechert and Heinz Braun, London: The Pāli Text Society.
The Book of the GRADUAL SAYING (Anguttara-Nikaya) or More Numberd Suttas (Vol.I), 1960, London: Luzac & Company Ltd.
The Commentary on the Dhammapada. Edited by H.C. Norman, 1970. London: Published for the Pāli Text Society by Luzac & Company, Ltd.
The Dhammapada Verses and Stories. Translated by Daw Mya Tin. 1990. (Reprint of Burma Pitaka Association Publication 1986). BIBLIOTHECA INDO-TIBETICA SERIES-XX, Sarnath, Varanasi: Central Institute of Higher Tibetan Studies.
The Majjhima-Nikāya. 1964. Edited by V. Trenckner, London: Luzac & Company Ltd.

for the Pāli Text Society.
The World of the Doctrine (Dhammapada). Translated with an introduction and notes by K.R. Norman. 1997. Oxford: The Pāli Text Society.

D. Sinhalese Sources

Niti Nighanduwa or the Vovabulary of the Law as it existed in the Last Days of the Kandyan Kingdom [NN]. 1880, Transl. by C.J.R. de le Mesurier & T.B. Panabokke, Colombo: The Government Printer.

E. English Sources

1. Historical Records

A List of the Officers of the Army [LOA] (Adjutant general's Office-21 January, 1839), Ordnance Medical Departments serving under the Presidency of Fort St. George, Madras: Asylum Press.

Blundell, E.A. 1836. An Account of Some of the Petty States lying of Tenasserim Provinces; drawn up from the Journal and Reports of D. Richardson, ESQ. Surgeon to the Commissioner of the Tenasserim Provinces, *Journal of the Asiatic Society of Bengal* [JASB], Vol.(No.68/October), Calcutta.

Buchanan, F. *Journal of Progress and Observations during the Continuance of the deputation from Bengal to Ava in 1795*, MSS. Eur. C.12, India Office records, London: The British Library.

Buchanan's Journal in Burman Empire, MS: Vol.I (Diary: 18th, April-7th, June, 1795), Vol. II (Diary: 7th, Hune 27th, November, 1795). Edinburgh: Colledge Library.

Cox, Hiram. 1821, *Journal of a Residence in the Burmhan Empire and more particularly at the court of Amarapoorah*, with an introduction by D.G.E. Hall. 1971, London: Gregg International Publishers Limited.

Crawfurd, John. 1829. *Journal of an Embassy from the Governor General of India to the Court of Ava in the year 1827*, in two volumes. London: Henry Colburn, New Burlington Street.

Correspondence for the Years 1825-26 in the Office of the Commissioner Tenasserim Division.

Dalrymple's Oriental Repertory 1791-7 of Portions Relating to Burma [DOR]. 1926. (published by Authority), Rangoon: Government Printing.

Davy, John. 1821. *An Account of the Interior of Ceylon and of its Inhabitants, with Travels in that Island*, London: Ongman, Hurst, Ress, Orme & Brown.

East India (10 August, 1869). Return to an Address of the Honourable The House of Common, "Copy of paper relating to the Route of Captain W.C., MeLeod from Moulmein to the frontiers of China and to the route of Dr. Richardson on his fourth mission to the Shan Provinces of Burmah, or extracts from the same. London, pp.3-147.

Gazetteer of Burma in two volumes, Vol.I & Vol.II (1980 reprint of 1880), compiled by

Authority, Delhi: Cultural Publishing House.

Gray, Lames. 1886. *Ancient Proverbs and Maxims from Burmese Sources; or Niti Literature of Burma.* London: Trubuner & Co.

Historical records of the Survey of India, Vol.I (18th century) [1945], Vol.II (1815-1830) [1954] & Vol.IV (1830-1843) [1958], Dehra Dun: The Office of the Geodetic Branch, Survey of India.

Journal of a Mission from the Supreme Government of India to the Court of Siam by Dr. Richardson. *Journal of the Asiatic Society* [JASB] 1840. Calcutta: Bishops College Press.

Malcom, Howard. 1839. *Malcom's Travels in Southeastern Asia:* Vo;.I (in two volumes)- *Burman Empire.* London: Charles.

Paper relating to the Burmese War [PBW] presented to both Houses of Parliament by His Majesty's Command, February 1825. London: The London Gazette Office.

Sangeromano, Father. Translated by William Tandy, 1966 (Fifth edition). *A Description of Burmese Empire.* London: Susil Gupta.

Scott, J. George. *Gazeteer of Upper Burma and the Shan States* in five volumes, Part.I-Vol. II. 1900. Rangoon: Government Printing.

Symes, Michael. 1800. *An Account of an Embassy to the Kingdom of Ava sent by the Governor-General of India, in the year 1795,* London: W. Bulmer and Co.

——. 1955. *Journey of the Second Embassy to the Court of Ava in 1802,* edited by D.G.E. Hall, London: George Allen & Unwin Ltd.

The Burney Papers. 1971 (Reprint of 1913). Vol. IV-pt.1 & 2. Bangkok.

The Dalhousie-Phayre Correspondence 1852-1856. 1932, eidited by D.G.H. Hall, London: Oxford University Press.

The East-India Register and Directory for 1823 [EIGD] (Second edition corrected to 16th, September 1823). London.

The East-India Register and Army List [EIRAL]. 1846. Madras.

The Tenasserim Provinces. *Calcutta Review* [CR]. 1847, pp.72-145.

Wilson, Horace Hayman (ed.). 1827. *Documents Illustrative of the Burmese War.* Calcutta: The Government Gazette Press.

Yule, Henry. 1968 (Reprint). *Narrative of the Mission to the Court of Ava in 1855,* London: Oxford University Press.

2. Legal Documents

Chan-Toon. 1899. *Leading Cases on Buddhist Law,* Rangoon: Hanthawaddy Press.

——. 1903. The Principles of Buddhist Law (2nd.ed.). Rangoon: British Burma Press.

Jardine, John. 1882-1883. *Notes on Buddhist law.* Vol.I-Viii. Rangoon: Government Printing and Stationary.

The Rangoon Law Reports. 1940. Rangoon: Government Printing.

Upper Burma Rulings [UBR] (1896-1922) Rangoon: Government Printing.

3. Secondary sources (including some Japanese sources)

Aoyama, Toru. 2016. Indianization in the Southeast Asia (in) *Joza Bukkyo Jiten* ("Encyclopedia of Theravada Buddhism") Edited by the Editorial Committee, the Society of Pasli and Buddhism Culture, Japan.: Tokyo: Mekon Publishing Co.Ltd.

Altekar, A.S. 1984 (Reprint). *State and Government in Ancient India*. Delhi: Motilal Banarsidass.

Ariyapala, M.B. 1968 (2nd. edition). *Society in Mediaeval Ceylon*. Colombo: Department of Cultural Affairs.

Aung Than Tun. 1961. The Burmese Customary Law. *The Guardian*, Yangon, pp.14-16.

—. 1981. Burmese Dhammathats (30th, November, 1981). *The Working People's Daily.*

—. 2003. *Myanmar Dhammathats*: Paradigm of Myanmar Social Framework. *Texts and Contents in Southeast Asia*, Pt.II. Yangon: The Tun Foundation Bank Literary Committee.

Aung-Thwin, Michael A. 1985. *Pagan-The Origin of Modern Burma*. Honolulu: University of Hawaii Press.

—. 1998. *Myth and History in the Historiography of Early Burma*. Singapore: Institute of Southeast Asian Studies.

—. 2017. *Myanmar in the Fifteenth Century—A Tale of Two Kingdoms*. Honolulu: University of Hawaii Press

Aye Kyaw. 1979, The Institution of kingship in Burma and Thailand, *Journal of the Burma Research Society* [JBRS], Vol.LXII, pt.I & II: 125-175.

Ba Han. 1965 (June). Burmese Cosmogony and Cosmology. *Journal of the Burma Research Society* [JBRS], XLVIII: 9-16.

Ba, Vivian. 1965 (February). The First Burmese Buddhist Catechism Composed for Europeans (1763). *The Guardian* Vol.XII No.2: 36-42.

Bode, Mabel Haynes. 1965, *The Pāli Literature of Burma*, Rangoon: Burma Research Society (Original Publication).

Bruce, George. 1973. *The Burmese Wars; 1824-1886*, London: Hart-David, Mac Gibbon.

Cassier, Earnest. 1966. *The Myth of the State*. New heaven: Yale University Press.

Charney, Michael. W. 2006. *Powerful Learning-Buddhist Literati and the Throne in Burma's Last Dynasty, 1752-1885*. Ann Arbor: Centers for South and Southeast Asian Studies, The University of Michigan.

Coedès, G. 1971 (First edition in English 1968). *Indianized States of Southeast Asia* (English translation). Honolulu: The University Press of Hawaii.

Desai, W.S. 1939. *History of the British Residency in Burma 1826-1840*, 1961, Rangoon: The University of Rangoon.

—. 1961. *A Pagent of Burmese Histroy*. Calcutta: Orient Longmans.

Dutt, Skumar. 1960. *Early Buddhist Monarchism*. Bombay: Asia Publishing House.

E Maung. 1970. *Burmese Buddhist Law*. Yangon: Sape-lawka Printing Works.

Feuhrer, A. 1883. Manusāradhammasattham, the only one existing Buddhist Law Book, compared with the Brahmanical Mānavadharmaśāttham. *Journal Bombay Branch of*

Royal Asiatic Society, XV: 329-338.

Forchhammer, Emil. 1885. *The Jardine Prize: An Essay on the Sources and Development of Burmese Law from the era of the first introduction of the Indian Law to the time of the British occupation of pegu*. Rangoon: The Government Press.

Frasch, Tilman. 1994. Some Reflection on the Burmese Dhammathats with Special Reference to the Pagan Period. In: *Tradition and Modernity in Myanmar*, edited by Uta Gärtner and Jens Lorenz, Berlin: Humbolt University, pp.57-71.

Furnivall, J.S. 1925. The Coronation of the Burmese Kings, *Journal of the Burma Research Society* [JBRS] Vol.15-pt.2 pp.142-143.

—. 1939. The Fashioning of Leviathan, *Journal of the Burma Research Society* [JBRS] Vol. XXIX (pt.1), Rangoon.

—. 1940. Manu in Burma: Some Burmese Dhammathats, *Journal of the Burma Research Society* [JBRS], Vol. 30 (pt.2): 351-370.

—. 1957. *Colonial Policy and Practice*. Cambridge: The University Press.

Furnivall, J.S. and Pe Maung Tin, Dr. 1960, *Zambu Dipa Okhsaung Kyan* ("Collection of Sittan"). Yangon: The Burma Research Society.

Godakumbura, C.E. 1966 (December). Relation between Burma and Ceylon. *Journal of the Burma Research Society* [JBRS] Vol.XLIX-pt.2. Yangon.

Gombrich, Richard F. 1994 (Reprint). *Theravāda Buddhism-A social History from Ancient Benares to Modern Colombo*, London: Routledge & Kegan Paul Ltd.

Grabowsky, Volker & Thurton, Andrew. 2003. *The Gold and Silver Road of trade and Friendship*. Bangkok: Sikworm Books.

Gywe, M.T. 1910, *A Treatise on Buddhist Law*. Mandalay: Upper Burma Advert- iser Press.

Hagesteijin, Renee. 1989. *Circles of Kings*, AM Dordrecht: Foris Publication.

Hall, D.G.E. 1955. *Michael Symes Journal of his Second Embassy to the Count of Ava in 1802*. London: George Allen & Unwin Ltd.

—. 1968. *Early English Intercourse with Burma 1587-1743*. London: Frank Cass and Co.Ltd.

—. 1974, *Henry Burney-A Political Biography*. London: Oxford Uni- versity Press.

Heesterman, J.C. 1957. *The Ancient Indian Royal Consecration*, The Hague: Mouton & Co. Printer.

Harvey, G.E. 1967 (New impression). *History of Burma*. London: Frank Cass & Co. Ltd.

Hazra, Kanai Lal. 1982. *History of Theravada Buddhism in South-east Asia with special reference to India and Ceylon*. New Delhi: Munshiram Manoharlal.

Hla Aung, 1969, Burmese Concept of Law, *Journal of the Burma Research Society* [JBRS] LII-pt.ii.: 163-172.

Hooker, M.B. 1978. *A Concise Legal History of South-east Asia*. Oxford: The Clarendon Press.

—. (ed.) *Laws of South-east Asia-Volume I-The Pre-modern Texts* (1986);-*Vol.II-European Laws in Southeast Asia* (1988), Singapore: Butterworth& Co. Ltd.

Htin Aung. 1962. *Burmese Law tales*, London: Oxford University Press.

———. 1966. *Burmese Monk's Tales*. New York: Columbia University Press.

Huxley, Andrew. 1994. The Reception of Buddhist Law in S.E.Asia 200BCG-1860 CE, *LA RÈCEPTION DES SYSTÈMES JURIDIQUES: IMPLANTATION ET DESTIN*, sous la direction de Michael DOUCET et Jacques VANDERLINDEN, Universite de Bruxelles (Centre de droit cmparé et d'histoire du droit) & Universite de Moncton Ecole de droit (Centre international de la common law en français), Bruylant/ Bruxelles.

———. 1994. Wills in Theravada Buddhist S.E. Asia, *Actes A Cause de Mort* (Acts of Last Will). Bruxelles: De Boeck Universite.

———. 1995. Buddhism and law-The View From Mandalay, *Journal of International Association of Buddhist Studies*, 18: 1, pp.47-95.

———. 1996a. Shylock's Bad Karma: The Buddhist Approach to Law, *Law and Critique* Vol. VII NO.2, pp.245-255.

———. 1996b. The Burmese Legal Professon 1250-1885, *L'Assistances Dans la Resolution des Conflicts* (Assiatance in Conflict Resolution), Bruxelles: De Boeck Universite.

———. (ed.)1996c. Thai, Mon and Burmese Dhammathats-who influenced whom? (In) *Thai law: Buddhist Law-Buddhist Law-Essays on the Legal History of Thailand, Laos and Burma*. Bangkok: White Orchid Press, pp.81-131.

———. 1996d. When Manu Meet Mahāsammata. *Journal of Indian Philosophy* No.24, pp.593-621.

———. 1997a. Studying Theravada Legal Literature, *Journal of International Association of Buddhist Studies*, No.20-1, pp.63-91.

———. 1997b. 'Traditions of Mahosadha': legal reasoning from Northern Thailand, *Bulletin of School of Oriental and African Studies* (University of London), Vol.60-pt.2, pp.315-326, London: Oxford University Press.

———. 1997c. The Importance of the Dhammathats in Burmese Law and Culture, *The Journal of Burma Studies* (Northern Illinois University). Vol.I, pp.1-17.

———. 1997d. The Village knows best Social Organization in an eighteenth Century Burmese Law code. *South East Asian Research* Vol.I (March), pp.21-39.

———. 2001. Positivists and Buddhists: The Rise and Fall of Anglo = Burmese Eccesiastical Law, Law & Society Inquiry. *Journal of the American Bar Foundation*, Vol.26, No.1, Chicago: The University of Chicago Press, pp.113-142.

———. 2007. Book review: on Michael Charney *Powerful Learning: Buddhist Literati and the Throne in Burma's Last Dynasty, 1752-1885*. Center for South and Southeast Asian Studies, Ann Arbor, MI, 2006, *South- east Asian Research* [SEAR] Vol.15 (November).

Ishii, Yoneo. 1975. *Jozabu Bukkyo no Seiji Shakaigaku* ("Political Sociology of the Theravāda Buddhism") Tokyo: Sobunsha.

———. 1983. Tai no Dentoho ("A Note on the Law of the Three Seals"), *Kokuritsu Minzokugaku Hakubutsukan kenkyuu Hokoku* (Bulletin of the National Museum of Ethnology), Vol.8-No.1: 18-32.

———. 1986. *Sangha, State and Society: Thai Buddhism in History*. Translated by Peter

Hawkes, Honolulu: The University of Hawii Press. [Original in Japanese: *Jōzabu Bukkyo no Seiji-shakai Gaku- Kokkyo no Kozo*, 1975, Tokyo: Sobunsha.]

—. 1986. The Thai Thammasat (with a Note on the Lao Thammasat), In: *The Laws of South-east Asia, Vol.I: The Pre-modern Texts*, edited by M. B. Hooker, Singapore: Butterworth & Co. Ltd., pp.143-203.

—. 1988a. Saninhoten-bon Pra Thammasat no Kosei ("The Structure of a Thai text of Phrathammasat in laws of the Three Seals of A.D.1805"), *Tōhōgakkai Sōritsu 40 shūnen Kinen Tōhōgaku Ronshu,* Tokyo: Tōhō Gakkai (The Institute of Eastern Culture), pp.111-123.

—. 1988b. Saninhōten no Kosei nitsuite ("Structure of the Thai Laws of the Three Seals of 1805"), *Tōhōgaku (Eastern Studies)*, No.74, pp.1-14.

—. 2000. Tonanajia-gaku Indobunka no Tonanajiateki Juyō ("Southeast Asia's Acceptance of Indian Culture"). *Tōhō-gaku (Eastern Studies)*, No.100, pp.188-196.

Ishizawa, Yoshiaki. 1986. Remarks on the Epigraphy of Angkorian Cambodia, In: *Laws of South-east Asia, Vol.I: The Pre-modern Texts*, edited by M. B. Hooker, Singapore: Butterwoth & Co. Ltd., pp.205-240.

Jayasekera, M.L.S. 1984. *Customary Law of Sri Lanka*. Colombo: The Department of Government Printing.

Judson's *Burmese-English Dictionary* [JBED]. 1966 (Second edition of 1953 Centenary edition). Rangoon: Baptist Board of Publication.

Judson, Edward. 1883. *The Life of Adniram Judson*. New York: Anson D.F. Randolph & Company.

Koenig, William J. 1990. *The Burmese Polity-1752-1819*, Michigan: Center for South and Southeast Asian Studies, University of Michigan.

Kyan. 1961. King Mindon's Councillors, *Journal of the Burma Research Society* [JBRS] XLIV-pt.1, pp.43-60 (in English); 61-80 (in Myanmar).

Kyin Swi. 1965. The Judicial System in the Kingdom of Burma, PhD. dissertation (Unpublished), London: University of London.

—. 1966. The Origin and Development of the Dhammathats, *Journal of the Burma Research Society* [JBRS], XLIX-pt.ii, pp.173-205.

Lammerts, Dietrich Christian. 2005. The Dhammavilāsa Dhammathat: A Critical Historiography, Analysis, and Translation of the Text, A Thesis (Master of Arts, Unpublished) presented to the Faculty of the Graduate School of Cornell University.

Langham-Carter, R.R. 1966. *Old Moulmein (875-1880)*, Moulmain: The Moulmein Sun Press

—. 1966. Some Episodes of the Burmese War-The Letters of Doctor Richardson, *The Army Quarterly*, Vol.LXXXXII No.2(July), pp.219-257.

—. 1966. David Lester Richardson – Diplomat and Explorer, *Journal of the Burma Research Society* [JBRS], XLIX-pt.2(December), pp.207-218.

Law, James.(Captain), History of tenasserim, *Journal of the Royal Asiatic Society* Vol. IV, pp.304-332; V, pp.141-263.

Lee, Orlan. 1978. *Legal and Moral System in Asian Customary law - The Legacy of the Buddhist Social Ethics and Buddhist Law*. San Francisco: Chinese Materials Center, Inc.

Lester, Robert C. 1973. *Theravada Buddhism in Southeast Asia*. Ann Arbor: The University of Michigan Press.

Lieberman, Victor B. 1984. *Burmese Administrative Cycles-Anachy and Conquest (c.1580-1780)*, Princeton: Princeton University Press.

———. 2003. *Strange Parallels Southeast Asia in Global Context, Vol.1 Integration on the Mainland*. C.800-1830. Cambridge: Cambridge University Press.

Lingat, Robert. 1949. The Buddhist Manu or the Propagation of Hindu Law in Hinayanist Indo China, *Annals of Bandarka Oriental Research Institute* No.30, pp.284-297.

———. 1950. Evolution of the Conception of Law in Burma and Siam, *Journal of the Siam Society* No.38(1), pp.9-31.

———. 1973. *The Classical Law of India*, translated from the French by J. Duncan M. Derrett, Berkeley: University of California Press.

Maung Maung. 1963. *Law and Custom in Burma and the Burmese Family*, The hague: Martinus Nijhoff.

Mendelson, E. Michael. 1975. *Sangha and State in Burma* ITHACA: Cornell University Press.

Myanmar-English Dictionary [MED]. 1993. Yangon: Department of the Myanmar Commission, Ministry of Education.

Maung Maung Gyi. 1983. *Burma Political Value-The Socio-political Roots of Authoritarinism*, New York: Praeger Publishers.

Myint Zan. 2000. Woe Unto Ye Lawyers: Three Royal Orders Concerning Pleaders in Early Seventeenth-Century Burma, *The American Journal of legal History*, Vol. XLIV, No.1, pp.40-72.

Nisbet, John. 1901. *Burma under British Rule and Before*, Vol.I & II, London: Westminster Archibald Constable & Co. Ltd.

Ohno, Toru. 1992. Myanmar Kokuritsutoshokan Shozō no Damavilāta Shahon ("The palm-leaf manuscript of the Dhammavilatha Dhammathat preserved at the Myanmar National Library"), *Ajiagaku Ronsou* ("The Collection of Treatises for Asian Studies") No.2, Osaka: Osaka University of Foreign Studies.

Okell. 1971. *A guide to the Romanization of Burmese*, London: The Royal Asiatic Society.

Okudaira, Ryuji. 1984a. Comparative Features of the Traditional Law of Sri Lanka, In: *Law and Culture in Sri Lanla - A Research Report on Asian Indigenous Law*, edited by Masaji Chiba, Tokyo: Research Group on Asian Indigenous Law, pp. 25-35.

———. 1984b. The Role of Kaingza Manuyaza, An Eminent Jurist of the Seventeenth century, in the Development of the Burmese Legal History, *Journal of Asian and African Studies*, No.27, pp.180-186. Tokyo: Institute of languages and Cultures of Asia and Africa.

———. 1986. The Burmese Dhammathat In: *Laws of South-east Asia Vol.I: The Pre-modern texts*, edited by M.B. Hooker, Singapore: Butterwoth & Co. Ltd.

———. 1987. Some Problems in the Study of the Burmese Legal Literature with Special Reference to the *Dhammatha'* [*Dhammathat*] or Traditional Law Texts. In: *Burma and Japan-basic Studies on Their Cultural and Social Structure*, edited by The Burma Research Group (Tokyo), pp.199-207.

———. 1989. Notes on the Burmese Dhammathats or Law Texts and Buddhist Polity in Burma, In: *The Formation of Urban Civilization in Southeast Asia*, edited by Yoshihiro Tsubouchi, Center for Southeast Asian Studies, Kyoto University, pp.53-81.

———. 1994. A Study on Foundation of the Konbaung Dynasty in Burma (Muyanmar) and Compilation on *Manugye Dhammathat* with special reference to the intention of inserting a Mythological Story on Sovereign Power in the Volume I. In: *Tradition and Modernity in Myanmar*, edited by Uta Gärtner and Jens Lorenz, Berlin: Humbolt University, pp.57-71.

———. 1996. A Hypothetical Analysis on "Theravada Buddhist State at its Height" Under King Badon with Special reference to *Manugye Dhammathat* (1782 Manuscript), *Tradition in Current Perspective*, Proceedings of the Conference on Myanmar and Southeast Asian Studies 15-17 December 1995, Yangon: Universities Historical Resaech Centre, pp.30-42.

———. 1999. The Role that the Dhammathat (law Book) played in the Theravada Buddhist State with Special Reference to the *Manugye Dhammathat* of Eighteenth Century Myanmar (Burma), *Tokyo Gaikokugo Daigaku Hyakushuunen Kinen Ronshuu (Essays in Commemoration of the Hundredth Anniversary of Tokyo University of Foreign Studies)*, Tokyo: Tokyo University of Foreign Studies, pp.465-485.

———. 2000a. Features of the Theravada Buddhist State Structure with Special Reference to the *Muddha Beiktheik* ("Supreme Coronation Ceremony") as Observed by King Badon in Eighteenth Century Myanmar, *Myanmar Two Milennia* (Part 3), Proceedings of the Myanmar Two Millennia Conference 15-17 December 1999, Yangon: Universities Historical Research Centre. pp.120-132.

———. 2000b. A Comaparative Study on Two Different Versions of the *Manugye Dhammathat*: A Leading Law Book in Eighteenth Century Burma (Myanmar), *Journal of the Asian and African Studies* No.59, Tokyo: Institute for the Study of Languages and Cultures of Asia and Africa (ILCAA), Tokyo University of Foreign Studies.

———. 2001a. Changes of The Role Which The Dhammathat (law Book) Has Been Playing in Myanmar History, *Views and Visions* (part I), Proceedings of the Views and Visions Conference 18-20, December 2000, 149-157.

Okudaira, Ryuji and Huxley, Andrew. 2001b. A Burmese tract on kingship: political theory in the 1782 manuscript of Manugye, *Bulletin of SOAS* (School of Oriental and African Studies), University of London, pp.248-259.

Okudaira, Ryuji. 2002. Biruma Houseishi Kenkyu Nyuumon ("Introduction to the Burmese Legal History" in Japanese), Tokyo: Nihon Tosho kankokai.

—. 2003a. Political Ideas of Eighteenth Century Myanmar, as seen in the *Manugye Dhammathat, Texts and Contexts in Southeast Asia* (part I), Proceedings of the Texts and Contexts in Southeast Asia Conference 12-14 December 2001. Yangon: Universities Historical Research Centre, pp.52-71.

—. 2003b. How Judges Used *Dhammathats* (law books) in Their Courts in 18th-19th Century Myanmar (Burma) with Special Reference to *Yezajyo Hkondaw Hpyathton, Journal of Asian and African Studies* No.66, Tokyo: Research Institute for Languages and Cultures of Asia and Africa (ILCAA), Tokyo University of Foreign Studies, pp.319-329.

—. 2005. Judicial Administration under the Reign of King Badon in 18th to 19th century Myanmar, *Essays in Commemoration of the Golden Jubilee of the Myanmar Historical Commission*, Yangon: Myanmar Historical Commission, Ministry of Education, Union of Myanmar, pp.82-108.

—. 2006. Manuscripts in the Studies of Pre-modern Legal History in Myanmar, In: *Enriching the Past Preservation, Concervation and Study of Myanmar Manuscripts*, edited by Teruko Saito & Thaw Kaung, Tokyo: The Centre for Documentation & Area- Transcultural Studies", Tokyo University of Foreign Studies.

—. 2014. Cases of Theft in 18th Century Myanmar (Burma) with Special Reference to the Atula Hsayadaw Hpython,. *Journal of Asian and African Studies*. Tokyo: Research Institute for Languages and Cultures of Asia and Africa.

Pearn, B.R.(ed.). 1937. A Burma Diary of 1810, *Journal of the Burma Research Society* [JBRS], XXVII- No.3, pp.283-307.

—. 1939, The State of Burma in 1790, *Journal of the Burma Research Society*, XXIX-No. 2, pp.250-256.

Pe Maung Tin.1960 (reprint of 1936 JBRS XXVI-No.1). Buddhism in the Inscription of Pagan. *Fiftieth Anniversary Publications No.2*, Selected Articles from JBRS, Rangoon: Burma Research Society.

Periodical Accounts Relative to the Baptist Missionary Society. 1807-1817, London.

Ray, Niharranjan. 1946. *Theravada Buddhism in Burma*, Calcutta: University of Culcutta.

Reid, Anthony. 1993. *Southeast Asia in the Age of Commerse 1450-1680, Vol.II: Expansion and Crisis*. New Haven and London: Yale University Press.

—. 1999. *Charting the Shape of Early Modern Southeast Asia*. Bangkok: Silkworm books.

Richardson, D. 1837. History of Labong from the Native Records consulted by D. Richardson, forming an Appendix to his journals published in the preceeding volumes, *Journal of the Asiatic Society of Bengal* [JASB] Vol.III (No.61), pp.55-57.

—. 1840. Journal of a Mission from the Supreme Government of India to the Court of Siam, *Journal of the Royal Asiatic Society of Bengal* [JASB] Vol. XIII (No.96): 1016-1036/Vol.IX-pt.1, No.97): 1-30/Vol.X (No.99: 219-250), Calcutta.

Saito, Teruko. 1997. Rural Monetization and Land-Mortgage *Thet-Kayit* in Konbaung Burma, In: *The last Stand of Asian Autonomies: Responses to Modernity in the Diverse States of Southeast Asia and Korea, 1750-1900*, edited by Anthony Reid, London:

Macmillan Press Ltd. pp.153-184.

Saito, Teruko & U Thaw Kaung. 2006. *Enriching Past-Preservation and Conservation and Study of Myanmar Manuscripts*, Tokyo: DATS, Tokyo University of Foreign Studies.

Sangermano, Father. 1966. *The Burmese Empire – a hundred years ago*, London: Susil Gupta (1st. edn. 1833, Roma).

San Shwe Bu. 1917. The Coronation of King Data-raja (1153-1165), *Journal of the Burma Research Society* [JBRS] Vol. VII-pt.2, pp.181-184.

Sarkar, H.B. 1985. *Cultural Relations between India and Southeast Asian Countries*. New Delhi: Indian Council for Cultural relations and Motilal Banarsidass.

Sakisyanz, E. 1965. *Buddhist Backgrounds of the Burmese Revolution*, The hague: Martinus Nijhoff.

Scott, J George. 1901. *Gazetter of Upper Burma and the Shan States*, pt.II-Vol.I, Rangoon: Government Printing.

Shwe Baw. 1955. *The Origin and Development of Burmese Legal Literature*, PhD. dissertation (Unpublished), London: University of London.

Smith, Donald Eugene.1965. *Religion and Politics in Burma*. Princeton: Princeton University Press.

Sparks, Major. 1860. *The Burmese Code*, Rangoon: Government Printing (1894, *A Manual of Buddhist Law being Sparks Code of Burmese Law* by Henry M. Lutter (2nd. edn.), Mandalay: The 'Star of Burma' Press.

Stadtner, Donald M. 2005. *Ancient Pagan*—Buddhist Plain of Merit. Bangkok; River Books.

Tambiah, H.W. 1968. *Sinhala Laws and Customs*, Colombo: Lake House Invest- ment.

Taylor, Robert H. 1987. *The State in Burma*, Honolulu: University of Hawaii Press. [*The State in Myanmar* (2009)]

Than Tun. 1958. Social Life in Burma A.D. 1044-1287, *Journal of the Burma Research Society* [JBRS]. Vol.XLI, pp.37-47.

—. 1959a. History of Burma, *Journal of the Burma Research Society* [JBRS], Vol. XLII, pp.47-69.

—. 1959b. The Legal System in Burma, A.D.1000-1300, *The Burma Law Institute Journal* (ii), pp.171-184.

—. 1960. History of Burma A.D.1000-1300, *Bulletin of the Burma Historical Commision* 1 (i), pp.39-57.

—. 1978. History of Buddhism In Burma A.D.1000-1300, *Journal of the Burma Research Society [JBRS]*, Vol.LXI-pt. i & ii, pp.1-266.

—. 1985, Checking Manugye (1782) with Manugye (1874) and Manuyin (1875), *Tonan Ajia Rekishi to Bunka* (Southeast Asian History and Culture), No.14, pp.28-43.

Thaung. 1959. Burmese Kingship in Theory and Practice Under the Reign of King Mindon, *Journal of the Burma Research Society* [JBRS], XLII-pt.2, pp.171-185.

Thaw Kaung. 2005. Excerpts from Myanmar Traditional Manuscripts and their Preservation and Conservation, *U Thaw Kaung-The Learned Librarian of Myanmar*,

Yangon: Myanmar Book Centre, pp.43-61.

Thurton, Andrew. 1997. Ethnography of embassy: anthropological readings of records of diplomatic encounters between Britain and tai states in the early nineteenth century, *Southeast Asian Research*, Vol.V (No.2/July9, pp.175-202, London: School of Oriental and African Studies, University of London.

Thant Myint – U. 2001, *The Making of Burma*, Cambridge: Cambridge University Press.

Trager, Helen G. 1966, *Burma through alien eyes*, Bombay: Asia Publishing House.

U Thein Hlaing. 2016. *Myanmar-English Dictonary of Ancient Myanmar Histroical Terms*. Yangon: Department of Historical Research and National Library.

Wayland, D.D. Francis. 1853. *A Memoir of the Life and labours of the Rev. Adniram Judson, D.D.* Vol.I London: James Nisbet & Co.

Williamson, A. 1929. *Shwebo District (Burma Gazetteer)*. Vol. A. Rangoon: Government Printing.

Wolters, O.W. 1982. *History, Culture, and Religion in Southeast Asian Perspectives*, Singapore: Institute of Southeast Asian Studies. [Revised edition 1999, Ithaca, New York: Cornell Southeast Asian Program Publications]

Yi Yi. 1961. Life at the Burmese Court Under Konbaung Kings, *Journal of the Burma Research Society* [JBRS], XLIV-pt.1, pp.85-129.

Zaw Lynn Aung. 2015. Study on *Mahasammata* Model of Kingshipin Mrauk U Period (1430-1784). *SUVANNABHUMI* Vol. No 2.

APPENDIX I

THE ROYAL LINE OF THE KONBAUNG DYNASTY [1752-1885]

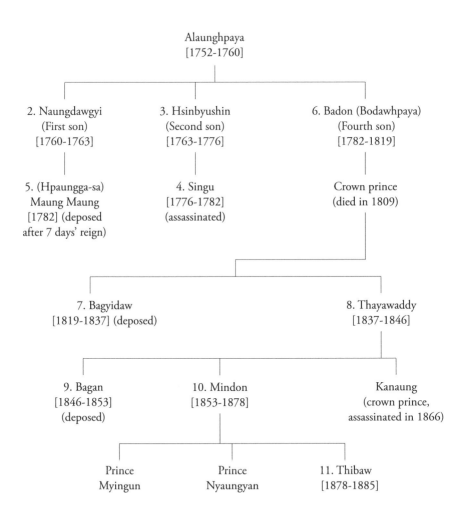

APPENDIX II

A BRIEF CHRONOLOGICAL TABLE OF THE KONBAUNG PERIOD [1752-1885]

1752   Fall of the Restored Taungu Dynasty by the attack of the capital city of Ava by the Mon rebels (11th, March). Founding of the Konbaung dynasty by U Aung Zeya (=King Alaunghpaya) (9th, April).

1753   Construction of the new capital city at Mok-hso-bo, later Shwebo (21st, June).

1754   Completion of the new palace construction at Shwebo (12th, September) and occupied by King Alaunghpaya (28th, October).

1755   Dagon renamed 'Yangon'(2nd, May).

1757   Fall of Hanthawaddy Bago (=Pegu), the capital city of Mons by the attack of the Myanmar troops led by King Alaunghpaya (12th, May). Commencement of constructions of Greater Shwebo (24th, October).

1760   King Alaunghpaya died in Kin Ywa on the way back from a campaign against Ayut'ia (11th, May). Prince Dabayin (Naungdawgyi) ascended the throne (7th, June). Sagaing (Mahājeyapura) made capital in August.

1763   King Naungdawgyi died (28th, November) and Prince Myedu ascended the throne (29th, November) and assumed the title of Hshinbyushin (Lord of White Elephant) (28th, June, 1770)

1765   New palace was constructed in Ava (23rd, June)

1765   Chinese invations to Myanmar four times (December, 1765/December, 1766/ January, 1776/October, 1776).

1767   Fall of Ayuthaya Kingdom by the attack of Myanmar troops (9th, June).

1776   King Hshinbyushin died (10, June) and Prince Singu ascended the throne on the same day.

1782   Prince Maung Maung (Hpaungga-sa) seized the throne from King Singu (5th, February). Prince Badon (famous for Bodawhpaya) killed [King] Maung Maung who ruled the country only for a week and took over the throne (11th, February).

1783   The King moved the capital city from Ava to Amarapura (12th, May)

1784   Myanmar troops led by the Crown Prince (Maha Upayaza) marched to Rakhine (Arakan) (16th, October) and conquered Rakhine on 20th, January in 1785.

1785   King Badon assumed the title of Hsinbyu-mya Shin ("Lord of White Ele- phants") (25th, February).

1785-1786   Military campaign against Thai twice (4th, July - 6th, February/ 7th, September -, but repulsed soon)

1795   Received Symes's mission (first embassy) to the court of Ava (14th, August)

APPENDIX II

1800   Arrival of Buddhist mission (six samanēra) from Sri lanka (5, June) and ordained as Buddhist monks (29th, November).

1802   Received Symes's mission (second embassy) to the court of Ava (14th, October)

1809   Crown prince (Maha Upayaza) died (29th, March) and Prince Sagaing, who was a grandson of theKing, succeeded Crown prince (6th, April).

1819   King Badon died (5th, June) and Prince Sagaing ascended the throne.

1824-1826   The capital city moved from Amarapura to Ava (3rd, March). The British declared war against Myanmar (First Anglo-Burmese war) (5th, March) and the war was over by conclusion of the Treaty of Yandabo (24th, February).

1829   Compilation of the Myanmar chronicle (*Hmanan Maha Yazawin-daw gyi*) started (3rd, May).

1830   Arrival of Major Henry Burney, the first British resident at Ava (17th, June).

1837   Prince Thayawadi occupied Ava and seized the throne (15th, May).

1846   King Thayawadi died and Prince Bagan ascended the throne ((17, November).

1852   British troops landed near Rangoon (Yangon) and the Second Anglo-Burmese war started (10th, January) and the British proclaimed annexation of Pegu District (20th, December).

1853   King Bagan abdicated the kingship to King Mindon (17th, February). King Mindon moved the capital city from Ava to Amarapura (20th, November).

1859   King Mindon ordered to build a new capital city of Mandalay (28, April).

1868   The Ti- Pitaka scriptures were inscribed on altogether 729 stones (4th, May).

1871   The Fifth Buddhist Synod started (15th, April) and finished (12th, September) in Mandalay.

1872   Visit of the First Envoys to Europe led by Kinwun Mingyi (22nd, January-2nd, May)

1878   King Mindon died (1st, October) and King Thibaw ascended the throne (8th, October).

1885   The Government of the British Burma sent an ultimatum to the Kingdom of Burma (22 October) and a reply to the ultimatum was sent back (27th, October)

1885   King Thibaw declared the war against the British (7th, November) and the British troops surrounded the Mandalay palace (28th, November). The King Thibaw and family went on board (5th, December) and exiled to India and the Konbaung dynasty fell.

* The relevant date of an incident is mainly based on ROB(III- IX) by Than Tun.

APPENDIX III

A LIST OF MAJOR MYANMAR DHAMMATHATS

Name of *Dhammathat*	Compilation-date M.E.	Compilation-date A.D.	Language & Style	Composer
Manu	—	—	—	(Rishi) Manu
Manawthaya (Manosara)	—	—	—	(Rishi) Manutheikka
Manutheikka (Manussika)	—	—	—	(Rishi) Manutheikka
Zali-min (Jali-min)	—	—	—	(Rishes) Thudewathukkadantha, etc.
Dutthabaung-min	—	—	—	(Highest monk)
Atitya-min (Atitra-min)	—	—	—	(Monk) Mahathinggawa
Pyumin-di (Pyu-min-hti)	—	—	—	Five Hsayas (teachers)
Dhammawilatha (Dhammavilasa)	455	1174	Pāli / Verse	(Monk) Dhammawilatha
Waru (Wagaru/Wareru)	643	1281	Pāli / Prose	(King) Waru
Pathada (Pasada)	607-704	1335-42		Kayin-ba
Dhammathat Kungya (Pyanchi / Lezaung-dwe	788	1426	Pāli / Prose	
Manuthara (Manusara)	—	—	Pāli / Verse	(Monk) Taunghpila & (Minster) Kaingza Manu Yaza
Shwemyin	991	1629		(Minister) Kaingza Manu Yaza
\<Mahayazathat\>	991	1629	Pāli-Myanmar / Prose	(Minister) Kaingza Manuyaza
Dhammathat Lezaung-dwè	—	—		(Monk) Nyana Dhammavilatha
Mingun (Manu-linga)	1012	1650	Pāli / Verse	(Monk) Dhammawilatha
Dhammathat-kyaw	1095	1733	Pāli / Prose	(Monk) Maha Buddhin-kura
Dhammawineikhsaya (Dhammavinicchaya)	1114-22	1752-60	Pāli	(Judge) Letwe Beiknanthu
Manugye (Manu-Akye)	1114-22	1752-60	Myanmar / Prose	(Minister) Bummazeya
Kandaw Pakeinnaka-linga	1120	1758	Pāli / Verse	(Monk) Lankathara (U Tun Nyo)
Shin Tezothara Shwe-myin	1112	1760	Myanmar (Trl. from Pāli)	(Monk) Thezothara (Tezosara)
Wunnadhamma (Vannadhamma) Shwe-myin (Manuthara)	1112	1760	Myanmar (Trl. from Pāli)	(Minster) Wunna Dhamma Kyaw Din

APPENDIX III

Manuyin (Manu Reng)	1129	1767	Pāli/ Verse	(Minister)Twinthin-taik (U Tun Nyo)
Wineikhsayayathi (Vinicchayarasi)	1129	1767	Pāli/ Prose	(Monk)Khemasara
Wineishsaya Pakathani (Vinicchaya Pakasani)	1133	1771	Pāli-Myanmar/ Prose	(Minister)Wunnadhamma Kyawdin
Manuthara Shwe-myin (Manusara Shwe-myin)	—	—		
Manuwannana (Manuvannana)	1134	1772	Pāli-Myanmar	(Minster)Wunnadhamma Kyawdin
Wineikhsaya Pakathani (Vinicchaya Pakasani)	1139	1777	Pāli/ Verse	(Minister)Yazabala Kyawdin
Yazabala (Rājabala)	1142	1780	Pāli-Myanmar/ Prose	(Minister)Yazabala Kyawdin
Hsondamanu (Sontamanu)	1143	1781		(Monk)Nandamala
Manu	1143	1781	Trl.to Pāli fromMyanmar	(Monk)Lankarama
Panam Pakeinnaka (Panam Pakinnka)	1143	1781	Pāli/ Verse	(Minister) Thiri Mahathihathu
Wineikhsaya (Vinicchaya-Kungya)	1165	1803		(Clerk for Royal Boats) Maung Pe Thi
Dayajjadipani	1173	1811	Pāli/ Verse	(Advocate)Candathu Cunduther
Waru	1184	1822	Pāli/ Verse	(Tutor to Poyal Family) U Shwe Po
Attathanhkeip Wunnana (Attasankhepa Vannana)	1203	1841		(Minister) Kinwun Mingyi U Kaung
Dhammatharamanju (Dhammasaramanju)	1207	1845		(Clerk)Theika Sithu Kyaw
Manuseiktaya (Manucittara)	—	—		
Shin Thapa	—	—	Pāli /Verse	(Monk) Shin Thapa

[Revised by this author based on Forchhmammer (1885), PTS (1903), Furnivall (1940) and Huxley (1993/1996)]

1) Pāli-Myanmar (Mon/Rakhine, etc.) =Nissaya: A word for word translation from Pāli to vernacular, such as Myanmar, Mon, Rakhine, Shan,etc.
2) *<Mahayazathat> is not Dhammathat, but Shaukhton (compilation of learned discourses by scholars or minsters or Hpyathton (collection of decisions by the court)
3) M.E.=Myanmar Era; A.D.=Christian era

APPENDIX IV

Location of the Manuscripts of the *Dhammathat/Hpyathton/Shaukhton*
at Major Libraries in and out of the Country

[ ] shows the rough number of each library collection

A. Myanmar

I. National Library (Yangon)
    [67] (As of June, 1979. There is no big change as of July, 2006)
II. The Universities' Central Library (Yangon)
    [146] (As of January, 2017. There are no big change as of 2007)
III. Universities Historical Research Centre [UHRC] (Yangon)
    [11](*pe*)+ [4](parabaik) Total=[15] (As of July, 2006 according to the List of the pe/parabaik Manuscripts)
IV. Resource Centre for Ancient Myanmar Manuscripts (RCAMM)
    [9](As of 2006)
V. The Library, Institute of the Pāli Buddhist Studies (Yangon)
    [5](*pe*) +[10] (*Parabaik*) Total=[15] (As of 1987. No change as of July 2006)
VI. The Library, University of Mandalay (Mandalay)
    [39] (As of February, 2007)
VII. The Library and Museum for Ancient Cultural Studies (Pitaka-taik hnit Shehaung Yinkye-hmu Thutethana Pya-daik, Taungdwingyi)
    [12] (As of 1987 there were about twelve *Dhammathat* existed.)

B. Out of the Country

I. The Library, Asiatic Society of Bengal (Calcutta, India)
   1. *Manuthaya Dhammathat* [No.24-Chapter I-16leaves/No.25-Chapter II-14 leaves/ No.26-Chapter III-101leaves]
   2. *Shinbyumyashin Dhammathat* [No.27-34 leaves]
   3. *Manuyaza Hpyathton* [No.28-56 leaves]
   4. *Manuthaya Shwemyin Dhammathat* [No.29-122 leaves]
   5. *Dhammathat Chok*[No.30-20leaves]
   6. *Shwemyin Dhammathat* [No.31-117 leaves]
   7. *Mahayazathat* [No. 32- 59/No.33-69]
   8. *Maha Pinnya Kyaw Hlaukhton(Shaukhton)* [No. 34-56 leaves]
   9. *Matika Ato-kauk Dhammathat* ("Table of contents of interpretation of the

APPENDIX IV

Dhammathats") [No.35 – 216 leaves]

(As of September, 1989. The number of [ ] described above shows the catalogue number of Myanmar manuscript. 'leaves' shows the number of palm-leaf.)

II. The British Library (London, United Kingdom)
  1. *Kaingza Shwemyin Dhammathat* (Part I-Thondara X): [No. Add. 12241] / [No. Add. 12242] /No.Add. 12250]<1134ME=AD1772.>
  2. *Thudhammasayi (Sudhammachari) Hpyathton* [No. Add.12244] <1145ME= AD1783>
  3. *Dhammathat* [No. Add. 12248] <n.d.>
  4. *Dhammathat Kyaw* [No.Add. 12249]<1187M.E=AD1825.>
  5. *Dhammawilatha (Dhammavilasa) Dhammathat* (Arakan script of Myanmar Version)[No. Add. 12254] <1111ME=AD1749.>
  6. *Wineikhsaya (Vinicchaya) Dhammathat (Wineithsaya-Thwang-Tara-mya Akyan)* [No.Add. 27458] <19c>
  7. *Manuyaza Hpyathton* [No.Or. 1029] <n.d.>
  8. *Dhammathat Linga* [No. Or. 2789] <n.d.>
  9. *Manu Akye (Manugye)* (Chapter I & II in parabaik) (No. 3447-A/B) <n.d.>
  10. *Dhammathat* (incomplete) [No. Or. 5048] <n.d.>
  11. *Yazabala (Rājabala) Dhammathat* [No. Or. 6452A] <1142ME=AD1780 or 1241ME.= AD1879.>
  12. *Dhamma Wineikhsaya (Dhamma Vinicchaya)* [No. Or.6456 B.] <1229. ME.=AD1867. or 1240ME=AD1878 .>
  13. *Dhammawilatha Dhammathat (Dhammavilasa Dhammathat)* [No. Or.11775] <n.d.>

(As of March, 1999. No. Add. shows the number of the Additional collection of the Oriental collection<Or.>)

III. Oxford University Bodleian Library (Oxford, United Kingdom)
  1. *Wineikhsaya Pakathani Linga (Vinicchaya Pakasani Lanka)* {Letwè Thondara} [MS. Burm. A, 10]
  2. *Thudhammasayi (Sudhammacari) Dhammathat* [MS. Burm. B, 10(R)] <n.d.>
  3. *Ko Zaung Gyop (Kyop) Dhammathat* [MS. Ind. Inst. Burmese 8]

(As of March, 1999)

IV. Cambridge University Library (Cambridge, United Kingdom)
  1. *Manuwunnana (Manuvannana) Dhammathat* (incomplete) [SCOTT LL 8 No.5]

(As of March, 1999)

V. Bibliotheque Nationale (BN) (Paris, France)
  1. *Mahayazathat*<1153ME=AD1791.>

2. *Dhammawineikhsaya (Dhammavinicchaya) Kyan* <1177ME=AD1815.>
   3. *Dhammathat Neitthaya (Nissaya)* <1194ME=AD1832.>
   4. *Dhammathat Hpyathton* <1197M.E.=AD1835.>
   5. *Dhammathat Hsatama-pain Sa-kyaw* <1196ME=AD1834.>
   6. *Sula Thambita Vini Dhammathat Kyan* <1196ME=AD1834.>
   7. *Kyeinsa Dhammathat Kyan* <1195ME=AD1833.>
   (Above list was made in accordance to the information given by Dr. Leider)

VI. Berlin National Library (Berlin, Germany)
   1. *Atula Hpyathton (Atula Phrat thumh)* (Atula Hsayadaw Rahan Yasa) <n.d.>
   (As of August, 1998)

Index

A

Abduction.......175
Abhiṣēka.......73, 77
Abhiseka.......73
Abhiṣeka Sadan.......77
adultery.......117, 175
Agati.......157
Aggan.......44
Aggañña Suttanta (=Sutta).......38, 121, 123, 170
Alaunghpaya.......30, 31, 45, 51, 61, 62, 63, 64, 67, 68, 69, 81, 82, 83, 84, 85, 86, 87, 88, 89, 95, 102, 120, 121, 123, 124, 125, 126, 127, 148, 149, 160, 162, 163, 164, 165, 166, 170, 171, 172, 173, 178, 182, 184, 186, 187
Alaungsidhu (=Alaungsithu).....51, 76, 166
Alaungsithumin Hpyathton....51
Amarapura.......53, 57, 63, 72, 77, 78, 92
Ameindaw.......163, 179
Amherst (=Kyaikkami).......90, 93, 94, 96, 150
Ana.......164
Anawyahta (=Anawrahta).......160
Anglo-Burmese war.......93
Apay.......115
Arbitration.......176, 177
Aryapala, M.B. 73
Assam.......92
Aśoka.......36, 37, 73, 77
Athi (=Athe).......175
Atin.......167, 168

Atitya.......48
Atitya Dhammathat.......48
Attayathi (=Attarasi).......59
Aṭṭathanhkeip (=Attasanhkepa) Wunnanakyan.......106
Atula Hsayadaw.......83, 87
Atula Hsayadaw Hpyathton.......51
Aung San Suu Kyi.......188
Aung-Thwin, Michael. 124
Ava (=Inwa).......52, 56, 57, 61, 62, 67, 71, 78, 83, 90, 92, 93, 94, 96, 120, 127, 128, 149, 163
Ayon.......167, 168
Ayuthaya.......62, 63, 64, 171

B

Badda Kaba (=Gaba).......107
Badon (=Bodawhpaya).......30, 32, 45, 50, 52, 54, 61, 63, 64, 65, 67, 68, 69, 70, 71, 72, 74, 76, 77, 78, 81, 82, 85, 91, 92, 102, 104, 106, 126, 127, 128, 148, 149, 151, 156, 160, 164, 165, 166, 167, 168, 169, 170, 171, 172, 173, 174, 175, 177, 178, 180, 181, 182, 183, 184, 186, 187
Badon Min Ayu Wada.......167
Badon Min Letswè.......167
Bagan (=Pagan).......30, 31, 37, 40, 43, 44, 47, 48, 49, 56, 58, 64, 68, 76, 120, 121, 122, 123, 125, 150, 160, 166
(King) Bagan.......85, 99, 106

Bagan Dynasty.......61, 106
Bagan U Tin.......50, 77
Bagyidaw.......65, 72, 74, 81, 92
Baker, George. 62, 66
Banyadala (=Binnyadala, Binya Dala)......61, 68
Baptist Mission.......95, 96
Bayin Ameindaw Pyandan.......163, 179
Bayinnaung.......150
Beiktheik.......123, 124
Be: dan.......115, 119
Blundell.......93, 94
Boddhisatta.......160, 163, 172
Brahmin (=Ponna).......77, 78, 79, 114, 132, 139, 140, 141, 152, 153, 174
Bṛhaspati.......42
British East Indian Company.......65, 66
Brooke, Henry. 66
Buddha.......31, 40
Buddhagotha (=Buddhagosa).......107
Buddhist State.......40
Burman Empire.......57

C

Cakkavattin.......119, 163, 164, 170
Cakkavatti-Sutta.......130
Calcutta (=Kolkota).......58, 77
Chapata (=Sappata).......160
Charney, Michael. 76, 164
Chengmai (=Zimme).......93
Chinese Shans of Kaingma.......65
Chittagong.......65
Code of law.......44, 52
Coedès, George. 38
Coronation ceremony.......73
cowherd.......43, 107, 109, 122, 123, 153, 161, 162
Cox, Hiram. 53, 54
Crawford, John. 54
Crown Prince.......63, 72, 78, 89, 92
Cūlavaṃsa.......42

D

Dabinshwedi (=Tapinshwehti).......121
Dagon.......62, 89
Danan.......44
Danu.......62, 134
Danyawadi (=Danyawaddy).......63, 76
Dattarāja.......77
Dawe (=Tavoy).......62, 64, 70, 71, 76, 93, 94, 95
Dawtha.......115
de facto.......69, 75, 124
de jure.......69, 75, 124
Dethan.......44
Dēvanampiya Tissa.......36, 73
Dhamma.......31, 40, 113, 171, 183, 187
Dhamma-niti.......128
Dhammasatthan (Dhammasatta).......42, 45, 55, 88, 122, 126, 165, 187
Dhammathat.......30, 31, 42, 44, 49, 51, 52, 53, 54, 58, 59, 83, 88, 89, 99, 103, 106, 107, 112, 114, 116, 122, 125, 126, 127, 128, 136, 137, 148, 149, 154, 155, 157, 158, 165, 171, 173, 177, 182, 183, 185, 186, 187
Dhammathat Kuncha.......59
Dhamma Wineikhsaya (Vinicchaya) Dhammathat.......87
Dhammawilatha (=Dhammavilasa) Dhammathat.......49, 54, 59, 60, 106, 107, 122, 128, 129, 130, 148, 149, 150, 151, 152, 155, 157, 158, 165, 171, 173, 177, 182, 185, 186, 187
Dhammayaza.......55, 76, 83, 124, 172
Dhammazedi.......160
Dharma.......36, 161, 183
Dharmaśāstra.......42, 43, 45, 55, 89, 155, 161
Digest.......86, 87, 88, 90, 103
Dīgha-nikāya.......122
Dupleix.......67

(King) Duttabaung.......48
Duttabaung Hpyathton.......48, 51

E
East Court.......174, 175, 180
East Indian Company.......65, 66, 92
Egayit (=Egarit).......119
Ekamsika.......168
ex-parte.......173, 184

F
Forchhammer, Emil. 42, 43, 49, 50, 51, 55, 83, 84, 88, 89, 90, 102, 103
Fort St. George.......66
Frasch, Tilman. 42, 47, 48, 49, 54
Furnivall, J.S. 44, 46, 49, 56, 77, 88, 93, 149

G
Gayuna.......116
Gazathana.......78
George II.......125
Gotama Siddhattha (=Siddarta).......40
Governor-General.......57, 65
Grabowsky, Volker.......93, 94, 95
Gywe, M.T. 97

H
Hantharwadi Bago (=Hanthawaddy Pegu) 61, 69, 84, 89
Hindu law.......43, 53, 155
Hkattiya.......38, 73, 106, 124, 172
Hkattiya-beiktheik.......74
Hkayaing-wun.......50
Hkon-daw.......181
Hkwè-bon.......47, 48, 171, 172
Hluttaw.......149, 174, 175, 176, 180, 184
Hmannan Maha-yazawin-daw-gyi (=Hmannan Maha Yazawingyi).......77
Hooker, M.B. 27, 30
Hpaungga-sa Maung Maung.......63, 164, 167
Hpaya-laung.......43, 108, 123, 125, 160, 162, 163, 170
Hpon.......164
Hpyat-sa.......51
Hpyathton.......51, 58, 177, 179
Hsinbyushin.......52, 63, 64, 68, 69, 164, 171, 184
Hsonda Manu.......59
Htin Aung.......46, 48, 153, 167, 168
Huxley, Andrew. 122, 123

I
Indianization.......38, 39
Inwa (=Ava).......56, 61, 78, 120, 163
Ishii, Yoneo. 31

J
Jardine, John. 53, 88, 102, 103
Jardine Prize.......103
Jātaka.......86
Jayasekera.......38
Judicial Commissioner of Burma.......102
Judson, Dr. Adniram. 96

K
Kachin.......62, 134
Kaingza Manuyaza (=Kaingza).......51, 86, 151, 160
Kaingza Manu Dhammathat.......184
Kaingza Manuyaza Hpyathton / Shaukhton(Hlyaukhton).......54, 86
Kaingza Shwemyin.......59, 106, 152, 182
Kala.......48, 121, 134
Kalan.......44
Kalyani Thein (=Kalyānī Sīmā).......160
Kandaw-Pakinnaka-linga Dhammathat (=Kandaw).......87
Karma.......121, 147, 163, 166
Kathe.......62, 134
Katyāyana.......42

Kawi Lekkana Dipani.......48
Kinwun Mingyi (U Gaung)......48, 90, 103
Kolkota (=Calcutta).......66, 77
Koenig, William, J. 64, 68
Konbaung Dynasty.......31, 43, 44, 54, 56, 61, 63, 66, 69, 83, 90, 92, 99, 121, 160
Konbaung Shwebo.......83, 84
Kozaung-gyop.......59, 84
Kśatríya.......124
Kudho-kan (Kramma, Kamma).......121, 161, 163, 164
Kyaikkami (=Amherst).......90, 93, 150
Kyannet.......59, 60
Kyauksa.......47, 111
Kyazwa.......47
Kyin Swi. 174
Kyone-wun Bumma Zeya.......83, 84, 86, 87, 89, 102, 123, 127, 186

L

Lampang (=Labaung).......93
Langham-Carter.......93, 94, 95, 96
Lawka Byuha Kyan.......149
Lawka Dipani Kyan.......158
Lawkathara-pyo.......128
Lawkawut.......182
Lawki Kyan (Book on worldly affairs) 77
Legal Maxim.......46, 52, 180, 182, 184, 185, 187
Let-yon.......164, 172
Letwe Beiknandhu (=Beinanthu).....83, 87
Letwè Nawyahta.......77
Lieberman, Victor, B. 62, 66, 83
Lieutenant Mcleod. 93
Lingat, Robert. 43, 44, 49, 86, 122, 126, 161, 162
Linzen.......134
Lower Burma.......99
Lumsden, J. 71

M

Madama (=Mouttama, Martaban).......62, 63
Madras (=Chennai)-Army.......66, 93, 94
Magada language.......107
Maha Bandula.......92
Maha Dhamma Thingyan.......81
Maha Dhammayaza (=a Great King of Law) 70, 83
Maha Dhammayaza Dhipati [Dibadi] (Hanthawaddy Pa-min).......61, 83
Mahathamada.......38, 40, 43, 73, 74, 75, 78, 106, 107, 108, 109, 114, 116, 119, 121, 122, 123, 124, 125, 136, 146, 157, 160, 161, 162, 163, 164, 170, 171, 172, 177, 186, 187
Mahāhamsa Jataka.......169
Mahāsammata (=*Maha Sammata*).......40, 43, 63, 123, 151
Mahasiriuttamajaya (=Mahathiri Outtama Thinjyan).......88
Maha Thiri Zeyathu.......48, 86
Mahawthada (=Mahosadha).......51
Mahā-vihāra.......36
Mahayazathat (-kyi).......44, 50, 51, 86, 87, 151, 160, 182
Maingy, A.D. 93, 95
Manawthara (=Manosara)......59, 106, 182
Manawthara (=Manosara) Dhammathat 84, 184
Mandalay.......50, 56, 58, 59, 98, 99
Manipur.......62, 76
Maniyadonabon.......128
Manouttheika(=Manussika) Dhammathat 49, 122
Manu.......38, 40, 44, 59, 73, 99, 106, 107, 108, 122, 161
Manu Dhammasatthan.......122
Manu Dhammathat.......54
Manugye (=Manu Akyay) Dhammathat [After 89, mostly abbreviation form

as *MD*].......38, 40, 43, 59, 73, 81, 83, 84, 85, 86, 88, 89, 90, 91, 92, 95, 97, 122, 123, 126, 148, 151, 156, 161, 163, 165
Manu-Kyetyo (=Kyetyo).......59, 60, 122, 128, 129, 130, 148, 149, 151, 155
Manuthaya (=Manusara) Dhammathat....106, 182
Manuthaya (=Manusara) Shwemyin......49, 54, 59, 99, 107, 148, 182
Manuthaya (=Manusara) Shwemyin Dhammathat......54, 99, 106, 148, 182, 184
Manuwunnana.......59, 99, 148
Manuyaza Hpyathton.......51, 54, 86
Manuyin (=Manu Reng) Dhammathat 59, 83, 84, 85, 88, 89, 99, 106, 122, 148, 161, 162
Maung Daung (=Htaung) Hsayadaw 71, 76, 77, 169
Maung Hmaing.......181
Mawgun.......77
Mawha.......79, 115, 152, 155, 156
Mawlamyine (=Moulmein).......93, 94, 95, 150
Mendelson, E. Michael. 167, 168
Messiah.......121
Metteya (=Arimetteya).......163, 167
Mindon.......74, 81, 98, 99, 103
Mingala Mandat.......78
Mingun Pagoda.......71, 167
Min Gyi Byu.......120
Mingyi Swa Sawke.......51
Min Kyin Taya.......164
Min Kyi Nyo.......121
Mintaya.......55
Mohawishsedani (=Mohavicchedani)....106, 148, 155, 164
Mo Hnin.......120
Mok-hso-bo.......62, 83, 88, 120, 164
Mon.......37, 40, 42, 43, 45, 48, 55, 56, 59, 60, 61, 62, 65, 66, 67, 68, 69, 80, 83, 84, 88, 95, 107, 114, 118, 123, 129, 149, 150, 160, 166, 169, 171, 180, 187
Mon Dhammasāt.......32, 42, 60
Mro-haung (=Myo-haung).......63
Muddha-beiktheik.......70, 71, 74, 75, 76, 77, 78, 80, 81, 82, 167, 169, 172, 178, 183
Muddha beiktheikta-min (Muddha-beiktheik-hkan-min).......77
Myanmar-ization (=Burmanization).......69
Myanmar Min Okchok-pon Sadan.......50
Mye-daing.......115, 138
Myitta.......68, 116
Myo-thugyi (=dhagyi).......50
Myo-wun.......50, 176
Myo-yon.......176

N

Naingan-daw.......30
Nai Pan Hla.......32, 60
Nārada.......42
Narameikha.......70
Narapatisidhu (Narapatisithu).......49, 76, 160, 166
Naungdawgyi.......32, 102, 164
Negrais Island (=Haing-kyi-kyun).......66
Ne Win.......188
Nirvana (=Nibbana, Neikban).......137
Nissaya.......86
Nīti-śāstra.......128, 171
Nyaungyan.......61, 121

O

Original Manu (=Manu Kyan Yin).......83, 85, 88
Ossa.......113, 117

P

Pāli-ization.......38

Papathat.......127, 131, 136, 165, 171
Parabaik.......47, 49, 54, 56, 58, 127
Pareikhkaya.......140
Pathein (=Bassein).......66
Pe.......47, 56, 97, 127
Phrathammasāt.......42
Phrathammasāt Būhan.......42
Pitakat Thon-bon.......78, 86
Pondicherry.......67
Preah Toammasah.......42, 45
Prince Sagaing.......92
Pyi (=Prome).......62, 92
Pyumin......48, 56, 106, 107
Pyumindi (=Pyuminhti) Dhammathat.....48

R

Rakhine (=Yakhine, Arakan).......45, 59, 60, 63, 65, 67, 69, 70, 71, 76, 77, 81, 92, 129, 148, 149, 150, 166, 168, 187
Rakhine Dhammathat.......60, 149, 150
Ramañña (=Mon) language.......107
Ratnasingha.......68, 69, 83, 84
Razawan (=Yazawin).......57
Richardson, David.......32, 85, 89, 90, 91, 92, 93, 94, 95, 96, 97, 99, 102, 103, 104, 106, 110, 113, 119, 148, 151, 153, 156, 157, 160, 161, 162, 170, 174, 186
Royal Duties.......55, 76, 110, 124, 130, 164, 165, 169, 171, 178, 183

S

Sagaing.......92
Sai Kham Mong.......32, 60
Sakka (=Indra).......118
Salin-myo.......83, 88
Sangermano, Vincent (Father). 53, 54, 57, 102
Sangha.......31, 37, 40, 41, 69, 75, 113, 114, 124, 126, 137, 160, 165, 167, 168, 186, 187, 188
Sawbwa.......62, 65
Second Taungu Dynasty.......61, 83
Sekkya-wade-min (=Cakkavattin).......118, 145, 163, 164, 166, 170, 171, 172
Seven Years War.......66
Shan.......45, 59, 62, 65, 69, 93, 94, 95, 134, 150, 166, 187
Shan Dhammathat (=Thammasat).......32, 60
Shaukhton (=Hlyaukhton).......50, 86, 182
She-yon.......174, 176
Shin Kyaw Dhu (=Thu).......51
Shinkyawthu Hpyathton.......51
Shinbyushin Thihathu (=Thihadhu)......120
Shwe Baw.......51, 150, 151, 152, 153, 154, 155, 182
Shwebo.......62, 68, 83, 84, 86, 88, 89, 102, 120, 123, 149, 164
Shwe-daik.......50, 151
Sihala Bikkhu Sangha.......160
Singu.......63, 68, 164
Sinhalization.......38
Sit-kè.......140
Sit-tan.......47, 52, 172, 173, 184
Sit-thugyi.......115
Siyinhton (=Hpyathton).......179
Symes, Michael. 57, 67, 70, 71
Syriam (=Tanyin).......66, 67

T

Tambiah, H.W. 42
Tanindhayi (=Tenasserim)......62, 70, 90, 93, 94, 104
Tapinshwehti (=Dabinshweti)......121
Taungu Dynasty.......56, 61, 69, 83, 150
Taya.......40, 119
Taya-thugyi.......111
Taylor, Robert H. 28, 30, 31
Taylor, Thomas. 66
Tezothara.......84, 85, 88

Thahte-thagywe.......77
Thalaing.......95, 96
Thalun.......45, 50, 51, 77, 86, 87, 150
Thamadi.......117
Thamaing (=Pitakat Thamaing Sadan)......48, 49, 51, 86
Thamanya Min......77
Than Tun.......32, 51, 104
Thathanabaing.......75, 78, 82, 167
Thaw Kaung.......56
Thayawaddy (=Thayarwadi).......74, 81, 94, 96
Thein Sein.......188
Thekkata Abhitheka Sadan.......76, 77
Thekkayit.......52
The National Library.......50, 57, 58, 99, 102, 103, 104
The second sun.......106, 108
Thenapati.......180
Theravāda Buddhism.......36, 37, 38, 40, 42, 73, 160, 187
Theravāda Buddhist State.......30, 31, 32, 36, 37, 40, 44, 46, 73, 81, 82, 122, 125, 126, 127, 160, 165, 166, 186, 187
Thet-pan Atwinwun.......77
Thibaw.......74, 99, 103
Thikya (=Dhaja).......118
Thiri Maha Zeyathu.......48
Thubhadya.......106
Thudhammasari (=Sudhammacari).......51
Thugyi (=Dhagyi).......138
Thu-gywe (=Dhagywe).......78
Thu-taw (=Thu-daw).......117
Treaty of Yandabo.......93
Trials by Ordeal.......174

U

U Aung Zeya.......62, 83, 120
U Kala.......48, 121
Universities' Central Library (UCL).......50, 57, 58, 99, 102
U Tin (=Bagan U Tin).......50, 77, 80
U Tun Nyo (the Twinthintaik-wun).......87

V

Vasettha.......38
Veda.......161
Vinaya Pitaka.......86
Vyavahāra.......42, 45

W

Wagaru (=Waru) Dhammathat (= King Wagaru's Manu Dhammasatthan)......59, 84, 99, 106, 122, 151, 152
War in Prassi.......67
War in Wandewash.......67
Widuya (=Vidhura).......51
Wineikhsaya Pakathani (=Vinicchaya Pakasani) Dhammathat.......99
Witness (Thet-the).......115, 116, 117, 118, 151, 152, 153, 165, 173, 181, 182
Wun.......68

Y

Yadanapura.......77
Yadanatheingha-myo.......88
Yājñavalkya.......42
Yakhine (Rakhine) Dhammathat.......81, 92, 149
Yandabo.......92, 93
Yandabo Treaty.......92, 93
Yandameik Kyaw Htin (=Din).......181
Yangon.......50, 53, 57, 58, 62, 63, 66, 67, 69, 89, 97, 99, 102, 103
Yathe (=Rishi) (hermit).......162
Yaza.......38, 124
Yazabala (=Rājabala).......59, 148
Yaza-beiktheik.......74, 94
Yaza-dhamma (=Yaza Dhamma).......164, 171

Yaza-niti (=Rāja-nīti).......171
Yazathat.......45, 47, 49, 50, 54, 87, 137, 151, 165, 173, 179, 183, 184
Yazawin.......57, 77, 120, 121, 163
Yazawut-taya Siyin-ye.......179
Yazawwada (=*Rajovada*).......128, 157
Yezajyo.......51, 181, 182, 183
Yezajyo Hkondaw Hpyathton.......51, 54, 181, 183
Yi Yi.......52, 56
Yodaya (=Ayuthaya).......134
Ywa-thugyi (=dhagyi).......50

Z

Zabudipa (=*Zambudipa*).......107
Zan.......52, 120
Zawgyi.......116, 145, 157
Zayat.......133
Zonda Hsayadaw.......83, 85, 88

[The above 'Index' shows vocabulary included only in the main body of this book.]

Ryuji Okudaira

After diplomatic service in the Japanese Ministry of Foreign Affairs from 1965 to 1981, he transferred to the Tokyo University of Foreign studies under the Ministry of Education as an Associate Professor in 1981 and was promoted to the Professorship in 1985. Since retirement from the University in 2002, he has been given the title of Emeritus Professor. His major field of studies is the pre-modern history of Myanmar, legal history and the structure of the 'Theravāda Buddhist State'. His major publications are (i) Burmese Dhammathat (in) *Laws of Southeast Asia* (Vol.I) edited by M.B. Hooker (1986), (ii) *Biruma Hoseishi Kenkyu Nyumon* ("Introduction to the Study of Burmese Legal History") in Japanese (2002), and (iii) several theses related to Myanmar political and legal history in the pre-modern period written in English.

Kingship and Law
in the Early Konbaung Period of Myanmar
(1752-1819)

A Study of the *Manugye Dhammathat* – an eighteenth century major law book

初版第1刷発行　2018年2月28日

定価8000円＋税

著者　奥平龍二Ⓒ
装丁　水戸部功
発行者　桑原晨
発行　株式会社めこん
〒113-0033　東京都文京区本郷3-7-1
電話03-3815-1688　FAX03-3815-1810
ホームページ http://www.mekong-publishing.com

組版　字打屋
印刷　株式会社太平印刷社
製本　株式会社新里製本所

ISBN978-4-8396-0309-0　C3022　¥8000E
3022-1802309-8347

JPCA 日本出版著作権協会
http://www.jpca.jp.net

本書は日本出版著作権協会（JPCA）が委託管理する著作物です。本書の無断複写などは著作権法上での例外を除き禁じられています。複写（コピー）・複製、その他著作物の利用については事前に日本出版著作権協会(http://www.jpca.jp.net　e-mail：info@jpca.jp.net) の許諾を得てください。